the
prawn cocktail
years

Simon Hopkinson &
Lindsey Bareham

the
prawn cocktail
years

MACMILLAN

contents

introduction

A few years ago, after a long day's session with *Roast Chicken and Other Stories*, we sat at the kitchen table and cracked open a nice bottle of Alsace. About halfway through we fell to talking about dishes we had loved and lost, those dishes that we had grown up with and memories of early restaurant outings. Before long our giggles turned to nostalgia and we started to scribble down a list of those fondly remembered dishes. They just came pouring out: Coquilles St-Jacques, Sole Véronique, Beef Stroganoff, Mixed Grill, Swedish Meatballs, Wiener Schnitzel, Chicken Maryland, Crêpes Suzette, Peach Melba and Profiteroles. And, of course, Prawn Cocktail.

Everybody, but everybody, loves Prawn Cocktail. We even tolerate a bad one – and we all know there are plenty of those. But the universal appeal of the Prawn Cocktail can be compared with another (more modern) ubiquitous favourite. The McDonald's hamburger is also highly addictive. The bun is ersatz and sweet, the meat is hardly your specialist chopped steak, the cheese is as far away from farmhouse Cheddar as you can possibly get and the pickle and ketchup are, well . . . just pickle and ketchup. However, the combination of all these components results in something so tasty that we are all hooked.

Prawn Cocktail is exactly the same: the shredded lettuce which sits at the bottom of the dish together with the pappy pink prawn in its sweet pink sauce somehow combines to deliver a dish which contradicts all the rules that constitute fine cooking.

So, it comes as no surprise that Prawn Cocktail remains the number one favourite 'starter' everywhere, from the plastic-clad menu of the café in the high street to the stiff vellum carte in the dining room of the five-star hotel – although there it may well still be referred to as Cocktail de Crevettes. In fact, Prawn Cocktail kicks off the triumphant trilogy that remains, according to opinion polls, the enduring favoured dining-out choice of a huge slice of the great British public. Prawn Cocktail, Steak Garni and Black Forest Gâteau is still It.

It's easy to laugh this off as yet another example of our lack of adventure and general wimpishness where food is concerned. But is there more to it than that? Is there a reason why these dishes have become so firmly embedded in the public consciousness?

One could hypothesize endlessly but it must surely be true that these are classic dishes which have stood the test of time. They may not always be prepared in the best possible way from the finest possible ingredients but it's easy to understand their appeal. If one bothers to prepare these and other dishes that predate the whim of fashion in food then it is a revelation how good they can be.

Dishes such as Spaghetti Bolognese, Chicken Kiev, Quiche Lorraine and Coq au Vin; dishes that were once exciting but have been slung out like old lovers, while we carelessly flirt with the flavour of the month. Our mission is to rehabilitate these old lags which have become scapegoats in a country now obsessed with culinary novelty.

The dishes we have in mind have no particular heritage. Some have their roots in Escoffier's classic cuisine, others are British nursery fare or greasy spoon stalwarts. More often than not, however, the recipes in question are what used to be called 'Continental' food that was served in the plethora of bistros and restaurants that sprung up in post-war, post-rationing Britain.

What all these dishes have in common is the potential for being truly excellent. Forget your prejudices for a moment and imagine freshly shelled prawns in a carefully made cocktail sauce, served on crisp shredded lettuce with a little cucumber and spring onion. The steak that follows should be cooked to a crust on the outside, pink and tender on the inside and eaten with properly made chips and the best Dijon mustard. The gâteau is a moist cake made with dark, bitter chocolate filled with kirsch-drenched cherries and whipped cream.

Inevitably, as we began to research and write this book, we stumbled upon archive material which put many of these recipes into their historical context. There are hundreds of others which we might have included but our selection is highly personal and they are all dishes that we have enjoyed eating and which we believe to be of genuine interest to the contemporary cook. They are also all dishes which were good ones in the first place. You will not, for instance, find Brown Windsor Soup, Steak Diane and Pêche Flambée amongst these pages because, in their time, they were every bit as unpleasant as the contemporary mish-mash that is flung together in the name of modern British cooking.

The purpose of this book is to redefine the Great British Meal and rescue other similarly maligned classic dishes from years of abuse, restoring them to their former status.

Simon Hopkinson and Lindsey Bareham, February 1997

the great british meal out

'A gin and tonic says a lot about you as a person. It is more than just a drink, it is an attitude of mind. It goes with a prawn cocktail, a grilled Dover sole, Melba toast and Black Forest gâteau.'

Nico Ladenis, *My Gastronomy,* **1987**

Prawn Cocktail, Steak Garni and Black Forest Gâteau has been the favourite British meal out for as long as one can remember. It's not surprising. It's delicious. The only trouble is, as with any popular food, familiarity breeds contempt.

Take that other ubiquitous Saturday-nighter, the Indian meal. Think of the countless times you've been served up greasy bhajis, dried-out tandoori and watery dhal, whereas you can probably count on one hand the occasions when the bhajis have been beautiful, the tandoori terrific and the dhal delectable. It's simply a question of good and bad cooking.

So it seems a shame that the Great British Meal Out has been singled out for such enduring ridicule. And, talking of ridicule, what on earth is wrong with grilled Dover sole?

prawn cocktail

Serves 2

You shouldn't muck about too much with a Prawn Cocktail. Starting at the bottom of the dish, you need the heart of a good lettuce, not the outside leaves. Any fresh lettuce will do but the heart of something like a Little Gem or similar would be most suitable. Shredding the leaves (chefs say chiffonade) is traditional and there's good reason for it: who wants whole lettuce leaves getting in the way of the prawns and their pink sauce?

Freshly boiled prawns from the British seaside are rare today, which is a pity, so the next best thing is whole cooked prawns. They will often have been frozen but their quality, once shelled and decapitated, is surprisingly good. Frankly, if you wish to use those tasteless, bulk-frozen little pink commas, then you have only yourself to blame.

Home-made mayonnaise is clearly ideal here but home-made tomato sauce is quite definitely not: the taste of fresh tomato does not a prawn cocktail make. However hard one tries, it is not possible to replicate the taste of Heinz tomato ketchup. No other will do. And as for that gin and tonic you're going to drink with it, try Tanqueray – it's stronger than Gordon's.

the heart of 1 large Little Gem lettuce, finely shredded

1 spring onion, white part only, very finely sliced

1 heaped tbsp cucumber, peeled, de-seeded and finely diced

4–5 tbsp of home-made mayonnaise (see page 24)

1 tbsp tomato ketchup

2–3 shakes of Tabasco

1 tsp cognac

tiny squeeze of lemon juice

200 g cooked, whole, shell-on prawns, peeled (reserve two, unpeeled, for garnish)

paprika

Divide the lettuce between two dishes, sprinkle over the spring onion and cucumber and pile the prawns loosely on top. Mix the mayonnaise, ketchup, Tabasco, cognac and lemon juice together to make the regulation pink.

the great british meal out   9

Spoon the sauce over the prawns and allow it to trickle between them. Dust sparingly with paprika. Hang one prawn over the side of each dish and attach a small wedge of lemon.

steak garni and chips

Serves 2

Perhaps the reason that 'a nice piece of steak' has always been the number-one choice for dinner out is that restaurant kitchens cook steaks better than we can at home. For one thing, they have better equipment – well-seasoned grills, which get very hot, deep deep-fryers and sharp knives – as well as sauces and garnishes, all at the ready. And they have waiters, too.

Have you ever tried to cook steak at home for six people? Two medium rare, one rare, two well done, and one cremated? And six portions of chips? Steak at home is a meal for two. If you want to feed six people with a nice piece of beef, then roast it.

Steak

There are two successful ways to cook a steak at home: grilling and frying in butter. When grilling, you need to use one of those cast-iron, stove-top, ribbed grill pans – using an overhead grill simply results in hot meat. These increasingly familiar pans must be extremely hot (this will take several minutes) before the meat gets anywhere near them. When stove-top grilling, it's the meat rather than the pan that is oiled. Conversely – and this may sound obvious – a fried steak should be gently cooked in constantly sizzling butter.

Preferred steaks for grilling are the more robust sirloin and rump, while tender fillet seems better for gentle frying, its texture turning meltingly soft and luscious.

Whether to season before or after? Advance seasoning extracts moisture and prevents the meat from developing that fantastically good charred and

steak garni and chips

crusted surface. Interestingly, however, when cooking buttery little fillets, they don't taste anywhere near as good if they haven't been seasoned first; perhaps it's something to do with the less aggressive mode of cooking.

And so to timing. It is difficult to give exact measurements here. Finger prodding is best. With a thick, rare steak a slight indentation is left in the surface; medium-rare gives but finally resists; medium is definitely getting bouncier; and with medium-well, the texture of the meat is becoming noticeably tight. Shoe leather comes to mind when describing well-done.

As far as size is concerned, this is entirely a matter for you. However, thick is best, as here one can control the degree of cooking far better than with a thinner piece of meat. 175–225g is a nice weight for a good steak.

Note: It is always a good idea to allow steaks – or any meat for that matter – to rest for a few minutes before serving. And anyway this will neatly co-ordinate with the final crisping of the chips.

Garni

Rather than use that inefficient overhead grill, you will get a far better result if you cook the 'garni' in a hot oven. It is quite extraordinary how many times one encounters barely warm, supposedly 'grilled' tomatoes, with mushrooms that manage somehow to be both shrivelled and almost raw. These are a feature of the cheap hotel breakfast buffet – you know, the type of buffet that is supposed to be for your convenience but is in fact for theirs.

2 tomatoes, halved horizontally   *salt and pepper*
2 flat black mushrooms   *cress*
a little melted butter

Brush the tomatoes and mushrooms with a little butter and season. Place in a small baking dish and cook in a hot oven (400°F/200°C/gas mark 6) for 20 minutes or until the tomatoes are blistered and puffy and the mushrooms sizzling. Garnish the 'garni' with cress.

Chips

Have your potatoes peeled, chipped, washed, dried and part-cooked before you even think about preparing the steaks. Here is the best way to go about it.

2 large floury potatoes, peeled   *salt*
groundnut oil for deep-frying

Cut the potatoes lengthways into your preferred thickness. Then wash them under cold running water, until the water is clear of starch, drain in a colander and wrap them in a tea-towel to dry.

Half-fill a chip pan or electric deep-fat fryer with oil and heat to 375°F/190°C (for those without a deep fryer or thermometer, this is when a scrap of bread turns golden after a couple of seconds). Cook the chips in batches so as not to overcrowd the pan, and fry for 6–7 minutes. They should be cooked through but only lightly coloured. Lift them out with the basket and allow them to drain. If you are improvising and don't have a chip pan use a slotted spoon. They can be held in this state for a few hours.

For the final crisping, increase the temperature of the oil to 360°F/185°C and continue cooking for between 30 seconds and 3 minutes. The time variance depends on the type of potato available at different times of the year. If, and it happens occasionally, the chips refuse to crisp, remove the basket from the oil, raise the temperature and cook for a third time. Drain on absorbent kitchen paper, sprinkle with salt and serve immediately.

black forest gâteau   *Serves 8–10*

Along with rather sad oranges in caramel, wilting profiteroles, gaudy sherry trifle and too-much-apple-in-it fruit salad, Black Forest Gâteau remains the school bully of the sweet trolley.

It's always there, isn't it, in the most prominent position, shoved in your face almost. 'And will Madam be having cream with that?' Yes, of course she will, we all do, poured from that silver-plated jug and drowning the already creamy black wedge into submission.

It's wolfed down day after day from Hastings to Hartlepool: dry sponge, cheap tinned cherries of a weird hue, ersatz cream and worryingly glossy icing. Neither waiter nor customer really cares whether it tastes good, how carefully it's been prepared or where it came from. Did it originate in the Black Forest? No, silly, it came from the local Happy Cake Company. That is, until now.

Of all the dishes in this book, this one seems to have plumbed the deepest depths. Who knows, perhaps once upon a time, somewhere in the very blackest bit of that forest, an old wood-cutter's wife knocked up a bit of chocolate cake, chopped it in half, threw in a few cherries, upended the kirsch bottle and filled the cake with cream. It was so good that word soon spread. So, of course, she bought a trolley, opened a restaurant, and the rest is history.

However loopy our mythical origin might be, the essence of a good Black Forest Gâteau lies in carefully chosen ingredients, lavishly assembled.

For the chocolate cake:
75 g best quality bitter-sweet chocolate, broken into pieces
100 g semi-salted butter
75 g soft dark brown sugar
1 tbsp golden syrup
175 g self-raising flour
25 g cocoa
2 large eggs, beaten
150 ml milk
––––

For the filling:
700 g (approximately) good quality bottled or canned pitted cherries in syrup
2 tbsp kirsch
––––

For the icing:
200 ml double cream
200 g best quality bitter-sweet chocolate, broken into pieces
––––
400 ml double cream

Pre-heat the oven to 325°F/170°C/gas mark 3. Butter a 20 cm wide × 5 cm deep loose-bottomed cake tin and fit a circle of greaseproof paper into the base.

Put the chocolate, butter, sugar and syrup into a heavy-bottomed pan over a low heat and stir until everything is melted and amalgamated. Allow the mixture to cool until it is tepid but still molten.

Sift the flour and cocoa into the bowl of an electric mixer or use an electric hand-whisk. Add the chocolate mixture using a spatula and start to beat slowly together. Combine the eggs and milk and slowly pour this in too. Whisk together gently, increasing the speed until the mixture is light and thick yet fluffy.

Spoon the mixture into the cake tin, smooth the surface and bake in the pre-heated oven for 35–40 minutes until firm and springy and when a skewer inserted into the middle of the cake comes out clean. Remove from the oven and leave to cool in the tin for around 30 minutes before turning out on a wire rack.

Drain the cherries in a sieve suspended over a bowl. Tip them into another bowl and measure off 200 ml of the cherry syrup. Add to this the two tablespoons of kirsch. With a serrated knife slice the cake horizontally into three discs. Place each disc on an individual plate and spoon the cherry syrup/kirsch mixture evenly over the three and leave to soak in. Meanwhile, heat the 200 ml of double cream until it is about to simmer and add the chocolate. Remove from the heat and stir gently until melted and very smooth. Pour into a bowl and allow to cool in the fridge while you assemble the cake.

Whip the 400 ml of double cream until thick. Spread one of the discs with half of it, cover with half the cherries, pressing them in lightly, cover with the second disc and repeat the process. Finally, put on the third disc and gently, with the palms of both hands, press all together.

Have a look at the chocolate cream mixture in the fridge, which should be stiffening. Give it a stir: it needs to be thick enough to spread, like icing. With a palette knife, cover the top and sides of the cake, spreading thickly until all the cream is used up. Leave to set in a cool place – preferably not the fridge as this can cause the 'icing' to weep slightly.

the fifties hotel dining room

'He always starts with soup whatever it is . . . He has half a bottle of Blue Nun Liebfraumilch whatever he's eating and she had a port to start with and then half a bottle of some kind of Sauternes. He has boiled potatoes with every lunch and either peas or carrots or, when it's in season, asparagus which he's very partial to. She picks her way about among the expensive dishes but usually has steak Diane because she likes the drama at the table.'

'A Certain Lack of Dignity', *The Bad Food Guide*, Derek Cooper, 1967

The Fifties Hotel Dining Room was home to Brown Windsor Soup. This was its birthplace and graveyard, where it simmered happily for many years before being usurped by young Turks such as Carrot and Orange and Curried Parsnip – new kids on the chopping block.

There was something about this dining room that could make one feel treated and depressed at the same time. Boiled cabbage must have been kept on a low heat twenty-four hours a day; there was always a crusted skin on the (half-used) little glass pot of Colman's mustard and there was the deaf waiter, not to mention the distantly rumbling dumb one. The only table-cloth was white, unless you were in the country where the table might have been polished mahogany. It would probably have been laid with well-worn shiny mats, with frayed green baize bottoms, depicting horses, haywains and hunting scenes. And the treat, incidentally, was simply the fact of going out to lunch.

This was also the home of the cruet set: dumpy little glass salt cellars and ground white pepper (no sign of pepper mills as yet), oil and vinegar flasks (the ones in endless embrace) for pouring over the plate of tired lettuce, curling cucumber slices and quartered tomatoes. The oil was any old stuff, pale, tasteless, not a whiff of olive – *that* was kept in the first-aid cupboard. And the vinegar was brown. Nobody ever used these condiments, of course, because what they really wanted was salad cream.

But back to that Brown Windsor. Only the British could come up with a name for a soup that instantly puts you off wanting it. Admittedly, the years of Brown Windsor were austere and post-war. However, just across the Channel, a French potato soup (Potage Parmentier) would have been lovingly made, carefully seasoned and a pleasure to eat: potatoes, onions and water never tasted so good. Once, even Brown Windsor might have been a decent bowlful: some recipes deliver up a classic consommé made with calf's foot, bones, beef stock and finished with Madeira. Delicious. But surely this is a different recipe? The fifties hotel-dining-room effort was quite clearly made from water, wallpaper paste and gravy browning. It had a whiff of old bones about it and the pinky-brown tint of stage makeup.

Other soups spoiled by Windsor's reputation became even easier to ladle out, thanks to the 'convenience' of can and packet: asparagus, tomato, oxtail and minestrone are probably the ones that most of us remember. In the timid fifties the only embellishment for those dreary soups would have been a tentative swirl of cream, while the minestrone wasn't improved by its dusting of cheesy-socks ersatz Parmesan. But that's enough about soup.

Possibly, the main problem with the fifties hotel dining room was ignorance seasoned with uninterest. The clientele didn't really care too much what they ate, and the management, who knew this, coasted along perpetuating the 'Well, nobody has ever complained before' syndrome.

Happily, there is much to resuscitate from those depressing days.

cream of celery soup

Serves 4

A thin, fibrous liquid, with an unappetizing beige hue and the merest hint of aniseed, constituted the fifties hotel-dining-room edition of Cream of Celery. Properly made, with a high proportion of celery, perhaps a little celeriac too, this is one of the finest British soups it is possible to eat.

50 g butter
1 small lovely head of celery, preferably with leaves, cleaned and chopped
2 small onions, peeled and chopped
1 tsp celery salt

1 potato or chunk of celeriac (about 225 g), peeled and chopped
900 ml light chicken stock
150 ml whipping cream
freshly ground white pepper

Melt the butter in a roomy pan and gently cook the celery and onions in it for 20 minutes or so until soft, but not coloured. Add the celery salt. Put in the potato or celeriac and the stock. Bring the mixture to the boil, check the seasoning to see if any further salt (plain) is needed, skim off any scum and simmer for half an hour. Liquidize well – that is, about a minute for each batch – as this accentuates the creaminess of the soup, then push it through a fine sieve. Return it to a clean pan, add the cream and pepper and reheat. Serve with croutons.

cream of tomato soup *Serves 4*

It is a curious thing that when you go to the bother of making a proper home-made tomato soup with very ripe tomatoes (essential), fresh herbs, decent home-made stock and cream, you end up with a soup that looks identical to and has an almost interchangeable consistency with what is very probably the world's most popular canned soup: Heinz Cream of Tomato. The taste, however, is quite different.

50 g butter
2 medium onions, peeled and finely chopped
2 celery sticks, finely diced
2 cloves of garlic, finely chopped
700 g very ripe tomatoes, skinned and
  chopped

pinch of sugar, salt and pepper
750 ml light chicken or vegetable stock
10 basil leaves
125 ml whipping cream

Heat the butter in a spacious heavy-bottomed pan (a Le Creuset would be ideal), and soften the onion and celery, allowing about 20 minutes for this. Towards the end add the garlic. Put in the tomatoes with the sugar, salt and pepper, let them melt and reduce a little, then add the stock. Cook for 15 minutes, adding the basil leaves for the last few minutes, then liquidize. Pass through a fine sieve into a clean pan. Stir in the cream, and gently reheat taking care not to let the soup boil. Taste and adjust the seasoning. Serve with buttery croutons.

Serves 6

oxtail soup

One of the finest consommés (see page 71) is fashioned from oxtail. The gelatinous qualities gained from its knobbly bone structure serve to enrich the initial broth, which is then clarified. Here, however, a more substantial soup is required, with shreds of oxtail meat being stripped from the bone and stirred into a thickened broth.

1 oxtail, cut into 2.5 cm pieces by your butcher	*3 sticks celery, chopped*
salt and pepper	*4 flat black mushrooms, chopped*
1 tbsp plain flour	*150 ml Madeira or port*
1 tbsp olive oil	*300 ml beef stock or canned consommé*
25 g butter	*1.75 litres water*
2 carrots, peeled and chopped	*1 tbsp redcurrant jelly*
2 onions, peeled and chopped	*4–5 tbsp extra Madeira or sherry*

Season the pieces of oxtail and roll them in the flour. Heat the oil and butter in a roomy stew-pan until frothing, turn the heat down a fraction and colour the oxtail all over until it is dark brown and crusted. Lift out the meat, pour off most of the fat and add the vegetables. Stir them around for about 10 minutes until coloured and then return the meat to the pan. Add the Madeira or port, the stock or consommé, water and redcurrant jelly.

Pre-heat the oven to 250°F/130°C/gas mark ½.

Now very gently bring the mixture to the boil, allowing a thick scum to form on top. When it is blanketing the surface, remove it with a large spoon. Once cleared, put a lid on the pan and place it in the oven for 3 hours.

Remove the oxtail pieces from the pot and allow them to cool on a plate. Strain the liquid into a clean pan through a colander and allow it to drip. Discard the vegetables, and pass the soup through a sieve. Now allow it to settle. Then lift off any fat from the surface with sheets of kitchen paper. Check the seasoning and add the extra Madeira or sherry.

Note: If left to cool overnight in the fridge, any fat may be easily removed in a stiff disc from the surface in one fell swoop.

Remove the oxtail meat from the bones and tear into shreds. Add as much of the meat to the soup as you wish, but do not add so much that it becomes more of a stew than a soup. (Any leftover meat would be wonderful fried up with onions and potatoes to make a delicious hash.) Reheat and serve in generous-sized bowls.

vichyssoise
Serves 6

Vichyssoise is sometimes so excessively enriched with cream that one wonders whether some chefs just pour seasoned chilled cream into a bowl and fling over a few snipped chives. Good Vichyssoise should be a glorious bowlful, soft as velvet with the taste of potato and leek at their most subtle.

By the way, it is often thought that Vichyssoise hails from France. Not so. It was invented by one Louis Diat (OK, *he* was French), chef of the Ritz Carlton, New York City, in the 1920s.

1 kg white part of leeks, trimmed, sliced	*250 ml milk*
* and washed*	*250 ml whipping cream*
500 ml light chicken stock	*pepper*
500 g potatoes, peeled and chopped	*small bunch of fresh chives, snipped*
1 tsp salt	

Simmer the leeks in the stock for 20 minutes. Add the potatoes and salt and cook with the milk for a further 15 minutes until the potatoes are tender. Liquidize, then strain through a fine sieve. Allow to cool, stir in the cream and correct the seasoning. Chill the soup for at least 4 hours. Serve in ice-cold bowls and garnish with chives.

Serves 6

asparagus soup

Asparagus soup should be pale green, limpid and creamy. The fifties hotel-dining-room version most certainly was not. Grey, thick and floury would be a more accurate description.

50 g butter
3 small leeks, trimmed, thinly sliced and
*   thoroughly washed*
900 ml light chicken stock
1 medium-sized potato, peeled and chopped
450 g sprue asparagus, trimmed of any
*   woody bits, washed and chopped,*

reserving 20 or so tips, for garnishing
*   the soup*
salt and white pepper
275 ml whipping cream
juice of ½ a small lemon
1 tbsp chives, snipped
cayenne pepper

Melt the butter and sweat the leeks in it until they are soft but uncoloured. Add the chicken stock, bring it to a simmer and cook gently for 30 minutes, covered. Add the potato and the chopped asparagus, and return to a simmer. Cook, uncovered this time, simmering slowly, for no more than 20 minutes. Check the seasoning. Briefly boil the reserved asparagus tips for about 2 minutes in a small pan of salted water. Drain and refresh in a bowl of iced water and put to dry on a clean tea-towel.

Ladle the soup, while still hot, into a blender and blend until it is very smooth, then push it through a fine sieve into a clean pan. Stir in the cream. Briefly reheat the soup with the cooked tips and lemon juice. Ladle it into hot bowls and sprinkle with chives and cayenne. This soup is equally good served ice-cold.

Serves 6

egg mayonnaise

In those distant days of the fifties hotel dining room, egg mayonnaise was all at once the daring option and the dull choice. It was invariably served on leathery lettuce leaves that nobody wanted to eat.

It needs the finest, freshest eggs, lightly boiled so the yolk remains soft

and the white springy. The eggs are then halved lengthways and cloaked with mayonnaise, which should cling to their curves like a satin négligé. A few choice leaves from the heart of a floppy garden lettuce, tucked around the eggs, becomes more than simply a garnish. The only other possible embellishment could be a criss-cross of anchovy fillets which add a savoury kick to what is otherwise a delicate and subtle dish.

9 medium eggs
3–4 floppy garden-lettuce hearts, leaves
    separated, washed and dried

———

For the mayonnaise:
2 egg yolks
1 tbsp Dijon mustard
salt and white pepper

300 ml groundnut oil
100 ml light olive oil (not extra virgin)
juice of ½ lemon
1–2 tbsp warm water

———

18 anchovy fillets, split lengthways
cayenne pepper

Put the eggs in a saucepan of cold water, bring to the boil and cook for 4 minutes. Refresh under cold running water for 3 minutes and then peel. Halve the eggs lengthways and lay out, cut side down, on a large white serving dish. Edge the dish with the lettuce leaves, tucking them in attractively.

To make the mayonnaise, ensure that all the ingredients are at room temperature. Place the egg yolks, mustard and a generous seasoning of salt and pepper in a mixing bowl and beat with a wire whisk until thick. Start to add the oils, one after the other, in a thin stream, beating continuously. Add a little of the lemon juice and then a little more oil. Continue beating, adding oil and juice in this way until both are used up and the mayonnaise is very thick and glossy. Adjust the seasoning. Whisk in a little warm water until the consistency is such that the mayonnaise will *just* cloak the egg. Spoon it over the eggs.

Use the anchovy fillets to make a criss-cross pattern over the top. Sprinkle with cayenne pepper. Eat with thinly sliced brown bread and butter.

oeufs en cocotte

Serves 4

At the legendary Lacy's restaurant in London, in the 1970s, chef Bill Lacy used to cook a charming egg dish. Its name was Oeufs en Cocotte Chez Nous. 'Our way with eggs' seems the neatest translation, and Bill's way was to bake the eggs gently in those familiar little brown and white pots, spoon over a modicum of meat glaze and finish the dish with a cap of sauce Béarnaise.

This reworked version of the classic baked egg was so good that it would seem churlish not to give the recipe here. However, should you wish to re-create the original plain-Jane Oeufs en Cocotte, just bake the eggs with some seasoned double cream and a leaf or two of fresh tarragon.

The meat glaze, which is essential to the recipe, is useful to have around. Once made (choose a day when you feel in the mood), it can be stored in the fridge for a few weeks or in ice trays in the freezer. It will add extra body to a gravy or sauce and, in the case of Lacy's Oeufs en Cocotte, only a small amount is needed to embellish and enrich.

Note: You will need to make the meat glaze well in advance of preparing Oeufs en Cocotte.

For the Béarnaise sauce:
2 tbsp tarragon vinegar
1 small shallot, peeled and finely chopped
½ tsp dried tarragon
2 egg yolks
150 g butter, melted

2 tsp fresh tarragon, chopped
salt and pepper
——
8 eggs
4 tbsp meat glaze (see overleaf)

In a small stainless-steel or enamelled pan, heat together the tarragon vinegar, shallot and dried tarragon until the liquid has all but evaporated. Remove from the heat and cool. Add the egg yolks and whisk them until they are thick. In a thin stream, pour in the butter, whisking all the time until the sauce is thick and glossy, leaving behind the milky residue that has separated from the melted butter as you pour. Pass the sauce through a fine sieve and stir in the fresh tarragon. Season and keep it warm.

Lightly butter eight ramekins and break an egg into each. Season, and place them in a large shallow pan filled with enough hot water to come two-thirds of the way up the sides of the dishes. Simmer to 'poach' the eggs until they are set – the whites firm and the yolks runny. Heat the meat glaze and spoon it over the tops of the eggs to coat them completely. Top with 1 teaspoon of the Béarnaise and serve. (You will find you have some sauce left over, but it is almost impossible to make smaller quantities of this.)

Meat Glaze

2–3 tbsp groundnut oil

900 g veal bones, preferably knuckle, chopped into small pieces by your butcher

450 g cheap, lean beef, such as chuck or shin, chopped into chunks

6 large flat black mushrooms

3 carrots, peeled and chopped

2 onions, peeled and chopped

3 celery sticks, chopped

4 garlic cloves, peeled and crushed

1 tbsp tomato purée

1 wine glass of white wine

1 wine glass of red wine

2 thyme sprigs

1 bay leaf

½ chicken or beef stock cube

2.3 litres cold water

Pre-heat the oven to 425°F/220°C/gas mark 7.

Drizzle the oil over the bones in a heavy-duty roasting tin, and move them around with your hands so that they are evenly coated. Roast in the oven until they are golden brown, turning them from time to time to prevent them scorching. This is important as burnt bits will turn a stock bitter. This should take between 30 and 40 minutes.

Remove the roasting tin from the oven to the hob and, over a moderate heat, put in the beef and turn it around with the bones until it is similarly browned. Add the vegetables, garlic and tomato purée and stir them around with the meat and bones until they are lightly coloured. Add the wines and, with a wooden spoon, scrape up any crusty bits from the bottom of the tin.

Allow it to bubble until it is well reduced, then tip everything into a large pot, rinsing out any left-behind bits with a little water. Put in the herbs and stock cube, and add the cold water. Stir together and bring very gently to the boil, then turn down the heat to a mere simmer. A great froth of scum will settle on the top, which must be removed with a ladle for as long as it is generated. The idea is to get rid of as many impurities as possible, which will include fat particles that also settle conveniently on the surface. The stock should cook, uncovered, for about 4 hours on the gentlest heat possible; little blips on the surface are all that should be visible.

With a large ladle, carefully lift the liquid and bones into a colander sitting over a clean pan and allow them to drain for a good 20 minutes until every drop has passed through. Throw away all the solids, and allow the liquid to settle completely so that any fat comes to the surface. Remove it with several sheets of kitchen paper by placing them directly on the surface of the stock then lifting them off immediately. This can be very successful, but if you want to do the best job possible, allow the stock to cool and place it in the fridge overnight so that any fat will solidify. Then it can be lifted off in a solid disc.

Place the clean stock on the heat and once again bring it slowly to the boil. Watch like a hawk for a thin blanket of creamy scum to form on the surface, and whip it off in one go with a large spoon or ladle – this is actually very satisfying! Turn down the stock to a simmer and from time to time look out for more scum to appear. Reduce gently until the stock has turned the colour of a conker, and is of a light and syrupy consistency. This meat glaze will be about a tenth of its original volume. Pour into a small porcelain or stainless-steel pot and cover it when it is cool. It will keep in the fridge for a couple of weeks or you can pour it into ice-cube trays and store it in the freezer.

Serves 4 # omelette arnold bennett

The English writer Arnold Bennett (1867–1931), who wrote *Imperial Palace* while he was staying at the Savoy in London, invented this omelette. He liked it so much that on his travels around the world he taught many hotel chefs how to make it. As a result, the dish passed into menu legend and became an international favourite.

It is a sublime combination of creamy eggs, smoked haddock and Parmesan and remains a speciality of the Savoy Grill, where it has pride of place among a short list of favoured first courses. Here, it is served perfectly round, its lightly burnished surface masking a gloriously soft and molten filling. The classic Omelette Arnold Bennett is made with both béchamel *and* hollandaise sauce as well as cream and it should be all at once eggy, creamy, smoky-fishy and with a hint of cheese. It needs neither embellishment nor accompaniment. The recipe is the original as cooked at the Savoy, and comes from *The Savoy Food and Drink Book.*

300 g smoked Finnan haddock fillets

275 ml milk

12 eggs

salt and freshly milled pepper

40 g unsalted butter

275 ml béchamel sauce (see page 50)

75 ml hollandaise sauce (see page 66–7)

50 ml double cream, whipped

20 g Parmesan, grated

Poach the haddock in the milk for about 3 minutes. Remove it from the pan and flake it.

Whisk the eggs, then add salt, pepper and half the haddock.

Heat an omelette pan, put in a quarter of the butter and swirl it around. Add a quarter of the egg mixture and cook very quickly, stirring constantly until the mixture is lightly set. Slide the omelette out on to a plate.

Mix the béchamel and hollandaise sauces together quickly. Add the remaining flaked haddock and fold in the whipped cream carefully. Cover the omelette completely with a quarter of the sauce. Sprinkle with a quarter of the Parmesan and glaze under a hot grill.

Repeat with the remaining mixtures to make three more omelettes. Serve immediately.

cold salmon mayonnaise *Serves 4*

Of all the dishes that are *not* so fondly remembered from this post-war period, one remains that could just possibly have been as good as – or even better than – it might be today.

This is because in the days before factory fish farming, cold salmon with mayonnaise was always made with the wild fish in season and there were no tasteless salmon. It was looked upon as a luxury to be offered a fine cut of truly pink, cold poached salmon.

It has to be said, however, that the so-called mayonnaise might well have been salad cream, and that the salmon is likely to have been woefully over-cooked. Furthermore, since its initial poaching, the fish had quite likely been kept hanging about for too long so that every last scrap was used.

But now that we have so much choice of anything and everything – and at any time of the year – would it not be nice to see this simple preparation of fresh *wild* salmon, served with properly made mayonnaise, offered on a table d'hôte menu, at a small hotel beside a river somewhere in Britain? The sad thing is, you just don't.

For the *court bouillon*:

1.1 litre water

2 carrots, peeled and sliced

1 large onion, peeled and sliced

1 celery stick, sliced

2 cloves

a few peppercorns

2 bay leaves

1 tbsp salt

2 tbsp white wine vinegar

——

900 g piece of wild salmon on the bone

——

1 quantity of mayonnaise (see page 24)

Put all the ingredients for the *court bouillon* in a large pan, preferably stainless-steel or enamel. Bring to the boil and simmer for 20 minutes. Slip in the salmon, bring back to the boil, switch off the heat, cover and leave for 20–30 minutes. The fish should easily be cooked through after this time, but a few minutes longer in the liquid is not going to spoil it.

Carefully lift out the salmon. Leave it to cool and, just before serving, remove the skin and lift the flesh from the bones. Serve the mayonnaise separately. Excellent with Cucumber Salad (see page 225).

Serves 4

coquilles st-jacques

The dish in question here is a classic of Parisian cookery. Its full name is in fact 'Coquilles St-Jacques à la Parisienne': 'coquille' means shell; coquille St-Jacques is the French name for scallops; and the mushrooms used in the duxelles surely refers to the celebrated *champignons de Paris*.

Many jokes have been made at the expense of this charming way with scallops, pointed directly at its ruff of piped mashed potato around the edge of the shell. Why this should be so, when one considers that most of us are fond of a nice fish pie, is a mystery. After all, this fluffy crusted border helps to hold in the sauce surrounding the scallop meat, adds a pleasing texture and, for heaven's sake, it pretties the dish.

Traditionally, the finishing touch to the surface of a classic St-Jacques is a coating of breadcrumbs and grated cheese – usually Parmesan. This is one of those rare occasions, along with Omelette Arnold Bennett (see page 28), where the combination of cheese with fish is, perhaps, no bad thing.

6 beautiful fresh scallops in the shell,
    cleaned by the fishmonger

——

For the béchamel sauce:
250 ml milk

½ small onion, peeled and chopped
1 bay leaf
4 black peppercorns
2 cloves
salt

25 g butter
25 g flour
freshly grated nutmeg
50 ml double cream

———

For the duxelles:
2 shallots, peeled and finely chopped
25 g butter
125 g white button mushrooms, thinly
    sliced

100 ml dry white wine
2 sprigs fresh thyme
a squeeze of lemon juice

———

1 tbsp freshly grated Parmesan
1 tbsp fresh breadcrumbs, made from a
    crust of stale bread
6 tbsp mashed potato (see page 88–9)

Take the given quantity of milk used in the following béchamel sauce recipe, and gently poach the scallops in it for 1 minute. Lift them out with a slotted spoon and allow them to cool on a plate.

Now make the béchamel sauce. Place the milk, onion, bay leaf, peppercorns, cloves and a pinch of salt in a saucepan. Simmer gently for a few minutes, turn off the heat, cover the pan and leave to infuse for 20 minutes. Meanwhile, melt the butter and stir in the flour, mixing to make a roux. Heat very gently for a couple of minutes to let the flour cook but without allowing the roux to colour. Strain the milk into the roux, whisking vigorously as the sauce comes to a simmer. Leave to cook over a very low heat, stirring every now and again for about 15 minutes. Season generously with nutmeg, add the cream and cook for a few more minutes until the sauce is unctuous and thickened. Cover the pan, to prevent a skin forming, and keep warm.

To make the duxelles, sweat the shallots in the butter until pale golden. Add the mushrooms and cook gently until completely wilted. Season with a little salt and pepper, pour in the wine, add the thyme and bring up to the boil. Simmer until almost all the wine has disappeared and the mixture is slightly sticky. Discard the thyme and squeeze in the lemon juice.

Spoon the duxelles into the bottom of four of the well-scrubbed scallop shells forming four little piles. Remove the pink corals from the scallops and dice them finely. Now slice each scallop into four and lay around the duxelles in a circle of six. Sprinkle over the diced coral.

the fifties hotel dining room 31

Pre-heat the oven to 425°F/220°C/gas mark 7 and also pre-heat an over-head grill. Ladle over the béchamel to blanket the scallops, sprinkle with the cheese and finally the breadcrumbs. Leave to cool and set in the fridge.

Meanwhile, fill a piping bag fitted with a star nozzle with the mashed potato. Carefully pipe it around the edge of each shell. Lay the shells on a baking tray and cook at the top of the oven for 20 minutes. Place under the grill for a few seconds to give a final gilding.

scampi with tartare sauce

Serves 4

Second to Prawn Cocktail, Scampi with Tartare Sauce is the most famously over-abused restaurant dish ever. Unlike Prawn Cocktail, which has a direct lineage to Escoffier, deep-fried scampi is derivative, perhaps singled out of a Fritto Misto (Italian mixed fried seafood) by some well-travelled chef. Made properly, however, it is a winning combination of sweet and juicy shellfish clad in a crisp, thin batter or breadcrumbs.

Its reputation has been ruined because some bright spark spotted its potential as a finger food and hit upon the idea of serving it up in a basket. Inevitably the batter jacket grew thicker and thicker, further compounded by a coating of bright orange breadcrumbs, the supposed scampi tail within this armour plating ending up the size of a pea.

These erosions to the original were, as is often the case, economy led. Scampi became – and remains – dangerously over-fished so our appetite for this tasty morsel led to the scampi tail of the original being replaced with reconstituted prawn scraps. Rumour has it that pieces of (once very cheap) monkfish, which has a similar texture though not, of course, flavour, were also used to simulate scampi. Typically, the home-made tartare sauce was also replaced – with unopenable individual sachets of a sticky, sweet gloop.

Note: Finding fresh scampi tails (also called langoustines or Dublin Bay prawns) is no easy thing. However, if you can locate them, the meat needs to be extracted from the shells, as you would peel a prawn. In good fishmongers and some of the better supermarkets, it is possible to find bags of frozen unbreaded scampi tails but they are nowhere near as good as the real thing. The obvious alternative would be to use shell-on king prawns, which are good, but are not the real McCoy.

For the tartare sauce:

1 quantity mayonnaise (see page 52)

1 dsp freshly chopped tarragon

1 tbsp freshly chopped parsley

1½ tbsp capers, drained, squeezed and chopped

1 tbsp gherkins, finely chopped

pepper

─────

oil for deep frying

generous bunch curly parsley, separated

into clumps, washed and thoroughly dried in a tea-towel

salt and pepper

500 g fresh shell-on scampi tails, shelled, or 400 g frozen tail meat, or shell-on king prawns, shelled

2 tbsp flour

2 small eggs, beaten

5–6 tbsp fresh white breadcrumbs

salt

lemon quarters

To make the tartare sauce, simply stir all the ingredients together. Heat the oil to 375°F/190°C (for those without a deep-fryer or thermometer, this is when a scrap of bread turns golden after a couple of seconds). Drop the parsley into the hot oil but BE CAREFUL! as fierce spluttering will ensue. Fry for about 30 seconds when it will have turned dark green. Drain well in the frying basket, turn on to a plate lined with kitchen paper and sprinkle with salt. Keep warm in a low oven.

Season the tails, then dip them first in flour, then egg and finally into the breadcrumbs. Drop in the scampi – possibly in two batches – and fry for no longer than two minutes, when they will be golden and crisp. Drain well on kitchen paper and pile on to a plate lined with a paper napkin. Sprinkle on the parsley and tuck in the lemon quarters. Serve the tartare sauce in pots for dipping.

sole véronique

Sole Véronique is another of the sadly tarnished restaurant classics that moved us to put together the recipes for this book in the first place. If memory prevails, this was one of the first lines in the repertoire of Alveston Kitchens, the Midlands-based firm who created a market in quick-frozen ready meals. They became known as boil-in-the-bag – such a winning description.

Fillets of Dover sole, gently braised in white wine, finely chopped shallots, a little lemon juice and cream, garnished with skinned and seeded grapes, should form the most delicate of fish dishes – a true example of a diminishing *haute cuisine*. Boiling already cooked fillets of mushy sole and tasteless grapes in a so-called cream sauce, all in a plastic bag, is possibly why a lot of people could never see the point of Sole Véronique.

For the fish stock:

3 shallots, peeled and sliced

100 g button mushrooms, sliced

25 g butter

200 ml dry white wine

the Dover sole bones, washed in cold water and drained

1 bay leaf

3 sprigs of fresh thyme

4–5 parsley stalks, chopped

6 peppercorns

a very little salt

2 large Dover soles, skinned and filleted by the fishmonger – ask him to keep the bones and chop them into small pieces

75 ml dry vermouth

300 ml double cream

squeeze of lemon juice

25–30 seedless white grapes, peeled and halved (sorry, but it really is worth doing and it makes the dish)

First make the fish stock. Sweat the shallots and mushrooms together in the butter until softened and not coloured. Pour in the white wine, add the fish bones, bay leaf, thyme, parsley stalks, peppercorns and salt. Bring gently to

sole
véronique

the boil, skimming off any scum that forms, then simmer uncovered for 20 minutes.

Pre-heat the oven to 350°F/180°C/gas mark 4. Meanwhile, using a rolling pin or meat bat, slightly flatten the sole fillets. Then take one, with the skin side innermost, fold each end over to the middle overlap and turn it over to reveal a neat-looking bundle. Repeat with the other fillets. Lay them in a lightly buttered oven dish and strain the fish stock over them through a fine sieve. Cover with foil and bake in the oven for 20 minutes.

Remove the fish from the cooking liquor and place on a warmed serving dish. Using the same foil, cover the fish loosely and keep warm in the oven, switched off and with the door ajar. Pour the liquor into the saucepan, add the vermouth, and boil hard to reduce it to approximately 6 tablespoons. Add the cream and lemon juice and gently reduce again, simmering until unctuous and with the consistency of thin custard. Tip in the grapes, warm through and pour over the fish.

Note: Sometimes there will be some residual juices from the fish after it has been kept warm in the oven. Check this just before the sauce is finally ready and if so, add these juices to the sauce.

chicken chasseur

Serves 4

Yet another classic that requires the Bareham–Hopkinson Stain Removal Service. Chicken, mushrooms and white wine never had it so bad – until now, that is.

8 plump chicken thighs	*6 shallots, peeled and chopped*
flour for dusting	*200 g button mushrooms, quartered*
salt and pepper	*400 ml dry white wine*
15 g butter	*4 sprigs thyme*
1 tbsp cooking oil	*1 bay leaf*

a squeeze of lemon juice

4 tomatoes, peeled, cored, de-seeded and
    diced

2 tbsp finely chopped flat-leaf parsley

Roll the chicken pieces in the flour and season generously with salt and pepper. Heat the butter and oil in a roomy, heavy-bottomed casserole dish – one of those oval Le Creuset pans would be ideal – and gently brown the chicken all over. Remove it from the pan and set it aside.

Add the shallots to the pan and sweat until golden, then put in the mushrooms. Cook for 5 minutes, stirring once or twice, pour in the wine and stir the mixture while it comes to the boil. Then return the chicken to the pan with the thyme and the bay leaf. Establish a gentle simmer, cover the pan and cook for 10 minutes. Remove the lid and cook for about 35 minutes until the sauce has reduced slightly and turned syrupy. Remove the thyme and bay leaf, add the lemon juice and adjust the seasoning with salt and pepper. Mix in the tomatoes and cook for 5 more minutes.

Stir in the parsley and serve.

chicken maryland

Serves 4

It seems that everyone of our generation to whom we have recently talked recalls the frankly weird Chicken Maryland with much affection – which made us wonder why it has not made more of an appearance on our increasingly eclectic restaurant menus. For when you think of crisply coated chicken joints (crisp-textured food is *numero uno* just now), fried bananas (fruity embellishments are bang on) and sweetcorn fritters (partnered with foie gras in the most chic establishments) as a combo, eclectic seems the description that immediately comes to mind.

However, Chicken Maryland remains as American as McDonald's: it is the luxury version of the most basic Southern Fried Chicken. Southern-states white-trash cooking has always been a touch weird to us Limeys, but it is based on sound principles – even if it's a bit high on the cholesterol count everything is fried in lard or hog fat.

8 chicken thighs, trimmed of messy bits of
    skin and fat
2 tbsp flour, seasoned with 2 tsp paprika, 1
    tsp black pepper and 1 tsp salt
2 small beaten eggs
100 g butter
75 ml sunflower or peanut oil
——

For the sweetcorn fritters:
100 g fresh sweetcorn, taken from fresh
    cobs, boiled in salted water until
    tender and drained
2 small eggs, separated

salt and pepper
1 tsp baking powder
50–75 g fresh white breadcrumbs
——

100 ml chicken stock (see page 47)
4 small bananas, peeled and sliced in half
    lengthways
50 g butter
a sprinkle of sugar
8 rashers thinly sliced streaky bacon
100 ml double cream
a squeeze of lemon juice
1 dsp chopped parsley

Dip the chicken thighs into the seasoned flour and then into the beaten egg. Shake off the excess egg, dip them into the flour again and lay them on kitchen paper. Take a deep frying pan large enough to hold all the chicken at once, with space to spare, and heat the butter and oil in it. Allow it to froth and put in the chicken pieces. Cook gently, making sure that the chicken continues to fry rather than letting it stew, which can easily happen if you are not diligent. The frying process will take around half an hour; turn the joints half-way through.

Meanwhile, mix together the sweetcorn, egg yolks and seasoning. Beat the egg whites until fluffy and gently fold them into the mixture. Add the baking powder and just enough breadcrumbs to form a thickish batter. Put to one side.

When the chicken is cooked, keep it warm in a low oven, suspended on a wire rack. Remove most of the oil from the chicken pan, including any stray crunchy bits, leaving just enough in which to fry the corn fritters (around 3–4 tablespoons). Drop tablespoons of the batter mixture into the fat and fry for a couple of minutes on each side until puffed and golden. Drain on kitchen paper and keep warm in the oven with the chicken.

Put the chicken stock on the heat and allow it to reduce by three-quarters.

Fry the bananas in the butter until golden, turning them regularly and sprinkling a little sugar on each side from time to time to aid their gilding.

Grill the bacon until crisp.

Keep both the bananas and the bacon warm too. (Although this may sound like cooking a big fry-up breakfast, it is the only way to go about making this rewarding dish!)

Add the cream to the reduced chicken stock and bring it back to the boil. Reduce until slightly thickened, add the lemon juice, check the seasoning and stir in the parsley.

Arrange the chicken on a big serving platter, together with the sweet-corn fritters, bananas and bacon. Spoon a little sauce over each chicken joint and serve the rest in a hot sauceboat. Tuck sprigs of curly parsley here and there, to brighten up what is essentially a beige dish.

mixed grill
Serves 2

Why anyone thought of doing a mixed grill as a restaurant dish is hard to understand for it is the most exacting of culinary operations. Assuming that one is going to go the whole hog, ingredients should include kidneys and liver (lamb's or, more luxuriously, calves'), a small piece of steak, a lamb chop, bacon rashers, sausage, grilled tomatoes and a fried egg. A slice of black pudding would also go down well.

However, the logistics of getting all these ingredients spot on can be a nightmare, even in the most efficient and well-staffed kitchen. Perhaps this is the reason rotten versions are so often encountered. But it is a perfect dish to cook at home, where there is all the time in the world to get it right, the ingredients carefully cooked in the right order, the meats allowed to rest in a warm oven and the all-important egg fried at the last minute.

2 nice thick lamb loin chops

salt and pepper

1–2 tbsp melted dripping or bacon fat

2 very small fillet steaks, cut from the tail
   end of the fillet

2 excellent quality pork sausages
   (Porkinson's are very good)

2 small tomatoes, halved

2 lamb's kidneys, split in half lengthways,
   cored

4 small rashers streaky bacon

2 small free-range eggs

2 sprigs curly parsley – the ubiquitous
   garnish

Pre-heat the oven to 400°F/200°C/gas mark 6, and pre-heat a stove-top ribbed grill.

Season the chops with salt and pepper (particularly with salt on the fatty edges) and brush them with melted dripping. Place them on the hot grill, fat side down, until they are crisp, then turn them on to their sides, cook for 1 minute on each and remove to a flat oven tray. Season the steaks, brush with dripping and grill them for 1 minute on each side. Put them beside the chops.

Take a heavy-bottomed frying pan that will also go in the oven and fry the sausages until they are golden all over. Now place the halved tomatoes beside them and season. Put the pan in the oven for 10 minutes, then put in the chops and steak alongside them, and continue cooking for a further 10 minutes.

Meanwhile, brush the kidneys with dripping and season. Lay them on the grill with the bacon. The kidneys only need to be coloured, which takes about half a minute on each side; the bacon, once crisp, can be kept warm in the oven. Add the kidneys to the tray with the steak and chops for the last 5 minutes of the cooking time.

Turn the oven down to its lowest setting, put the tomatoes and sausages on the tray with the kidneys, chops and steak, and use the frying pan to cook the eggs.

Divide everything between two hot plates, garnish with the sprig of parsley (on top of the tomato is a good place to put it) and eat at once with ketchup and freshly made English mustard.

gammon and pineapple

Serves 4

This is a period piece, if ever there was one, and its name conjures up images of an oval plate arranged with a thick slab of fibrous pink meat edged with a frill of fat (if the frill hadn't been nicked – as often happened – the gammon slice turned it into a gammon boat) topped with a couple of tinned pineapple rings. The inevitable accompaniment was chips, invariably made from extruded, reconstituted potato, and frozen peas. Tomato ketchup rather than English mustard was the favoured relish.

This is always going to be a controversial dish, however carefully the combination of gammon and pineapple is cooked, but there is no reason why tender, salty meat and fresh, sweet pineapple should not be as delicious as, say, duck with orange or roast pork and apple sauce. This is one dish that we have had to re-invent.

500 g piece of boneless gammon or shoulder

2 carrots, peeled and diced

2 small onions, peeled, each stuck with
    4 cloves

2 sticks celery, chopped

2 bay leaves

3–4 sprigs fresh thyme

12 peppercorns

1 large, ripe pineapple, skin removed

4 tbsp pure maple syrup

watercress

Place the gammon in a large pan and cover it with cold water. Bring it slowly to the boil, lift out the gammon and discard the water. Rinse the meat under cold running water and return it to the pan. Re-cover it with cold water and add the vegetables, herbs and peppercorns. Bring it to a simmer and gently cook for 1¼–1½ hours. The meat is ready when it is tender enough to be pierced right through with a skewer. Lift it out and leave it to cool on a plate.

Pre-heat an overhead grill. Remove the skin from the ham, but leave the layer of fat intact. Cut into eight 0.5 cm thick slices and snip the fatty edges, just into the meat, in a few places with a pair of scissors. Then lay it

gammon and pineapple

on a large flat baking tray. Now cut eight slices of pineapple in the same way, removing the core with a small biscuit cutter, and lay each piece on a slice of gammon. Using a pastry brush, generously paint the pineapple and exposed gammon with the maple syrup. Place the baking tray under the grill and leave it until richly glazed and burnished. Then slide the gammon and pineapple slices onto a hot oval platter and decorate with watercress.

tournedos rossini

Serves 2

It is very interesting to note how the times they are a-changing. For some strange reason, Tournedos Rossini lost all credibility some time around the beginning of the 1980s and was banished from all but the most 'inter-national-airport-hotel-gourmet-restaurant' type of *à la carte* menu.

It is, always has been and always will be a near perfect combination of ingredients that make up a Tournedos Rossini. It's rich man's food for sure: the neat tower of tender fillet steak, the rich disc of foie gras that sits on top, the syrupy Madeira sauce, the buttery crouton under the steak and the final thick slice of black, black truffle that crowns the dish. It is such a great looker, with its black on pink, glistening under a sheen of mahogany sauce, that it seems incomprehensible that it ever lost favour.

If you are lucky enough to live in an area where you can buy freshly prepared foie gras then do just that. Otherwise you're going to have to do your own; tinned block foie gras is not worth buying. You will need to start preparing it at least three days before you make the Tournedos Rossini. Clearly there is going to be far too much liver for this dish from the amount specified, so use the rest another time as a first course.

100 ml Madeira, less 1 dsp

2 tbsp meat glaze (see page 26–7)

½ tsp arrowroot, slaked in 1 dsp Madeira

2 circles bread, cut from a white loaf

2 × 150 g steaks from a well-hung fillet

2 slices foie gras (see page 44)

the fifties hotel dining room   43

First make the sauce. Put the Madeira in a small pan and reduce it by three-quarters. Add the meat glaze and allow it to melt into the Madeira. Stir the arrowroot mixture before adding it to the Madeira and meat glaze, then heating it through until it has thickened. Keep it warm.

You will notice that there is a fair amount of yellow fat from the foie gras in its cooking dish. Take a spoonful of this, melt it in a small frying pan and fry the croutons on both sides until they are golden brown. Lay them on kitchen paper to drain.

Heat a ribbed grill pan until it is very hot. Brush the steaks on each side with a little oil and season with salt and pepper. Place on the grill pan and cook for 1 minute; turn them through 90 degrees and cook for a further minute. Turn them over and repeat the process. Lower the heat and continue cooking for another 2 minutes on each side. This will give you a rare steak; cook for a few minutes longer for a medium steak. A well-done fillet steak is hardly worth eating.

To assemble, put a crouton in the middle of each hot plate and lay the steak on top. Warm the sauce through, whisking in a teaspoon of foie gras fat until the sauce is glossy. Cut two slices of foie gras from the terrine and trim them into a shape that will fit neatly on top of each steak. Pour over the sauce and serve immediately.

Note: If you happen to have a cooked black truffle lying around in the fridge (doesn't everyone?), then cut two slices from it and place on top of the foie gras before pouring over the sauce.

Foie gras

The following method of preparing foie gras comes from Michel Guérard's *Cuisine Gourmande*. It is so clearly descriptive (SH first learnt to do it some fifteen years ago from these instructions) for a job so fiddly that it would seem appropriate to pass it on. You may not have come across *quatre-épices* before, but it is easy to make: simply grind together 125 g white peppercorns, 10 g cloves, 30 g ground ginger, 35 g whole nutmeg.

1 fresh foie gras – around 600 g
½ tsp salt
¼ tsp white pepper, finely ground
nutmeg
a pinch of quatre-épices

½ tsp sugar
1 tbsp Madeira or medium-dry sherry
1 tbsp port
½ tbsp cognac or Armagnac

Day 1. When you buy fresh foie gras it is normally vacuum-packed in plastic. Allow it to come to room temperature. Then put it to soak for 1 hour in a basin of water at blood-heat. This cleans it as well as making it soft and easier to deal with. Drain the liver and, with your hands, separate the larger from the smaller lobe. Using a small sharp knife, cut open each lobe to reveal the network of veins inside. With the point of the knife, loosen each vein from the liver, working progressively towards the base of the lobe. Detach them by pulling them carefully away from the lobe, loosening them further with the knife if necessary. Very carefully, scrape away the greenish part, which may have been left by the gall-bladder and will have a bitter taste.

Arrange the two opened lobes in an earthenware dish, season with salt, pepper, nutmeg, *quatre-épices* and sugar, and moisten with the alcohols. Let the liver marinate for 12 hours in the fridge, turning it once or twice.

Day 2. Take the liver out of the fridge 1 hour before you want to start cooking it, and arrange the lobes as nearly as you can in their original shape. In a terrine, place first the large lobe, then the small one, and press them down firmly.

Pre-heat the oven to 300°F/150°C/gas mark 2. The oval earthenware dish in which the livers were marinated can be used as a bain-marie; wash it thoroughly and put in 2 cm water. Heat it to 158°F/70°C in the oven. Keeping the oven at the same temperature, place the terrine, without its lid, in the bain-marie. Cook for 40 minutes, during which time the temperature of the water in the bain-marie must on no account fall below or rise above 158°F/70°C. Keep checking with a thermometer.

Take the bain-marie and terrine out of the oven. Remove the terrine from the bain-marie, cover it with its lid and allow it to cool slowly, at room temperature, for 2–3 hours. It should then be kept in the refrigerator overnight, before serving.

Serves 4

braised celery

Along with the aforementioned Tournedos Rossini, this supremely good dish was also deemed unfashionable. It was nudged aside, making way for a welter of crunchy mange-tout, barely cooked infant carrots, and French beans all the way from Kenya.

Braised Celery is an elaborate preparation from the repertoire of Escoffier. Here, the celery has to be pared down to its heart, peeled (very important to peel celery when it is to be cooked as there is nothing worse than stringy bits stuck between the teeth), then slowly cooked in the oven with chicken stock and a few dried mushrooms for added flavour. Christmas lunch would be a fitting time to serve it.

200 ml hot chicken stock (see below), not too salty

10 g dried porcini mushrooms

50 g butter

4 celery hearts (the ones in packets from supermarkets are ideal), the outer stalks peeled

1 tbsp white wine vinegar

1 small clove garlic, bruised

50 ml Madeira or *medium sherry*

pinch celery salt

freshly milled white pepper

1 dsp parsley, chopped

Pre-heat the oven to 350°F/180°C/gas mark 4.

Pour the chicken stock over the dried porcini and leave them to soak for 15 minutes. Melt the butter in an ovenproof cast-iron dish. Gently stew the celery in the butter, colouring it lightly, then add the vinegar. Allow the liquid to bubble and reduce it to almost nothing, before adding the stock and swollen porcini. Bring it to the boil and slip in the clove of garlic, together with the Madeira or sherry and seasonings. Cover the dish with its lid or foil and place it in the oven for 40 minutes to 1 hour. Check from time to time that liquid is still there, turning down the heat and adding a little more stock if it starts to get at all dry. The finished look should be syrupy and golden brown. Conversely, if the dish looks a bit wet, remove it from the oven and reduce the liquid swiftly over an open flame. Discard the garlic clove before serving and sprinkle with parsley.

Chicken Stock (makes 1.75 litres)

900 g chicken wings or carcasses, roughly chopped

3 sticks celery, chopped

3 leeks, trimmed, cleaned and chopped

1 medium carrot, peeled and chopped

2 small onions, peeled and chopped

3 garlic cloves, crushed

4 ripe tomatoes, peeled and chopped

1 Knorr chicken stock cube

3 sprigs fresh thyme

2 bay leaves

8 black peppercorns

6 sprigs parsley

2.8 litres water

Put all the ingredients into a large pan, bring to a simmer, skim off any froth and cook at the merest blip for 3 hours. Pour the stock through a colander into a clean pan and leave it to drain for 15 minutes. Remove any fat from the surface with several sheets of absorbent kitchen paper, or chill overnight in the fridge and remove the disc of fat that will have formed. Strain the stock through a fine sieve and cool. It will keep in the fridge for a few days, or you could pour it into cartons to freeze.

Serves 4

carottes vichy

Poor old carrots, forever the British make-do vegetable; and looked upon only marginally better than boiled cabbage. When Carottes Vichy appeared on the fifties hotel-dining-room menu as a dish of glossy, glazed carrot slices garnished with finely chopped parsley, it was at least something different to do to carrots.

Carottes Vichy are so called because the area of the Bourbonnais in which the springs of this famous spa flourish is also famous for its root vegetables. To be totally authentic this dish should be made with a splash of Vichy water, although tap water would do just fine. It goes without saying that the dish is only worth making with the best-flavoured carrots, and to get the desired glaze, just-tender texture and the right balance of buttery sweetness, it needs careful cooking.

450 g carrots, peeled and finely sliced on the diagonal
150 ml Vichy water
salt

40 g butter
1 scant tsp sugar
1 tbsp very finely chopped parsley

Put the carrots in a pan and pour on the water; they should be just covered. Add a pinch of salt, the butter and sugar. Bring gently to the boil, stirring at first while the sugar dissolves, then boil more vigorously until the carrots are tender and the liquid reduced to a glossy, colourless glaze. Adjust the seasoning, stir in the parsley and serve.

creamed spinach

Serves 4

There are two schools of thought on Creamed Spinach: in the first, the spinach is cooked long and slow with butter until dark and slimy, and in the second the spinach is cooked briefly, then finely chopped and folded into a creamy béchamel sauce.

Although quite different in taste and texture, each is special in its own way. The former develops a natural 'creaminess' from the slow cooking and a deep and intense flavour not normally associated with fresh green leaf vegetables. The latter preparation, however, has a fresher taste – due to its quick cooking – and is then 'creamed' with the béchamel. We give recipes for both.

Creamed spinach 1

1.4 kg young spinach, washed and dried
150 g butter
salt and freshly ground white pepper

Stuff the spinach into a stainless steel or enamel saucepan and place it over a low to medium flame, pushing the leaves down and using a lid to hold it if necessary. After a few minutes, remove the lid and stir the spinach around to stop it catching on the bottom. Continue to cook until it has flopped evenly, smells aromatic and the colour is beginning to darken. Stew very gently until almost all the liquid has evaporated, allowing as long as 20 minutes.

Add the butter, a chunk at a time, letting each piece be absorbed before adding the next. Continue until it is all used up and the spinach is *fondant* and almost a purée. This operation should take about 15 minutes. Season with salt and pepper.

Creamed spinach 2

For the béchamel:

275 ml milk

2 cloves

1 small onion, peeled and chopped

salt

50 g butter

50 g flour

75 ml double cream

freshly grated nutmeg

pepper

————

1.4 kg spinach, washed, briefly blanched in salted boiling water, drained, refreshed in very cold running water, squeezed out with your hands until completely dry and finely chopped

Heat together the milk, cloves, onion and a little salt. Simmer for a few minutes, then cover and allow the flavour to mingle for about 30 minutes. In another pan, melt the butter, stir in the flour to make a roux, and cook it gently for a minute or two. Strain the milk into the roux and vigorously whisk them together until the sauce is smooth. Set it to cook on the lowest possible heat. You may think at this point that it is very thick but this is intentional so the sauce has enough body to hold the chopped spinach in suspension. Do not cover the pan. Stir the sauce from time to time with a wooden spoon and cook for about 15 minutes. Mix in the cream, nutmeg, pepper and chopped spinach thoroughly. Check the seasoning and heat through for a few minutes.

Serves 6

russian salad

In *Ma Cuisine*, Escoffier says, 'Take equal quantities of carrots, potatoes, French beans, peas, truffles, capers, gherkins, sliced and cooked mushrooms, lobster meat, and lean ham – all cut julienne fashion, and add some anchovy fillets. Cohere the whole with Mayonnaise sauce: dish, and decorate with some of the ingredients of the salad, together with beetroot and caviar.'

In some editions of the book the final garnish of caviar is not mentioned and tongue is also added as one of the earlier ingredients; chopped egg

should surely be included, and perhaps cauliflower, even. Ah well, over time recipes have a habit of undergoing metamorphoses, even instigated by the creators themselves.

The cookery bible, *Larousse Gastronomique*, adds sausage and includes the tongue, but omits the ham and caviar. Constance Spry's recipe seems legitimate – she also suggests including chicken – although, along with others, she deemed the trio of lobster, truffle and caviar a mite excessive. Who on earth would ever dream of including truffle and caviar in the same dish? Certainly lobster has a place here and, if throwing caution to the wind, a smear of caviar would not go amiss.

For the mayonnaise:
2 egg yolks
salt and freshly ground white pepper
1 tsp Dijon mustard
a squeeze of lemon juice
200 ml vegetable oil
1 tbsp white wine vinegar
75 ml light olive oil (pure, not virgin)

——

For the salad:
the first seven ingredients should be cut into thin strips (julienne)
75 g carrots, cooked
75 g potatoes, cooked
75 g French beans, cooked

75 g celery or celeriac, peeled and cooked
75 g ham, cooked
75 g salt tongue, cooked
6 gherkins
75 g peas, cooked
1 level tbsp small capers, drained and lightly squeezed dry
1 lobster, cooked, weighing approx. 450 g, shelled, flesh removed and diced
1 medium-sized beetroot, freshly cooked, cut into thin strips
2 large hard-boiled eggs, shelled and grated
1 level tbsp chopped chives
6 small tsp caviar (optional) or 6 anchovy fillets split lengthways – don't use both

First make the mayonnaise by whisking together the egg yolks, seasoning and mustard until thick. Squeeze in the lemon juice and start to add a few drops of the vegetable oil, whisking all the time, until the mixture is very thick and sticky. Now add a little of the vinegar to loosen it and carry on adding the oil, a little faster now, in a very thin stream. Once the mixture starts to thicken again, add a little more vinegar and then revert to the oil, and so on, finishing the mayonnaise with the olive oil. Check the seasoning and add any extra drops of vinegar if necessary: this mayonnaise should not be too bland.

In a large bowl, gently stir together the first ten salad ingredients with enough of the mayonnaise for the mixture to cohere loosely (you may have some mayonnaise left over, but it will always get eaten). Divide it between six shallow bowls or small soup plates, making neat piles. Scatter strips of beetroot around the edges (mixing in the beetroot earlier will cause unsightly pink bleeding) and sprinkle with some of the grated egg and chives. If you are using caviar, spoon it into the centre of each pile; if not, criss-cross the top of the salad with the anchovy. Serve with thinly buttered, crisp hot toast.

english salad

Serves 4

These days, when we are used to making salads from a wide choice of leaves and think nothing of cooked – or raw – vegetable salads, it is hard to imagine that right up until the early seventies, the English would quite happily put up with salad made from limp lettuce, sliced cooked beetroot, sliced unskinned cucumber, quartered tomatoes, quartered hard-boiled egg and, perhaps, a few spring onions. It wasn't 'dressed' with vinaigrette – most people didn't know what that was – but was served with a bottle of Heinz salad cream. This was poured over individual portions at the table and salad was unthinkable without it.

The best version of English Salad was invariably made at home from the heart of a just-dug lettuce, just-pulled onions and just-picked tomatoes and cucumber. If the beetroot didn't come from the garden or allotment, it was carried home from the greengrocer, just cooked and often still warm, wrapped in newspaper. It was in the fifties hotel dining room – and elsewhere – that its awful reputation was compounded. Here it languished for hours in a warm kitchen before it was eaten, until those water-logged, bruised outer lettuce leaves had wilted, the cucumber slices curled at the edges and the beetroot begun to bleed into the egg. What a pity. It is high time the English Salad was revived and given the respect it surely deserves. Here's how to do it properly.

For the salad cream:
6 hard-boiled eggs, separated; the yolks
    sieved into a bowl, the whites coarsely
    chopped
2 tsp sugar
salt and cayenne pepper
2 rounded tsp dry English mustard
1½ tbsp tarragon vinegar
1 tbsp fresh tarragon, coarsely chopped
275 ml double cream

———

For the salad:
2–3 Little Gem lettuces, or hearts of Cos
    lettuce, separated into leaves, washed
    and dried
6 small, ripe tomatoes, peeled and
    quartered

12 slender, spanking fresh spring onions,
    trimmed and left whole
12 radishes, washed, halved and put into
    ice-cold water for 30 minutes, to crisp
4 large eggs, placed in cold water, brought
    to the boil and cooked for 5 minutes
    exactly, refreshed under cold running
    water for 3 minutes, peeled and cut
    into quarters
12 small new potatoes, boiled with a sprig
    of mint, halved and added to the salad
    while still warm (optional)
4 small beetroot, peeled and sliced
½ cucumber, peeled and not too thinly
    sliced

To make the dressing, whisk together the egg yolks, sugar, seasoning, mustard and vinegar. Add the tarragon and cream and mix thoroughly.

Arrange the ingredients for the salad in a large shallow dish to give a natural look. Sprinkle over the chopped egg whites and spoon over the cream dressing in dribbles and swirls. Serve straight away.

peach melba

Serves 4

The great impromptu dessert. Legend has it that Dame Nellie Melba, the legendary Australian soprano, lent her name to this concoction, which had been thrown together by Escoffier in a fit of passionate expression, to celebrate the singer's performance in Wagner's *Lohengrin*.

Escoffier's original recipe is simple and to the point: 'Poach the peaches in vanilla-flavoured syrup. Dish them in a timbale upon a layer of vanilla ice-cream, and coat them with a raspberry purée' (*The Savoy Food and Drink Book*). This bears little relation to the nasty tinned peaches with synthetic ice-cream and raspberry jam that was most likely to feature on the fifties hotel-dining-room menu.

2 fresh ripe peaches (preferably white ones)
175 g caster sugar
275 ml white wine

175 g fresh raspberries
vanilla ice cream (see page 59)

Fill a large pan with water and bring it to the boil. Drop in the peaches and blanch them for 10 seconds. Lift them out and allow them to cool. Peel off their skins, halve them and set them aside on a plate. Put the sugar and wine in a saucepan that will take the peach halves tightly. Bring it to the boil and simmer for 5 minutes. Drop in the peach halves and poach gently for 10 minutes. Leave them to cool in the syrup.

Lift out the peach halves and put them on a plate. Reduce the syrup by half. Whizz the raspberries in a blender, with the syrup, then pass the purée through a fine sieve into a bowl and chill.

Take four chilled glass dishes, put a scoop of vanilla ice-cream in the base of each, perch a peach half on top and generously cover with the raspberry purée.

fresh fruit salad

There's no place in this book for the sort of fruit salad that contains chunks of green-skinned apple and pithy pieces of orange. You know the sort of thing; it's a standard sight on the dessert trolley, usually in a cut-glass bowl, complete, perhaps, with a few tinned lime-green grapes and strange pink cherries. Sometimes a flaccid strawberry or a furry slice of banana might still be lurking about after too many top-ups. The syrup is watery, the sad fruit almost floating in it and there is always that bashed-up old silver ladle stuck in the bowl, day in, day out. That was the usual standard of fruit salad on the fifties hotel-dining-room trolley.

pears

grapes – peeled is luxuriously good but
    they must be pipped

melon

fresh lychees

strawberries

raspberries

passionfruit pulp

mango

pineapple

peaches

banana, but it should be added just before
      serving

All the above fruits can be used in any way you wish but too many varieties together is gilding the lily. As a general rule, 'less is more' is the maxim when it comes to making fresh fruit salads. For example, the combination of melon, pear and grapes is a winner; so too – though perhaps in a more exotic fashion – is the trio of mango, lychee and passionfruit, especially when embellished with chopped stem ginger.

A small amount of home-made sugar syrup is always nice to have around when you are thinking about a fresh fruit salad. It can be made in a trice and, once prepared, can be stored in the fridge in a screw-top jar.

Sugar syrup

300 g granulated sugar
200 ml water
100 ml fruity white wine (Alsatian
  Gewürztraminer is good here,
  particularly if you are going to
  include lychees, as its fragrance echoes
  their flavour)

3 cardamom pods
2 small bay leaves, torn
1 blade of mace
2 cloves
4–5 strips pithless lemon peel

Whisk all the ingredients together in a non-reactive saucepan and set it over a low heat. Bring it to a simmer and cook gently for 5 minutes. Cool, strain and store. Use as needed.

meringue glacé and hot chocolate sauce

Serves 4

Do you remember those whiter than white meringues which had a plaster of Paris texture that, when pressured with a fork, shot off on to an adjoining table, which, for some unaccountable reason, was often occupied by a lady of a certain age, usually with a blue-rinsed concrete hair-do and no sense of humour? Well, you'll be glad to hear that the results of the following recipe bear no resemblance to those chalky numbers.

These meringues turn out a pale coffee colour with a slightly crackled surface, and are chewy-soft and sticky within. When they are partnered with really good vanilla ice cream and a welter of chocolate sauce, the result is so seductive that it would probably cause that crabby old lady to reach over, whip it out from under your nose and tuck into it herself.

Make the meringues as squiffy as you please, using a tablespoon to form their shape. Or, if you are into nozzles and piping bags, this therapeutic

meringue glacé and hot chocolate sauce

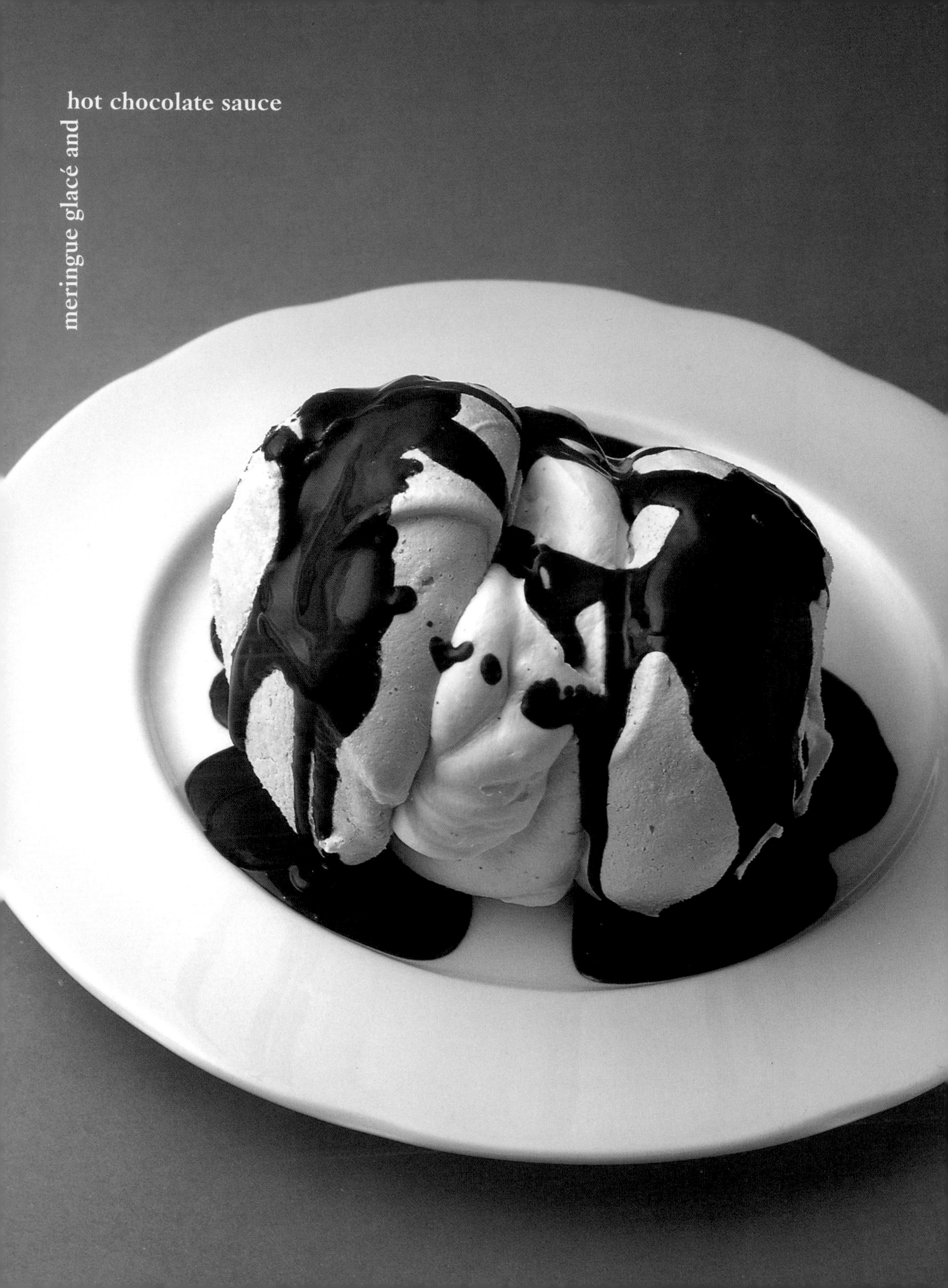

squeezing and oozing may be the direction you might like to pursue. The old-fashioned method of preparing a non-stick baking tray, which we give below, is still the best – whatever people say about baking parchment.

For the vanilla ice cream:
600 ml milk
1 vanilla pod, split lengthways
7 egg yolks
250 g caster sugar
750 ml double cream

——

For the meringue:
4 egg whites
a pinch of salt
225 g caster sugar
a little butter, softened

plain flour

——

For the chocolate sauce (which will make plenty):
200 ml whipping cream
150 g best quality bitter chocolate, broken into small pieces
40 g unsalted butter

——

For the whipped cream:
400 ml double cream
2 tbsp caster sugar

First make the ice cream. Heat together the milk and vanilla pod, and whisk vigorously as it comes to the boil, bashing and scraping the vanilla pod so that its seeds flow into the milk. Cover, remove from the heat and allow to infuse for 30 minutes. Beat together the egg yolks and sugar, pour the flavoured milk on to this mixture (including the vanilla pod) and mix well. Return the custard to a saucepan over a gentle heat, and stir constantly but gently until the sauce has the consistency of thin cream. Whisk vigorously at this point to homogenize and then strain into a cold bowl. Add the cream and leave to cool. When cold, turn into an ice-cream maker and freeze according to the manufacturer's instructions.

Pre-heat the oven to 275°F/140°C/gas mark 1.

Using a scrupulously clean mixing bowl, whip the egg whites with the salt until they are soft but hold a peak. Beat in half the sugar, a tablespoon at a time, until the mixture is glossy and stiff. Now fold in the rest of the sugar, using a large spatula, with authoritative scoops rather than mimsy movements: the air must be contained, but the sugar must be mixed in thoroughly.

Lightly grease a flat baking tray with the butter and sift over a spoonful of flour. Shake around a bit to disperse it in an even coating and then tap off the excess (the kitchen sink is the most contained area and affords the least mess).

Spoon out the meringue mixture in whichever form suits your mood and bake it in the oven for about 1½ hours. The point at which the meringue reaches a pale coffee hue is about right. Leave it to cool for a few minutes before removing it from the baking tray. Store in an air-tight container until ready for use.

To make the chocolate sauce, warm together the cream and chocolate over a very low heat. Once melted and completely smooth, whisk in the butter until the mixture is smooth and glossy. Keep it warm.

Whip the double cream with the caster sugar until thick.

To assemble the meringues, put a scoop of ice-cream on each well-chilled plate. Take two meringues and sandwich the ice-cream between their flat sides, gently squashing them together. Spoon or pipe the cream over the gap and hand the warm chocolate sauce separately.

Serves 6

trifle

Everyone loves a home-made Trifle. Decent sherry should be used or even some rich Marsala. Sponge cake is usual, but you can also use ratafias, macaroons or Italian amaretti biscuits which we prefer. We don't recommend using shop-bought sponge fingers, as their flavouring often smacks of the cheaper end of the bottled vanilla extract spectrum.

The next three layers of the Trifle may invoke strong argument, but in our opinion they should be composed of home-made custard, very, very good quality jam and lightly sweetened, whipped cream. Jelly is an abomination; fresh fruit is too tart and seems somehow alien to the confection.

The custard, however, is probably the most important layer of all. It must be made with eggs, vanilla, sugar and cream and be thick enough to set in a layer. No glacé cherries or hundreds and thousands, please, just angelica and silver balls. This is classy Trifle.

200 ml whipping cream

200 ml milk

½ vanilla pod, split lengthways

12 amaretti biscuits, or *160 g of*
macaroons or *ratafias*

5 tbsp sweet sherry

1 tbsp cognac

4 tbsp raspberry jam, warmed

4 egg yolks

1 egg

1 rounded tbsp caster sugar

275 ml double cream

1 tbsp icing sugar

angelica and silver balls to decorate

Scald the whipping cream and milk with the vanilla pod, give it a quick whisk to disperse the vanilla seeds. Cover the pan and leave the mixture to infuse. Lay the biscuits in the base of a deep glass dish. Spoon over the sherry and cognac, leave it to soak in, and then spoon over the warmed jam. Beat the egg yolks and the egg with the sugar. Strain the vanilla-flavoured cream over the eggs and mix together. Pour back into the cream pan and cook very gently over a low flame until the custard has thickened; this is like making Crème Brulée (see pages 244–5), so be careful of over-cooking. However, be brave, because if the custard is not cooked enough, it will not set. You can safely take it as far as the odd blip, and when this happens, whisk vigorously to disperse the hot spots. Strain it immediately over the soaked biscuits and put the dish in the fridge for at least 4 hours, or overnight.

Whip the double cream with the icing sugar until it is just holding peaks. Pile on top of the jam in a swirly way and decorate with the angelica and silver balls. Chill once more until ready to eat.

'Here is the food of the Reform Club – grouse à la Rob Roy, ribs of beef à la George IV, and most famous of all, lamb chops Reform – breaded chops served with a brown sauce, flavoured with pickles and redcurrant jelly. Like other foreign chefs in England, Soyer had to adapt his style to the tastes of his masters, who preferred square meals with plenty of meat and game, culminating in that quintessentially English dish, the savoury.'

Anne Willan, *Great Cooks and Their Recipes*, 1977

The dishes in this chapter seem to have a timeless appeal. Some, such as Fish Cakes, Cod with Parsley Sauce, and Bread and Butter Pudding, are currently enjoying a revival in popularity. You can glance at the menu in any number of contemporary London restaurants and see dishes like these. What is interesting, however, is that they are now being carefully made, from scratch, to a particular recipe, accurately cooked and expertly sauced. They will taste good, too – sometimes sublimely so.

We often visit this sort of restaurant with the sole intention of tucking into something such as the speciality fish cake. It seems quite normal now, and so much so that fish cakes have become an essential listing in many of the best places. However, it was not always thus. No, the fish cake was eaten at a gentleman's club because, well . . . just because it was there. The food in these institutions was never a reason for securing membership – 'Good heavens, George, you must join Bertles, the toad-in-the-hole they serve there is the best in London!' Quite the contrary, in fact. It was all a bit vulgar to be too concerned about what you ate. Yet the gentleman's club is renowned for its menus.

The most important element of the food served in all these places is its familiarity. Colonel Hufton-Tufton doesn't want Johnny Foreigner mucked-about grub. Generally speaking, when he is away from his wife and other female influences, a chap is looking for comfort food.

Perhaps it was all Nanny's fault. Take cauliflower cheese, for example. That is the sort of thing she might have knocked up in the back nursery. And it would also have been Nanny who fiddled with a fish cake for tea.

Downstairs, in the main kitchen, Cook was probably rustling up fish pie for the staff supper, fashioned, inevitably, from the same leftover cod and boiled potatoes as the fish cake. So it is entirely understandable why a simple fish cake or pie, macaroni or cauliflower cheese are some of the most cherished dishes to be found in the dining room of the gentleman's club.

Other favourites might have been on the weekly dinner rota at school – shepherd's pie, for example, was probably Monday. Amongst all these British stalwarts (most of which involve mashed potato and/or cheese sauce), however, there are several notable exceptions. As well as all that stodge and gravy, some of the grander, older club menus show a nod towards times past and a continental influence: Oeufs en Gelée, for example, and classically made consommé – or 'clear soup'. Of these, the most infamous is Lamb Cutlets Reform, created by the great Alexis Soyer, chef at the Reform Club in Pall Mall from 1837 to 1850. In his day, he was regarded as the greatest chef to have visited these shores and it has been said that, then, the food at the Reform Club was the finest London had ever seen.

According to André Simon, in his *Dictionary of Gastronomy*, Lamb Cutlets Reform consists of breaded cutlets, garnished with thin strips of carrot, truffles, ham, slivered whites of hard-boiled eggs, served with a piquant *poivrade* sauce. Strips of gherkin and beetroot are not uncommon additions to this – frankly – quite awful dish. One would rather cherish a memory of the extraordinary things that Soyer did to truffles and ortolans (not to mention his invention of the stock cube).

There are also the seasonal specialities, such as asparagus, gulls' eggs and game, and also, of course, dishes that reflect past colonial glories, the days of Empire, the Raj: we're talking mulligatawny and kedgeree here. And rice pudding, maybe because the men of the mess missed it so. In fact, the officers' mess was simply the gentleman's club at one remove and a second home to the Great British Pudding – the sort that involves suet and needs plenty of lubrication from custard.

Last, but by no means least, for this is an area of excellence, the gentleman's club is one of the few places to offer a full list of that quintessentially

British speciality, the savoury, with their quaint and sometimes perplexing names like Angels and Devils on Horseback and Scotch Woodcock.

It is 'The Club', then, where overgrown schoolboys go to be looked after (nannied) to play hide and seek from their wives (truancy and deceit) and to have a chin-wag with dear old Bertie (get pissed). Well, we are, of course, talking Wodehouse and Wooster here. With this in mind, 'the fairer sex' now having a stilettoed heel most firmly in the door, perhaps the food will start to lose its school-dinner look and a few more sophisticated dishes will nudge out the old retainers. Conceivably, in years to come – and perhaps it is already happening – there will be a complete turn-around. The clubbers will be eating an elegant little warm salad and the groovers in the bars and restaurants will play merry hell if they don't get their fish-cake fix.

asparagus
Serves 4

There cannot be many ingredients more seasonally British than fresh asparagus. Its season is mercifully short so does not allow room for foreign impostors to sully this brief early summer treat. Of course, this is how we would like to imagine the asparagus season but in these days of extended seasons with the importation of inferior spears from all over the world, our six-week gorge, which should be keenly observed, sadly no longer is.

Members of the Club would like their asparagus to be straightforward – none of those witty little tortured piles here, thank you very much. And thank heavens for that. This is one ingredient that needs simple, subtle treatment and surprisingly swift cooking.

There are four traditional sauces. Melted butter is possibly the first choice for hot asparagus; vinaigrette with cold. Hollandaise sauce is for gourmet members. However, the recipe for cooked salad cream, although probably unheard-of in the Club, would almost certainly have been in the repertoire of the country-house cook – and deserves a place here too. It is

the gentleman's club   65

a sadly forgotten, old-fashioned English salad dressing, but once Joe Heinz thought to bottle the stuff, and turned it into one of his 57 Varieties, it became for ever Salad Cream. The comparison ends there.

24 asparagus spears
salt

Trim the asparagus and, if necessary, peel the ends. Bring a very large pan of water to the boil, add salt, and when the water is bubbling vigorously, throw in the asparagus. Boil rapidly until the spears are tender to the point of a knife – check after 3 minutes. Drain them carefully and pile them on to a serving dish. Hand the chosen sauce separately.

Vinaigrette (makes about 350 ml)

pinch caster sugar

salt and pepper

2 tbsp red wine vinegar

2 tbsp smooth Dijon mustard

4 tbsp tepid water

150 ml groundnut or other flavourless oil

150 ml olive oil

Put the sugar, salt, pepper, vinegar and mustard in a blender. Add the water and blend together. With the motor running, pour in the oils, one after the other, in a thin stream until homogenized. You are aiming for the consistency of pouring cream so if it seems too thick, thin it with a little more water.

Hollandaise (makes about 450 ml)

225 g butter

3 egg yolks

juice of lemon

salt and freshly ground white pepper

Melt the butter in a small pan and leave it to settle. Remove the frothy scum with a spoon, then carefully pour off the clear butter into a bowl, leaving behind the milky residue. Keep it warm. This is now clarified butter.

Take either a small stainless steel pan and set it over a thread of heat, or a bowl and put it over a pan of barely simmering water. Put in the egg yolks and whisk them with a splash of water until they are thick. Add the clarified butter in a thin stream, whisking all the time until the sauce has the consistency of mayonnaise. Add the lemon juice and season with salt and pepper. Serve warm.

Lemon Butter (makes about 350 ml)

juice of 1 large lemon
2 tablespoons water

125 g butter cut into small chunks
salt and pepper

Place the lemon juice and water in a small pan and heat gently until slightly syrupy and reduced by about two-thirds. Lower the heat to a mere thread and whisk in the butter, bit by bit, until it is thoroughly amalgamated and the texture of the sauce turns creamy. Season, adding a final squeeze of fresh lemon, and serve warm.

Cooked Salad Cream (makes about 400 ml)

5 tbsp milk
2 dsp sugar
1 tsp dry mustard powder, mixed with a
    little milk

1 tsp salt
soft butter, size of a walnut
2 eggs, well beaten
3 tbsp malt vinegar

Place the milk, sugar, mustard, salt and butter in a basin. Stand over a saucepan of just simmering water. Stirring well, add the eggs carefully. Pour the vinegar into the bowl in which the egg were beaten, making sure that any of the remaining egg is rinsed with vinegar. Add this to the sauce mixture and stir it constantly until it has thickened. Serve cold. Any left over can be stored in a screw-top jar in the fridge, where it will keep well for a week or so.

the gentleman's club   67

Serves 4

oeufs en gelée

Oeufs en Gelée Stendhal has been on the menu at the Connaught Hotel in London's Mayfair since time immemorial. Here, a perfectly soft-boiled egg is suspended in a rich jelly with strips of ham, tongue, gherkin and truffle (possibly tarragon too). It is truly *haute cuisine* of the highest calibre. Yet however delicious this sophisticated version surely is, its origins are simpler.

'Eggs in Jelly' – for that, prosaically, is what it is – smacks of garish buffet work or those *salons culinaires* (chef's showtime) where everything is covered in shining aspic, decorated to the nines with flower shapes made from vegetables and cut-out bits of mock truffle. Underneath, though, all these exhibits taste like cardboard – a triumph of design over content.

Carefully made, the simple Oeuf en Gelée is really nothing more than a peeled soft-boiled egg set in a clear amber jelly, which should be made from a good consommé, prepared with a pig's trotter so that it gels, and plenty of tarragon. It is a beautiful and harmonious trio. The familiar flavour of eggs with tarragon, trembling jelly and runny yolk combine to make this charming hors-d'oeuvre a class act, particularly when it is eaten with crisp Melba toast.

For the jelly:
500 g chicken wings
1 pig's trotter, split lengthways by the
    butcher
1 litre water
250 ml dry white wine
1 onion, peeled and chopped
1 carrot, peeled and chopped
2 sticks celery, chopped
3 cloves
3–4 thyme sprigs

2 bay leaves
½ chicken stock cube
——

For the clarification:
200 g raw skinless chicken meat
2 egg whites
1 onion, peeled and chopped
1 carrot, peeled and chopped
4–5 sprigs fresh tarragon
75 ml dry sherry
——

oeufs en
gelée

8 small eggs
12 tarragon leaves
1½ tbsp tarragon vinegar

For the Melba toast:
6 slices white bread – any sort will do

Put all the ingredients for the jelly in a large pan and bring it gently to the boil, removing any scum as it forms. Cook at the gentlest simmer for 3 hours. Drain it through a large colander set over another large pan. Pick out the pieces of chicken and also the by now misshapen trotters – if you can be bothered, the meat from these can be used to make delicious brawn-type potted meat, set with some leftover jelly.

After draining, and once the stock has settled, lift off any fat from the surface with several sheets of kitchen paper and allow it to cool completely.

Put all the ingredients for the clarification into the bowl of a food processor. Work them to a purée and, with your hands, mulch it into the liquid. Set the stock pan over a low heat and allow it very slowly to come to a simmer.

When the first signs of froth and scum appear, and the clarification mulch begins to solidify, a trickle of stock will appear through it. Allow this to happen in several places, then turn off the heat. Leave it for a few minutes, then repeat the process twice more. Finally, allow the mixture to simmer over the lowest possible heat for 40 minutes. Switch off the heat and let it settle for 10 minutes.

Wet an old tea-towel or square of muslin and use it to line a sieve. Suspend the sieve over a roomy bowl or pan and, with a ladle, pull back the crust and carefully pour the now clarified stock from underneath. Leave to drip and under no circumstances consider pressing the solid matter as this will cloud the jelly.

Cover the eggs with cold water and bring them to the boil. Cook for exactly 3 minutes then refresh under cold running water for 3 minutes. Shell them carefully – the yolks will be soft – and roll them over a tea-towel to dry them thoroughly: you do not want any excess water around once the eggs are in the jelly as this may prevent the jelly setting.

Choose a glass dish (or individual ones) that will take the eggs neatly, but with enough space to allow the jelly, once it is poured over, to cover them completely. Add the tarragon leaves and vinegar to the jelly and pour it over the eggs. Put the dish into the fridge to set for at least 3 hours.

To make the Melba toast, first light an overhead grill. Toast the bread in a toaster until *just* starting to colour. Remove it and quickly cut off the crusts. Then, while the toast is still hot, slide a sharp serrated knife horizontally through the middle to make two even thinner slices. It is important that all the toast is hot when you perform this trick as once it has cooled it doesn't work. Place under the grill, cut sides uppermost, and watch carefully as they curl, which will be a matter of seconds. They *do* burn easily.

consommé

Serves 6–8

Properly made, a Consommé is one of the finest elixirs. At its worst, it is a thin, watery liquid masquerading as 'beef tea', for sustaining invalids and to comfort the elderly. Most often made from beef or chicken, the production of a true Consommé is one of the most magical of cooking tricks. What initially looks so unpromising – a pan of murky stock – gently transforms itself into a limpid liquid of absolute clarity with a resultant savour that beggars belief.

For the stock:

2 tbsp vegetable oil

900 g oxtail, cut into slices and trimmed of almost all its fat

900 g chicken wings, chopped up a bit

1 large carrot, peeled and chopped

2 sticks celery, chopped

2 leeks, trimmed, sliced and washed

2 garlic cloves, bashed

2 large onions, peeled and chopped

300 g flat black mushrooms, chopped

a few black peppercorns

1 chicken stock cube

2 sprigs fresh thyme

2 bay leaves

½ bottle dry white wine

3 litres water

———

8 fresh tomatoes, chopped

2 beaten egg whites

100 g lean beef, minced

6 tbsp Madeira or Amontillado sherry

Heat the oil until it is smoking in a large, heavy-bottomed stew-pot. Put in the oxtail and fry it until it is a rich, deep brown. Remove it to a plate and reserve it. Add the chicken wings to the pot, fry for a couple of minutes until golden, then remove them and set them aside. Now tip up the pan, spoon out almost all the fat and add the next six ingredients. Stir them around for a few minutes until they are lightly coloured and add the peppercorns, stock cube and herbs. Pour in the wine and water, bring it to the boil, skim off any scum that appears on the surface and leave the mixture to simmer for 2 hours on a very low heat, or even uncovered in the oven (275°F/140°C/gas mark 1).

Strain the stock through a roomy colander and allow it to drip for 10 minutes or so. Then pass it through a damp, folded sheet of muslin into a large clean stainless steel or enamelled pan. Remove any fat from the surface with several sheets of kitchen paper, or put the stock to chill overnight in the fridge, where the fat will set to a hard disc that can be whipped off in a trice.

Now simmer the stock and reduce it gently, once again skimming the surface of any scum that may form. When the stock measures about 2 litres (this does not have to be dead accurate), remove it from the heat and leave it to cool until lukewarm.

In a roomy bowl, mulch together the tomatoes, egg whites and beef with your hands. Tip it into the stock and gently stir them together. Put the pan on to a moderate heat and return it to the merest simmer for 40 minutes. During this time, make sure that the mulched mixture does not stick to the bottom; feel around with a wooden spoon, perhaps, but try not to disturb the minced meat crust that forms on the surface too much.

This is the clarification process: the egg whites and the natural albumen in the meat are collecting into themselves all the impurities in the stock while the meat and tomatoes are flavouring it. As the stock gently blips through the crust it should be a clear golden colour. After the 40 minutes is up, make a hole in the crust with a spoon and lift some of it away. Now, using a ladle, transfer the Consommé that lies beneath through a muslin-lined sieve into a clean pan. Collect all you can. Check the seasoning and add the Madeira or sherry. The Consommé is now ready to serve. Discard the crust; it has done its work.

mulligatawny

The exact origin of this beguiling, gently curried soup is unclear. There are certainly enough versions of it and it has long been claimed as their own by both British and Indian cooks; even Eliza Acton recorded a recipe for it as long ago as the mid-nineteenth century. It was perhaps something that the Indian cook-wallah assumed that the unitiated British palate could cope with, as it was both a little spicy and also the ever-familiar 'soup'.

Should it be thick or thin, or should it, perhaps, approach a dish of sloppy dhal? Who knows? The various versions over which we have pondered include ingredients such as chopped apple, carrots, sweet chutney, sultanas and rice in the stock, sometimes all at once. Even in the officers' mess this might have been thought of as being closer to a curried rice pudding than a savoury soup.

Mulligatawny is essentially a spiced meat stock and the following recipe is, we think, a winner, even though some might think it wildly inauthentic. The most important thing is that a decent Mulligatawny – as with any soup – should be made with fine ingredients, using a proper meat stock, and be sensitively spiced so that it excites rather than bullies the tastebuds.

2 onions, peeled and finely chopped

2 small leeks, trimmed, cleaned and thinly
    sliced

50 g butter

1 tsp turmeric

1 tsp cumin

1 dsp garam masala

salt

400 g can chopped tomatoes

1.4 litres well-flavoured chicken or lamb
    stock

75 g red lentils

5–6 curry leaves or 2 bay leaves

4 cardamom pods, lightly crushed

zest of 1 lime

juice of 2 limes

½ tsp dried chilli flakes

200 g coconut milk (½ can)

2 tbsp fresh coriander, chopped

4 garlic cloves, peeled, sliced and cooked
    gently in 50 g butter until golden

Gently fry the onions and leeks in the butter until pale golden. Add the turmeric, cumin, garam masala and salt, and cook slowly for 3–4 minutes. Tip in the tomatoes and cook again for 5 minutes. Pour in the stock and stir in the lentils, curry or bay leaves, cardamom and lime zest. Simmer gently for 30 minutes, skimming off any scum that rises and stirring occasionally until the lentils are tender and have somewhat thickened the soup. Now stir in the lime juice, chilli flakes and coconut milk. Simmer for a further 5 minutes. Finally, stir in the chopped coriander and the garlic, including the butter in which it was cooked, and serve.

potted shrimps

Serves 6

Of all the dishes on the menu at, say, Boodles', White's or the Reform Club, Potted Shrimps remains, above all, cherished by the members. But we like to put things in little pots – pâté, fish paste, ham – don't we? It is so soothing to spread something buttery and savoury on hot toast.

Think, for a moment, of that slim, crisp slice of toast, with its crumbly, melting, shrimpy butter, those tiny pink tails, which are irritatingly always falling off, doused with the essential squeeze of lemon. Add a dusting of cayenne pepper, a crisp lettuce leaf and a glass of chilled Chablis, and you have one of the most pleasing assemblies imaginable.

There is a niggling anxiety for the future of the Potted Shrimp. What is going to happen when a new generation of shrimp peelers decide that this is just not the sort of job they wish to do for the rest of their lives? We have relied on their mothers, grandmothers and great-grandmothers to perform this tedious task for as long as we can remember. Will the potted shrimp become a rarefied treat, only available to nimble-fingered folk who are prepared to peel their own?

350 g peeled brown shrimps
175 g best quality unsalted butter
salt
1 tsp cayenne pepper

1 tsp ground mace
a generous scraping of nutmeg
juice of 1 lemon

In a large frying pan, melt 100 g of the butter. When it is hot but not frothing, tip in the shrimps and stir them around until they are heated through. Sprinkle with a little salt and stir in the spices. Squeeze in the lemon juice and remove the pan from the heat.

Take six ramekins and divide the buttery shrimps between them, making sure you collect an amount of liquid and butter equal to the quantity of shrimps in each pot. Gently press down with the back of a spoon so that the shrimps are as submerged as possible. Place in the fridge until cold. Then melt the remaining 75 g butter and spoon over the tops to seal. Return the ramekins to the fridge where they will be fine stored for up to four days.

Serves 6–8

cauliflower cheese

Of all the soundly British nursery favourites in our collection – and there are many – none is more familiar or more abused than Cauliflower Cheese.

It is its very familiarity – a bit like mashed potato or a traditional British breakfast – that results in it being regarded as an 'ordinary' dish which gets thrown together in a make-do way with little regard for getting it right.

Cauliflower is a member of the cabbage family, and Mark Twain was right when he said that cauliflower is nothing but cabbage with a college education. Originally, this distinctive-looking white vegetable with its frame of bright green leaves was bred for its flowers and it is these knobbly curd-like clusters that present a problem for the cook: how to end up with tender stalks and stems without cooking the 'flowers' to a pulp. It is for this reason that cauliflower is usually broken into florets before it is cooked and why the sight of a whole cooked cauliflower is rare.

We give two recipes for Cauliflower Cheese. One is the familiar divide-up-the-florets-pour-on-the-sauce-sprinkle-it-with-breadcrumbs-to-get-a-crunchy-topping, while the other is a more elegant dish when the

cauliflower cheese

cauliflower is served whole – white-on-white – with its creamy cheese sauce clinging like the icing on a sweet bun.

Perhaps because of its colour, early recipes recommended cooking cauliflower in milk; it would seem likely that the Victorians added cheese to disguise cauliflower's cabbagey flavour. The cheese sauce given here is assertive but not overpowering, and is made with tasty Lancashire cheese and a well-seasoned béchamel.

570 ml milk
1 small onion, peeled and chopped
1 bay leaf
2 cloves
salt
50 g butter
50 g flour
freshly grated nutmeg
100 g Lancashire cheese, grated

1 medium-large head cauliflower, leaves
*   trimmed and core removed*
salt and white pepper
——

For Crusted Cauliflower Cheese:
ingredients as above, plus a knob of butter,
*   and 50 g grated Lancashire cheese*
*   mixed with 25 g fresh breadcrumbs*

First make the sauce by placing the milk, onion, bay leaf, cloves and a pinch of salt in a saucepan. Simmer it gently for a few minutes, then turn off the heat, cover the pan and leave it to infuse for 15 minutes. Meanwhile, melt the butter and stir in the flour, mixing to make a roux. Cook very gently for a couple of minutes to let the flour cook but without allowing the roux to colour. Strain the infused milk into the roux, and bring the sauce to a simmer, whisking vigorously. Leave it to cook over a very low heat, stirring every now and again, for about 15 minutes. Season generously with nutmeg, stir in the grated cheese and cook for a few more minutes until the cheese has melted and the sauce is thick and creamy. Cover the pan, to prevent a skin forming, and keep it warm.

Meanwhile, fill a saucepan that can hold the cauliflower snugly with 7.5 cm water. Bring the water to the boil, add salt, and lower the trimmed cauliflower into the water. Put on the lid and boil hard – the stalks and leaves will be in the water and the florets will steam – for about 20 minutes, check with a skewer after 15 minutes, until the cauliflower is tender. Remove it carefully to a colander and drain *very* thoroughly.

To serve, place the cauliflower on a hot serving dish and pour over the hot cheese sauce.

For the Crusted Cauliflower Cheese, make the cheese sauce as above. Pre-heat the oven to 400°F/200°C/gas mark 6. Remove the cauliflower's outer stalks, and divide the cauliflower into equal-sized florets. Drop them into a large pan of vigorously boiling salted water and boil for 4 minutes. Drain thoroughly in a colander, saving a little of the cooking water to dilute the cheese sauce if it seems too thick. Use some of the butter to smear a suitable oven-proof dish. Put in the florets, cover with the cheese sauce, sprinkle over the breadcrumbs and reserved cheese, dot with butter and bake in the oven for about 25 minutes or until golden, crusted and bubbling around the edges.

cod with anchovy and egg sauce, or parsley sauce

Serves 4

Contrary to most uses of anchovy in cooking – where it is most likely to be found partnering continental meat, egg or vegetable dishes – here, in this traditional English sauce, the nuance of preserved and salted fish, for once, seems to be bang on and is surprisingly fitting when served with a plainly cooked piece of cod.

This style of sauce is probably seen as unfashionable just now: flour-thickened, no little wine and fish-stock reductions, not 'mounted' with butter or finished with tomato concassé. There is nothing wrong with these delicately fashioned restaurant fishy lotions but, conversely, this pale pinky white sauce with flecks of yellow egg and green parsley marries so well with those big flakes of fish, one wonders why it is not given the status it deserves.

Parsley sauce, on the other hand, *is* having a renaissance. Vibrant green flooded plates of it have increasingly been seen once more on restaurant tables everywhere. But, as far as we are concerned, this, our most cherished of fish sauces, has never been far away.

450 ml milk

1 small onion, peeled and chopped

2 cloves

1 sprig thyme

1 bay leaf

freshly grated nutmeg

little salt and pepper

40 g butter

25 g flour

100 ml double cream

½ tbsp anchovy essence

4 anchovy fillets, finely chopped

2 hard-boiled eggs, peeled and grated

2 tbsp chopped parsley

*4 × 150 g pieces unskinned cod or
        haddock fillet*

squeeze of lemon

Heat together the first seven ingredients and bring to a simmer. Cook very gently for 5 minutes, switch off the heat, put a lid on the pan and leave the mixture to infuse for 30 minutes.

Melt the butter in another pan, preferably with a thick base, and stir in the flour to make a roux. Strain the flavoured milk onto this, stirring constantly, and bring to a simmer. If you have one of those useful heat-diffuser pads, set the pan on this and allow to cook gently over a thread of heat, for about 20 minutes. Add the cream, anchovy essence and fillets, grated egg and parsley. Check for seasoning.

Steam or poach the cod fillets for about 5–7 minutes until just firm. Remove the skin and lay the fish on kitchen paper to drain away any excess cooking water. Just before you pour the sauce over the fish, stir in the lemon juice.

Parsley sauce

1 large bunch flat-leaf parsley, leaves only

75 g butter

175 ml whipping cream

salt and pepper

Tip the parsley leaves into a pan of boiling water, cook for 30 seconds, drain in a colander and rinse thoroughly under very cold water. Squeeze dry in a tea-towel. Boil together the butter, cream and seasoning, put it into a blender with the parsley and purée until the mixture is smooth and bright green. Do not overblend for fear of the sauce separating and always make sure the cream and butter are really hot.

Serves 4

fish cakes

Fish Cakes are quite often the consequence of leftover cooked fish and are none the worse for that. They can be made with almost any fish but the British tradition is with cod, sometimes haddock and, after a salmon with mayonnaise, a 'luxury' version such as the following recipe. This is ironic as cod is now more expensive than farmed salmon.

There is no secret to making a good Fish Cake but the best ones favour a high proportion of fish, lightly crushed (rather than mashed) potato, a generous seasoning and lots of chopped parsley. To get the desirable softly crusted surface, the Fish Cakes are dipped in flour before frying; we prefer not to have to do battle with the more usual armour of egg and breadcrumbs.

250 g potatoes, cooked and crushed with a fork	*grated rind of 1 lemon*
	8 tbsp double cream
250 g salmon, cooked and flaked	*2 egg yolks*
1 small bunch spring onions, trimmed and finely chopped	*1 tbsp anchovy essence*
	flour
4 hard-boiled eggs, shelled and chopped	*25 g butter*
2 tbsp chopped parsley	*2–3 tbsp oil*

In a large bowl, carefully but thoroughly mix together the potatoes, salmon, spring onions, hard-boiled eggs, parsley and lemon rind with your hands.

Gently whisk the cream, egg yolks and anchovy essence, then carefully fold it into the potato/salmon mixture, but don't over-mix for fear of curdling the cream. Form into 8 cakes with neat sides and flat tops, then chill for about 30 minutes until firm. Roll each one evenly in the flour.

If you have a large enough frying pan, cook all the Fish Cakes in one go, otherwise do them in two batches of four. Heat together the butter and oil until it is foaming and carefully put in the Fish Cakes. Turn down the heat a little and fry for 4–5 minutes on each side until golden brown and well crusted. Serve the Fish Cakes with Tartare Sauce or Hollandaise Sauce (see pages 33 and 66–7).

fish pie   *Serves 6*

Fish Pie has a place in the heart of every English person. No fancy flavours here, just a creamy sauce with chunks of familiar white fish under a crusted surface of nicely browned mashed potato. Well, that's how a good one should be. However, all too often this quintessential comfort dish fails to live up to our rose-tinted memories. Too many school versions, invariably made with meagre quantities of inferior fish that swam in a thin, watery sauce with hard, dry, lumpy potato, have put countless people off fish pie for life.

What it *should* be is a handsome, generous dish, shopped for particularly and cooked with attention to detail. This might seem an obvious thing to say and, of course, it applies to all cooking, but, in the case of poor old fish pie, it is too often thought of as a lowly dish and just gets, how shall we say, chucked together.

The best fish to use is cod or haddock (perhaps a mixture of fresh and smoked haddock) with a few prawns added for texture as well as flavour. There must be no bones – these will ruin the most carefully made fish pie – and the béchamel sauce must be thoroughly cooked to avoid a floury taste.

350 g cooked whole prawns, in shell

700 ml milk

1 medium onion, chopped

1 bay leaf

salt

500 g cod fillet

500 g smoked haddock

1 large bunch flat-leaf parsley, leaves only,
    chopped

75 g butter

75 g flour

white pepper

———

For the mash:

1.5 kg floury potatoes, peeled

75 g butter

25 ml milk

Remove the shells from the prawns and place them in a pan with the milk, onion, bay leaf and a pinch of salt. Bring to the boil, establish a simmer and cook for 10 minutes. Turn off the heat, cover the pan and leave it for 15 minutes.

Lay the fish, skin side down, in a single layer in a shallow pan or heat-proof dish. Strain over the milk and simmer, turning the fish after 5 minutes, and cook until it is lightly but not completely cooked. Lift on to a plate. When it is cool enough to handle, ease the fish off the skin in chunks, taking care to remove any bones, and place in a large bowl with the shelled prawns and chopped parsley.

Make a sauce for the fish by melting the butter in a small pan. Stir in the flour, adding the fishy milk, whisking as you pour, to make a smooth thick sauce. Simmer very gently for 15 minutes, using, if possible, a heat-diffuser pad, and season with salt and plenty of white pepper. Pour the sauce over the fish. Carefully mix everything together, transfer the mixture to a suitable pie dish and put it to cool and firm up in the fridge so that when the mashed potato is piled on top it doesn't sink into a sloppy mixture.

Pre-heat the oven to 350°F/180°C/gas mark 4. Cook the potatoes in salted water, drain well and mash with the butter and milk.

When the fish mixture is good and firm, spoon over the mash, decorating with a fork if you wish, and bake in the oven for 30–40 minutes or until the top is nicely crusted and golden.

kedgeree

Serves 4

Basmati rice is the thing to use for this Anglo-Indian dish, which was once a feature of the country-house breakfast sideboard. These days, it has slipped out of fashion, but it makes occasional appearances on enlightened menus, and is also regarded by some as a spirited way of making a little bit of fish go a long way; perfect for Saturday lunch.

A freshly made Kedgeree is a satisfying dish and to be authentic should be made with smoked haddock. The current fashion for using fresh salmon in a Kedgeree seems a nonsense, as it is the smoky flavour combined with curry spices that makes the dish. We offer two versions: each is completely different and both are slightly controversial. In one the fish and rice are bound together in a sloppy, lightly curried sauce and the top is decorated with hard-boiled eggs. The other is closer to a pilau, with the fish baked in large chunks within the spiced rice, and then flaked and forked into a loose pile together with chopped egg, chillies and fresh coriander.

Wet Kedgeree

300 g basmati rice, rinsed

450 g smoked haddock (the thicker the piece the better)

1 bay leaf

4 black peppercorns

350 ml milk

40 g butter

1 large onion, peeled and finely sliced

1 level tbsp curry powder

1 level tbsp flour

100 ml single cream

salt and pepper

juice of ½ a small lemon

small bunch chives, finely snipped

3 hard boiled eggs, peeled and quartered lengthways

a few sprigs of flat-leaf parsley

Place the rice in a saucepan with 450 ml water. Bring it to the boil, cover and then turn down to the merest thread of heat, preferably on a heat diffuser pad. Allow it to cook for 15 minutes without removing the lid, then turn off the heat and leave it to steam for 5 minutes before peeping. The rice should be light and fluffy, having absorbed all the water. Tip it out on to a tray and fluff it up with a fork so that it dries out.

Meanwhile, place the smoked haddock in a shallow pan, add the bay leaf and peppercorns and pour over the milk. Simmer gently for 10 minutes and remove the fish to a plate. Peel the skin off the fish, flake it into big chunks, taking care to remove all bones, and keep warm.

Melt the butter in a small pan and cook the onion over a gentle heat until limp and golden. Stir in the curry powder and flour and continue stirring for a minute or two to allow them to cook. Strain the milk into the mixture, stirring vigorously as the sauce comes to a simmer. Leave to cook over a very low heat, stirring every now and again, for about 15 minutes. Add the cream and bring the sauce back to a simmer. Adjust the seasoning with salt, pepper and lemon juice. Stir in the chives and flaked fish.

Have ready a warmed serving bowl. Tip the rice into the bowl and gently fold the sauce into the rice. Decorate the top with slices of boiled egg and sprigs of parsley.

Dry Kedgeree

50 g butter

1 tbsp curry powder

300 g basmati rice, rinsed and drained

150 g sweetcorn kernels, preferably cut
    from a freshly cooked cob

450 ml chicken stock

½ tsp saffron threads

2 bay leaves

450 g smoked haddock, skinned and any
    small bones removed (the thicker the
    piece the better)

2 large mild green chillies, de-seeded and
    finely chopped

salt

15 g butter

2 medium eggs, beaten

4 spring onions, trimmed and thinly sliced

1 heaped tbsp chopped fresh coriander

1 lemon, cut into quarters

Pre-heat the oven to 350°F/180°C/gas mark 4.

dry kedgeree

In a shallow, lidded ovenproof pan, melt the butter and put in the curry powder. Allow to sizzle very gently to cook the spice, then add the rice and sweetcorn and fry very gently, turning them in the spiced butter until well coated. Pour in the stock, saffron and bay leaves and bring it to a simmer. Slip in the smoked haddock, burying it in the rice. Put on the lid, slide the pan into the oven and bake for 15 minutes.

Meanwhile, mix the chillies and salt to taste into the beaten egg. Melt the butter in a non-stick frying pan and pour in the egg. Allow it to set over a low heat, effectively making a flat omelette. Once set, flip over and cook the other side; each side of the omelette should be pale golden. Tip onto a chopping board, allow it to cool slightly and then cut into ribbons with a sharp knife.

Now remove the rice and fish from the oven. *Do not remove the lid* for 10 minutes. Remove the lid and, with two forks, lift and separate the rice and at the same time flake the smoked haddock. Quickly mix in the omelette, spring onions and coriander. Serve immediately from the dish. Hand the lemon separately to squeeze over at the last minute.

Serves 4

macaroni cheese

Everybody loves Macaroni Cheese and it is a dish which stays with us all through our lives. There is very little to get wrong here but a few pointers will help to make this familiar yet sometimes disappointing dish into superior comfort food.

Macaroni Cheese gets its name from the tiny curls of tubular pasta called *macaroni* but it becomes a better dish when made with *penne* because the cheese sauce is able to flow inside this larger-sized pasta. As almost all the joy of eating Macaroni Cheese comes from its creamy sauce, it is worth going to town on the seasoning and investing in an assertively flavoured cheese; an occasion to splash out on good mature Cheddar or Lancashire – *not* a time to make do with a plastic pack of plastic cheese.

Purists will wish for no further embellishment to this nursery favourite but it is pleasing to add silky-soft onion or leeks to the mixture. Instead of the more usual unpeeled slices of tomato that pretty the top of a Macaroni Cheese, whole roasted tomatoes served alongside it are much nicer.

For the cheese sauce:
400 ml milk
1 bay leaf
salt and pepper
25 g butter
25 g flour
1 tbsp English mustard powder
100 g mature Cheddar or Lancashire,
    grated
150 ml double cream
small bunch of chives, snipped

freshly grated nutmeg
————
350 g penne
a large knob of butter
1 large onion, sliced, or *2 medium leeks,*
    white and pale green parts only,
    trimmed, thickly sliced and washed
4 tbsp freshly grated Parmesan
4 tomatoes, halved horizontally
a little melted butter

Heat together the milk, bay leaf, salt and pepper, and simmer for 5 minutes. Remove the pan from the heat, cover it and leave the mixture to infuse for 30 minutes. Melt the butter and add the flour to make a roux. Stir in the mustard and strain in the milk. Whisk thoroughly as it comes to the boil and simmer gently for 10 minutes. Stir in the cheese and heat through until it melts. Add the cream and chives, and season with nutmeg.

Pre-heat the oven to 400°F/200°C/gas mark 6. Cook the pasta for 8 minutes in boiling salted water, and drain thoroughly. Meanwhile melt the knob of butter in a spacious pan and cook the onion, or leeks, over a gentle heat until softened.

Mix the pasta, onion, or leeks, and sauce together and pour into a shallow baking dish. Scatter over the Parmesan. Also, brush the tomatoes with a little melted butter, season well and arrange in a separate dish. Cook both in the oven for 20–30 minutes until the macaroni is blistered and golden and the tomatoes are puffed up and scorched in places.

the gentleman's club   87

Serves 4

shepherd's pie

Frankly, there has always been a great deal of pointless discussion over whether Shepherd's Pie is made with lamb or beef. It would seem clear, that as a shepherd looks after sheep, then his pie should be made from that animal. The other dish using meat and mashed potato, which is made from beef, is curiously called Cottage Pie (heaven knows why), and, more often than not, the beef is minced up from a leftover roast joint. The resultant texture is somewhat pasty, but that seems traditional.

There is no reason why a Shepherd's Pie cannot also be made from a cooked lamb joint but it turns out better and juicier when made from raw minced meat. Incidentally, the addition of tomato ketchup in the mince is *de rigueur* in our school, as is an excessive amount of butter in the mash.

2 tbsp dripping or lard

1 large onion, chopped

1 celery heart, finely chopped

3 medium carrots, grated

1 bay leaf

leaves from 4 sprigs of thyme

salt and black pepper

750 g good quality minced lamb

1 level tbsp flour

2 tbsp tomato ketchup

1 dsp anchovy essence

150 ml water

For the mash:

1.5 kg floury potatoes, peeled, cut into even-sized pieces, and rinsed

25 ml milk

100 g butter

black pepper

freshly grated nutmeg

extra butter

Heat most of the dripping in a heavy casserole and fry the onion over a medium heat for a few minutes. Add the celery, carrot, bay leaf and thyme, season with a little salt and pepper, cook until the vegetables are tender and transfer them to a plate. Add the remaining dripping to the pan and briskly fry the meat, stirring until it changes colour. Sprinkle over the flour, stirring it in thoroughly, add the ketchup, anchovy essence and then the water. Cook for a few minutes and then return the vegetables to the pan. Leave to simmer for 30–45 minutes until thick and nicely amalgamated. Adjust the seasoning. Remove the pan from the heat, tip the contents into a suitable shallow earthenware dish and leave to cool.

Boil the potatoes until they are tender. Drain them and mash them with the milk and butter to make a fluffy but firm mash. Season with black pepper and nutmeg. Spoon the mashed potatoes over the cooled minced meat, fork up the potato and dot with butter.

Pre-heat the oven to 360°F/180°C/gas mark 4. Bake the pie for 30 minutes until the top is golden and crusted and the meat is beginning to bubble up around the edge.

toad-in-the-hole *Serves 2*

In her book *Classic British Dishes* Marguerite Patten gives a recipe for luxury Toad-in-the-Hole in which the ingredients almost constitute a complete mixed grill buried in batter: lamb's kidneys, bacon, lamb cutlets and the traditional sausage. Other references mention leftover cooked meat from a joint and another recipe insists that just chops or cutlets were the original idea. However, the mention of Toad-in-the-Hole to most people simply means sausages cooked in a big dish of crusted Yorkshire pudding.

A couple of controversial ideas for improving a good toad – and making it much tastier – are: add sage to the batter and coat the sausages with tomato ketchup before submerging them. However, in this instance, the sausages must be skinned or the ketchup just slides off. This is just an idea, you understand; the die-hard traditionalists among you might feel apoplectic even considering such a notion.

It is also well worth searching out really good sausages if you want to eat really good Toad-in-the-Hole.

8 thick pork sausages – the best you can
buy – skinned

4 tbsp Heinz tomato ketchup

2 small eggs

100 g plain flour

100 ml milk

4–5 sage leaves, chopped

salt and plenty of pepper

75 ml fizzy mineral water (not in the
original recipe, but the bubbles help to
lighten the pudding)

3 tbsp beef dripping or bacon fat

Put the sausages into a dish and spoon over the ketchup, rolling them in it until well coated.

Pre-heat the oven to 425°F/220°C/gas mark 7.

Put the eggs into a mixing bowl (or use an electric hand whisk; the more you whisk, the lighter the pudding) and beat until they are really thick. Add a little of the flour and then some of the milk to loosen the batter. Alternate these two ingredients until they are used up, and beat until smooth. Season, and then mix in the water. Leave the batter to rest for 15 minutes.

Take a heavy, preferably cast-iron roasting dish (one that will sit happily on a naked flame as well as being suitable for the oven – an oval Le Creuset, 35 cm long, 25 cm wide and 5 cm deep, is ideal), place on a high flame and heat the chosen fat until it is smoking. Pour in all the batter and immediately arrange the ketchup-smeared sausages in it. Put the pan in the centre of the oven and bake for about 30 minutes until puffed, crisp and a rich golden brown. Serve without delay, with extra ketchup if desired. Not the sort of dish that requires the accompaniment of a nicely dressed green salad.

Serves 4

treacle tart

There is a tendency towards fancy nonsense when it comes to making a Treacle Tart – ground nuts in the pastry, lemon zest in the breadcrumbs and a pointless pastry lattice on top. All you need is fresh breadcrumbs made from slightly stale bread, a blind-baked shortcrust pastry case, more golden syrup than you thought possible, and a generous squeeze of lemon juice. This is what makes the best Treacle Tart.

To achieve the required slightly gooey yet firm texture for the filling, the breadcrumbs must be loosely but generously loaded into the pastry case, which should be warm to help settle the golden syrup. A tang of acidity from the lemon provides the perfect counterbalance to all this sweetness. It is wonderful served warm with clotted cream but for those with a very sweet tooth – us included – there is also something rather special about home-made custard or vanilla ice cream.

200 g plain flour

a pinch of salt

75 g cold butter, cut into pieces

2–3 tbsp cold water

175 g fresh white breadcrumbs

7–8 tbsp golden syrup

juice of ½ a lemon

Pre-heat the oven to 400°F/200°C/gas mark 6.

Stand the tin of golden syrup in a pan of boiling water (this just makes it easier to pour).

Sift the flour into a large mixing bowl with the salt. Add the butter and quickly rub it into the flour until the mixture resembles heavy bread-crumbs. Add the water, a little at a time, and use a knife to stir it up into a clump. Knead it a couple of times, pat into a ball, cover and set aside for 30 minutes.

Flour a work surface and roll the pastry until you can cut a circle to fit a 25.5 cm tart tin. Wrap the dough round the rolling pin and loosely drape it over the tin, lifting the edge of the dough with one hand and pressing it into the base and up the side of the dish with the other hand; this prevents shrinkage. Trim off the excess dough and use scraps to plug any tears or cracks. Loosely cover with a large sheet of foil and fill with pastry beans or rice. Cook in the middle of the oven for 10 minutes. Remove the foil, lower the oven temperature to 350°F/180°C/gas mark 4, return the tart to a lower shelf and cook for a further 5 minutes.

Tip the breadcrumbs into the hot tart case – they should come almost to the edge of the pastry – and spoon over the golden syrup, working from the outside in. Allow the syrup to sink down and saturate the bread – you don't want any pools of syrup remaining but, equally, you don't want blonde patches – and then squeeze over the lemon juice. Cook in the middle of the oven for 25–30 minutes until the filling has set and turned a light toffee colour. Allow the tart to cool for 5 minutes before serving.

Serves 4–5

rice pudding

There would be an outcry, we suspect, if Rice Pudding with strawberry jam were to be removed from the menu of the gentleman's club. This is a favourite dish from nursery and school days, and epitomizes what is meant by a nursery pudding: something bland, milky, filling and sweet. The sweetness, in this instance, comes from that spoonful of runny strawberry jam, which has to be eked out to last the bowlful.

The British way of making Rice Pudding is to cook what we call pudding rice (round grain) in slightly sweetened vanilla-flavoured creamy milk. This is baked very slowly in the oven until the rice swells, its starchy content thickening the reducing milk. It is ready when most of the liquid has been absorbed and the pudding takes on a wobbly, almost jelly-like look. The ultimate treat for many rice-pudding lovers is the skin that forms across the top of the pudding, looking like a thin, delicate pale golden tarpaulin.

50 g butter
75 g caster sugar
100 g round grain rice
1 litre milk

1 vanilla pod, split lengthways
150 ml double cream
a pinch of salt

Pre-heat the oven to 275°F/140°C/gas mark 1. Melt the butter in a flameproof casserole and add the sugar. Stir it around and heat gently until it is straw-coloured and gooey. Add the rice and continue stirring until it looks puffy, pale golden and syrup-sticky. Add the milk, which will seethe, with the rice/butter/sugar mixture setting into lumps. Fear not. Feel around with a wooden spoon and disperse these lumps because as the milk heats it will dissolve them. Add the vanilla pod, squashing it around a bit so that it releases its little black seeds. Now add the cream and salt and bring it to the simmer. Place in the oven for 3–3½ hours or until the pudding is just starting to set but still slightly liquid-looking in the centre; as it cools, it will finish cooking in its own heat. Serve lukewarm or cold but not hot from the oven, as milk puddings have little flavour if served piping hot.

spotted dick and custard   *Serves 6*

This traditional British pudding proved an elusive creature when it came to investigating its history. One source mentioned that it might have also been called 'Spotted Dog'. Maybe this was its original name and the dog was called Dick. Who knows? It would seem we had a national habit for giving daft names to puddings: Whim-Wham, Sussex Pond, Apple Hat, Plum Duff and other loopy nomenclature too silly to mention.

But whatever its provenance, a Spotted Dick remains a well-loved favourite with children and adults alike. This currant-spotted, canary-yellow sponge slowly steams away giving off wafts of sweet fruity scents, so beguiling that one is tempted to get in there long before the pudding has finished cooking.

Custard is a must here, but we also think that some warmed golden syrup trickled over each serving makes it doubly gorgeous.

The following recipe comes from Sara Paston-Williams' book *Traditional Puddings*, published for the National Trust in 1983. She uses butter instead of suet, pointing out that it makes for a lighter pudding. However, if you wish to use suet, then go ahead, as it *does* give a more authentic density to the pudding.

spotted dick and custard

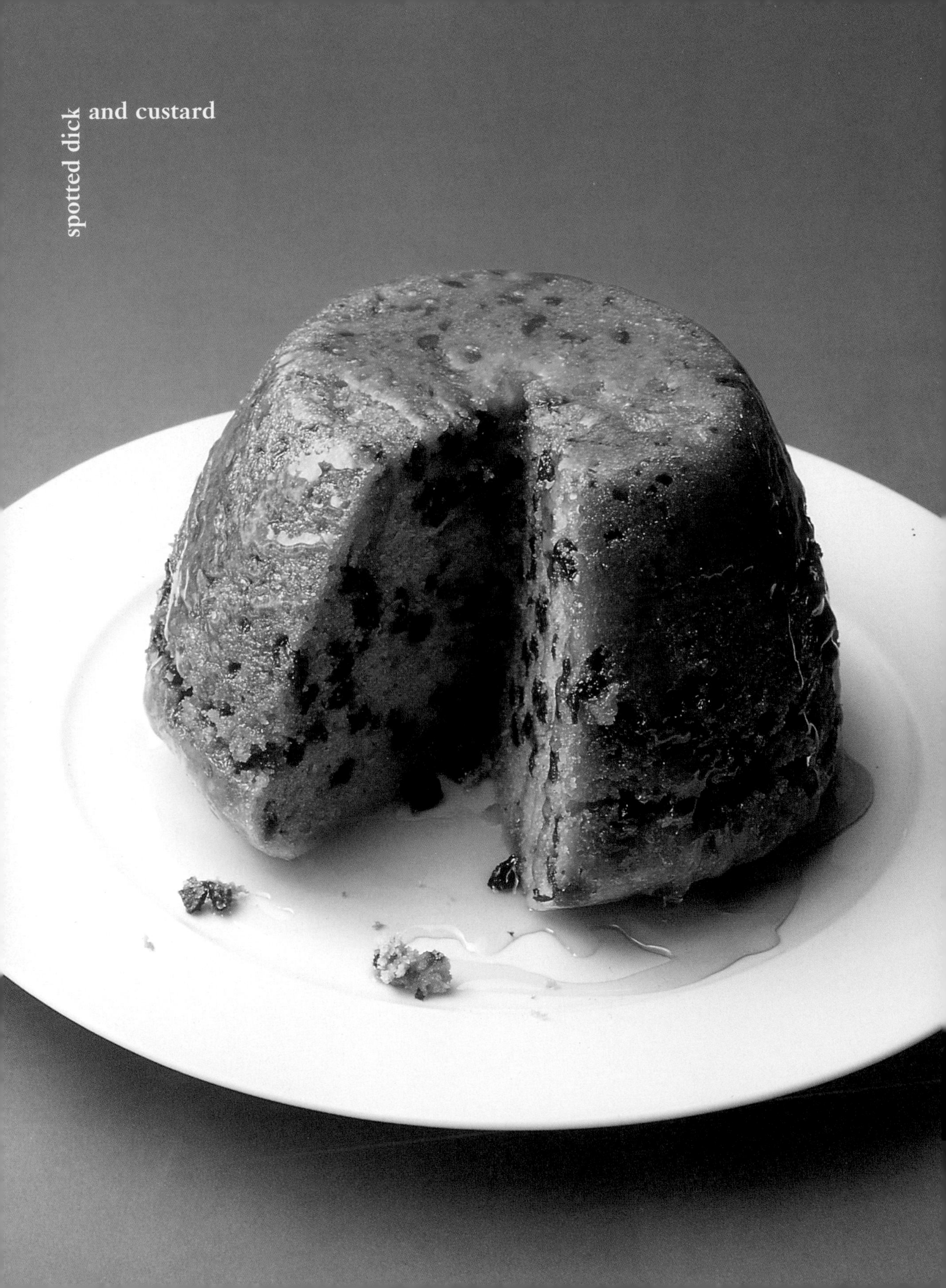

225 g self-raising flour
a pinch of salt
125 g butter or suet
2 heaped tbsp caster sugar

175 g currants
2 eggs
1–2 tbsp milk

Butter well a 750 ml pudding basin. Sieve the flour and salt into a bowl. Rub in the butter or suet and stir in the sugar and currants. Beat the eggs, add them to the bowl and mix until smooth. Then add enough milk to give a dropping consistency. Pour the mixture into the buttered basin, cover it with buttered kitchen foil, making a pleat across the centre to allow the pudding to rise. Tie securely with string and steam for 1½–2 hours (nearer 2 if you are using suet) or until well risen and firm.

Turn out on to a warmed serving dish and serve with custard and some warmed golden syrup.

Custard

275 ml milk
½ vanilla pod, split lengthways
4 egg yolks

50 g caster sugar
75 ml double cream

Heat the milk with the vanilla pod in a heavy-bottomed saucepan. Remove from the stove and whisk for a few seconds to release the vanilla seeds into the milk. Leave it to infuse for 10 minutes and remove the vanilla pod (wash it and keep for re-use). Briefly beat together the egg yolks and sugar and strain the warm milk over them, whisking as you go. Return the mixture to the saucepan and cook over a very low heat, with a heat-diffuser pad if possible, until limpid and lightly thickened. Some say it should coat the back of a wooden spoon, but it should be taken further than this, almost until there is the odd simmering blip on the surface. When you think it is ready, add the cream, give a final vigorous whisk to amalgamate it and pour it into a warmed jug.

Note: If you are unlucky enough to curdle the custard, give it a quick blast in a blender.

bread and butter pudding

Serves 4–6

Quite possibly, the first Bread and Butter Pudding was no more than a bowl of stale crusts softened with hot milk and sprinkled with sugar (delicious!). Over the years, however, it has evolved into a rich and luscious custard pudding, which billows and puffs around slices of bread. The bread is laid out like overlapping roof tiles, and part of the joy of a good pudding is when these pointy edges get slightly crusted. It is important too, that the sultanas, which are strewn between the slices, remain submerged and hidden, to be left in peace to swell and soften rather than sitting on the top getting burnt and bitter.

It is tempting to serve Bread and Butter Pudding hot from the oven but it is far better left for at least 15 minutes and eaten warm with cold thick cream.

400 ml milk
1 vanilla pod
2 tablespoons caster sugar
approximately 75 g soft butter
125 g white bread, medium sliced, crusts removed

75 g sultanas
3 large eggs
freshly grated nutmeg
350 g good quality marmalade
200 ml whipping cream

Pre-heat the oven to 325°F/160°C/gas mark 3.

Bring the milk slowly to the boil with the vanilla pod, giving it a good bashing to release the tiny seeds, and simmer gently for 5 minutes. Remove the pan from the heat, stir in the sugar until it dissolves, and cover with a lid to infuse while you deal with the bread.

Butter a 1-litre shallow ovenproof dish. Spread the bread with butter, cut it in half diagonally, then into quarters. Arrange the slices in the dish and distribute the sultanas between them.

Whisk the eggs in a bowl. Remove the vanilla pod (which can be saved and re-used) and whisk in the milk and whipping cream. Pour the eggy milk over the bread, making sure that all the sultanas remain covered. Dust the surface with grated nutmeg and dot with any remaining butter. Leave the dish to stand for 20 minutes.

Heat the marmalade in a small pan until it turns liquid. Pour through a sieve to catch the peel. Using a pastry brush or spoon, smear the top of the pudding with a generous glaze of marmalade. Bake for 35–40 minutes until the custard has set and the top has billowed and turned golden with crunchy bits where the bread has poked through the custard. Allow it to settle and cool slightly. Serve the remaining strained marmalade in a jug to be spooned over each helping, along with cold, thick cream.

Note: You could, if you wish, chop the strained peel and add it to the pudding with the sultanas; alternatively the sultanas could be soaked in hot rum or whisky – or either alcohol could be added to the marmalade sauce.

jam roly-poly

Serves 6

'Oh, goody! Dead Man's Leg!' cries the schoolboy, as he joins the queue at the serving hatch. 'Brilliant! Dead Baby!' shrieks another, their grotesque descriptions uttered with unashamed greedy joy.

Both these exclamations refer to steamed Jam Roly-Poly suet pudding. This old favourite is now a rarity in the school canteen, as is the sauce that went with it. Sweet white sauce is the prosaic description, but it was wonderful: slightly floury, faintly dairy tasting and it usually came with a flap of thick white skin that clung to the lip of the battered aluminium pouring jug – that's if you were lucky enough to be first in the queue.

The Roly-Poly, with its oozing spread of jam weeping through the damp suet, has a textural quality that is really something: all at once light and fluffy, sweet and dense. And, with a lubrication of that sauce, it's classy as hell. This pudding is actually quite refined and sophisticated, and it seems odd that it is almost alone in *not* being one of the cherished steamed puddings that have recently enjoyed a renaissance in the smartest restaurants.

175 g self-raising flour

1 level tsp baking powder

a pinch of salt

50 g fresh white breadcrumbs

150 g grated suet

6–7 tbsp milk

5 tbsp warmed strawberry jam

a little extra milk

Mix together the flour, baking powder, salt, breadcrumbs and suet in the bowl of a food mixer. Work together briefly until all is the consistency of the breadcrumbs. Add milk a little at a time until the pastry is soft and doughy, but not sticky. Allow to rest for 30 minutes in a cool place. Roll out to a rectangle 20 cm wide and approximately 0.5 cm thick. Spread it with jam up to 1 cm from the edge, then brush this edge with milk. Roll up, tweaking the edges together as you go. Loosely wrap the roly-poly in very well-buttered greaseproof paper, tie the ends with string and also (again, loosely) at two places along the roll. Steam for 3 hours. Unwrap it carefully and cut it into thick slices. Serve with:

Sweet White Sauce

500 ml milk

50 g butter

40 g plain flour

a tiny pinch of salt

75 g caster sugar

75 g double cream

1 tsp pure vanilla extract

Put the milk into a pan and heat until it is hot but not boiling. Meanwhile, in a heavy-bottomed saucepan, melt the butter but do not allow it to froth. Stir in the flour until well blended. Cook over a very gentle heat for 2–3 minutes. Now carefully pour in the milk, whisking all the time. Allow it to come to a gentle simmer and stir for a few minutes with a wooden spoon until the sauce is smooth and lightly thickened. Add the salt and sugar, and if you have a diffuser pad, set the pan on this and let the sauce cook very gently for a good 10 minutes, stirring occasionally. Pour in the cream, add the vanilla extract, gently reheat and serve.

devilled herring roes on toast

Serves 2

The disappearance of Devilled Herring Roes as a favourite English savoury is almost certainly because, these days, their season is no longer reflected on the fishmonger's slab. Instead of being offered as a spring speciality (in May you might be lucky enough to be offered herrings with their roes intact), roes tend to be frozen at sea and remain so until they emerge from the deep freeze. They are readily available, often in a semi-defrosted state lying in a plastic dish looking like plump, headless grubs. However, once seasoned with cayenne and powdered with flour, they fry up a treat, a thin crusty layer offsetting their incredible creaminess.

The toast should be a thick, crisp, crustless slice so that it soaks up the buttery, fishy juices. Also, herring roes should be eaten with plenty of lemon juice and a generous seasoning of Maldon sea salt. Although traditionally served as a savoury, a dish of Devilled Herring Roes makes an excellent light supper.

200 g herring roes

cayenne pepper

flour for dusting

2 tbsp clarified butter (see page 66)

25 g fresh butter

2 thick slices white bread, crusts removed

Maldon sea salt and extra cayenne

1 small lemon, cut into quarters

Blanch the roes for 20 seconds in boiling water. Drain, pat them dry on kitchen paper and season with cayenne. Sift the flour onto a large plate and roll the roes through it. Heat the clarified butter in a frying pan until it is very hot and lay out the roes in a single layer without crowding. They will instantly shrink and splutter; turn down the heat slightly and cook for a couple of minutes without moving them. Turn them over and repeat the process on the other side until the roes are evenly crusted and gilded. Lift them out and drain on kitchen paper. Tip away the clarified butter and replace it with the fresh butter. Allow it to froth slightly before returning the roes to the pan, turning them to coat them nicely with the butter.

Toast the bread and pile the roes on top with any buttery juices. Dust with extra cayenne and sea salt and serve immediately with the lemon.

angels and devils on horseback

Serves 10 for canapés, serves 6 as a savoury

There has been controversy as to whether the 'angels' should be chicken livers but this has never been proven and as far as we are concerned they have always been oysters. The origin of the name 'devils', on the other hand, is surely a certainty: prunes are black as hell and bloated, particularly if they have been pre-soaked in tea that has had a generous slug of Armagnac added to it.

Bacon and shellfish together has always been a good idea (think of scallops and bacon), but the combination of a briny, juicy oyster clad in crisp, salty bacon is incredibly savoury. It truly is almost heavenly.

Devils are no less satisfying – although they are not quite in the class of Angels (well, they wouldn't be, would they?). However, in their lowlier way, they are also jolly nice: sweet, salty, soft and succulent – in fact, devilishly good.

For the Angels:
40 medium-sized rock oysters
cayenne pepper
40 very thin rashers rindless streaky bacon
    (Italian flat pancetta, as opposed to the
    big round sausage type, is excellent)

For the Devils:
40 stoned prunes, soaked in warm tea
    flavoured with a little Armagnac
40 almonds, toasted whole and skinned
40 very thin rashers rindless streaky bacon

Ask your fishmonger to shuck the oysters, or do it yourself if you can but make sure that whoever does it collects the juices with the oyster meat. Discard the shells. Pick out the oysters one by one from their juices and rinse

them briefly under a slow-running cold tap in case there are any clinging bits of shell. Place them in a saucepan and strain the juices over them using a very fine sieve. Gently poach them for 1 minute until they have just stiffened, then strain. Put the oysters on a plate and allow them to cool. Sprinkle each with cayenne pepper and wrap in a slice of bacon, making sure you keep the join underneath. Heat an overhead grill and cook until they are crisp and brown. Serve hot, secured with a cocktail stick for ease of eating.

For them little Devils, simply shove an almond inside each prune, then wrap and cook them in the same way as for the Angels.

Serves 4

scotch woodcock

Scotch Woodcock – heaven knows why it is named thus – is the most savoury of eggy treats. Perhaps a canny Scot thought that scrambled eggs on toast with some anchovies might deceive somebody as a reasonable substitute for that now increasingly rare, and sensationally delicious, game bird.

Use the very best and freshest eggs and the finest anchovies you can find for a dish such as this, as these small luxuries will make the Woodcock especially good. Brioche for the toast, rather than ordinary bread, is also worth searching out from an enterprising baker.

75 g best butter
6 very fresh free-range eggs and 2 egg yolks
6 tbsp double cream
a little salt and plenty of pepper
1 tbsp snipped chives

4 thick slices white bread, toasted and buttered, crusts removed, or toasted brioche, unbuttered
8 anchovy fillets (Spanish ones are particularly good)

Melt the butter in a wide non-stick pan or frying pan. Beat together the eggs and yolks with the double cream and seasoning. Cook very gently, using a wooden spoon, until wet and curdly – or however you like your scrambled eggs to be. Stir in the chives, spoon the eggs on top of the toast and crisscross with the anchovies.

welsh rabbit

Serves 2

As yet, in the Gentleman's Club, there is no sign of bruschetta and crostini nudging aside our own tradition of something on toast; the most familiar of which is surely Welsh Rabbit.

According to Jane Grigson's *The Observer Guide to British Cookery*, there is evidence of its popularity in the sixteenth century and she surmises that it was so called – later gentrified to rarebit – because to the Welsh and other Celtic folk, cheese on toast was proudly claimed to be as fine a treat as a real rabbit. It was made from hard English cheeses – Cheddar, Double Gloucester, Cheshire and Lancashire.

The recipe given here is far richer than the original due to the addition of egg yolks, which cause it to puff and swell as it turns golden. The mustard powder and spiced condiments simply effect a tastier dish. The recipe uses what seems like a silly amount of stout; however, the rest of the bottle is drunk with the Rabbit.

25 g butter	*75 g mature Cheddar or Double Gloucester*
1 tsp English mustard	*or Cheshire or Lancashire, grated*
Worcestershire sauce	*2 egg yolks*
4 shakes Tabasco	*2 thick slices bread*
2 tbsp stout or Guinness	*cayenne pepper*

Place the butter, mustard, Worcestershire sauce, Tabasco and stout or Guinness in a small pan and heat it through. Add the cheese, stirring as it melts, without letting the mixture boil. Remove the pan from the heat and leave it to cool to room temperature. Beat in the two egg yolks. Toast the bread on one side, spread the untoasted side thickly with the mixture and cook under a pre-heated grill until blistered and bubbling. Dust with cayenne and serve immediately, with the bottle of Worcestershire sauce near at hand.

the continental restaurant

'Chi-chi writers sneering at caterers who provide simple inexpensive meals at the expense of traditional haute cuisine underestimate both public demand and changing taste. The brightly lit classless popular catering establishment is rapidly replacing the old dirty dingy "café round the corner". These writers would not dream of giving the old establishment consideration; but the modern popular rendezvous demands – and gets – their attention.'

The editor of *Hotel and Restaurant Management*, January 1964, from Stephen Mennell, *All Manners of Food*, 1985

This is possibly the most difficult chapter to categorize. Although the term 'continental' is rarely used now to describe a style of restaurant and its cooking, the meaning, in a way, could not be more ironically appropriate to today's often pseudo-eclectic school of cooking.

The description 'continental' harks back to the days before we joined the Common Market and to the mid-fifties, when it was rare to come across a restaurant that concentrated on one particular country's cooking. Yes, there *were* French restaurants, of course, some decent Italian ones, and a concentration of Chinese around the docks of Liverpool and the East End of London, but that was about it. To most of us 'continental' meant foreign food.

Invariably these places had a Middle-European flavour about them, often with a touch of German, Greek, French and Italian – an 'all dishes to all nationalities' type of menu. Although they were often quite homely in their way, some menus couldn't shake off a snob French tradition so there would be *hors d'oeuvres*, *les potages*, *les entrées*, etc., which were often listed before, rather than alongside, the native cuisine of the owners. It is amusing to note that in those days, and until fairly recently, every restaurant paid homage to France with a selection of popularized classics – a sort of 'best of' – such as Scampi Mornay and Caneton à l'Orange, sometimes even to the extent of semi-translating some of their own dishes. Why, for instance, as we found on one old menu, was Greek stifado described as stifado *de boeuf*?

Places like these played an important part in our introduction to food from countries other than France. Many tended to be owned by post-war immigrant families, who had brought with them a small repertoire of dishes that may have been everyday fare to them, but were exciting and novel to us. Remember, this is long before the days of pink blancmange masquerading under the name taramasalata. The chef – or, more often than not, the jolly good cook – was an essential part of the family package. He or she would have been a cousin, brother or sister-in-law perhaps, and Granny probably helped with the washing up – she would also have kept a beady eye on the paprika piquancy in the pot of Goulash.

It was these peasant dishes, such as Goulash and Moussaka, for example, which were the 'sophisticated' things to choose. They might not have always been expertly cooked, but what they lacked in finesse was compensated for by authenticity of ingredients. For instance, the noble sweet paprika in Goulash, the good olive oil to fry aubergines in Moussaka and real curd cheese in the Cheesecake.

Another of the principal reasons for writing this book was to rejoice in the fine dishes that restaurants such as these provided. In this time of unfocused magpie world cuisine, and the relentless search for new ingredients and new ways of cooking them, would it not be welcome to come across a cosmopolitan menu that offered some of these fondly remembered favourites?

Serves 6

borscht

The classic Russian recipe for Borscht often provides a meal in itself, packed with meat and vegetables swimming in a deep red broth, traditionally served with miniature pasties called *pirozhki* made with yeast dough and filled with meat from the pot. Although this might be considered peasant style, it is certainly not something that is simply thrown together: beetroot, beef, other vegetables and seasonings need to be spot on to create a harmonious potful.

It can also be turned into the most sophisticated soup and is glorious when served cold and jellied. Its colour is quite magnificent and should preferably be served in pristine white soup plates for the most dramatic effect. Beef stock is the traditional flavour in the cooking liquid, although duck stock can be particularly fine too – the perfect use for a leftover carcass from a roast. Incidentally, you can make a very passable chilled Borscht using canned beef consommé for the stock.

You may think that making Borscht is a real palaver, particularly the chilled version, but just wait until you taste the result. Incidentally, the beef is not essential to the success of the first recipe and is entirely optional depending on whether you wish to serve this hearty soup as a complete meal or not.

Traditional Borscht

500 g piece beef brisket, which is a little bit fatty, or *leaner silverside*
500 g raw beetroot, scrubbed
2 litres chicken stock (see page 47)
1 medium onion, halved and very finely sliced
3 garlic cloves, peeled and pounded to a paste with a little salt
1 large carrot, peeled and diced
75 g butter
4 ripe tomatoes, peeled and chopped

600 g potatoes, peeled, diced and rinsed
½ small white cabbage, cored and shredded
3 tbsp balsamic vinegar (not traditional but perfect here)
salt and freshly ground black pepper
juice of ½ a lemon

———

Garnish:
150 ml soured cream, thinned with a little milk
1 tbsp chives, freshly snipped

Place the meat and beetroot into a large pot with the stock, bring it slowly to the boil and skim off any scum that rises to the surface. Partially cover the pan and simmer very gently for 2 hours, checking from time to time with a skewer as to whether the beetroot are tender; they should take about an hour – remove them when they are done. During the last 30 minutes of cooking, check the beef with a skewer to make sure that it is really tender. Remove it to a plate to cool, then cut it into small chunks. Also, peel and dice the beetroot.

Meanwhile, in a large pan stew together the onions, garlic, and carrot in the butter until they have softened. Add the tomatoes, potatoes and cabbage, and stir them around with the other vegetables until the cabbage is starting to wilt. Then pour in the stock and add the beef and beetroot. Bring the pan to a simmer and check the seasoning. Add the vinegar, bring it back to a simmer and allow it to cook for a further 30 minutes. Finally, stir in the lemon juice.

Serve in deep soup bowls, with the soured cream and chives stirred together and handed separately in a bowl.

Jellied Borscht

2 tbsp vegetable oil

450 g chicken wings, roughly chopped

500 g slice of beef shin, cut in one thick
    slice across the bone (make sure your
    butcher prepares it like this)

1 large carrot, peeled and chopped

2 sticks celery, chopped

2 leeks, trimmed, cleaned and sliced

2 garlic cloves, crushed

a little salt

a few black peppercorns

1 peeled onion, stuck with 3 cloves

2 sprigs fresh thyme

2 bay leaves

2.5 litres cold water

——

For the clarification:

4 fresh raw beetroots, peeled and grated

2 wineglasses port

2 beaten egg whites

200 g lean minced beef

——

3 cooked beetroots

1 tbsp red wine vinegar

150 ml soured cream, thinned with a little
    milk

paprika

1 tbsp snipped chives

In a heavy-bottomed stew-pan, heat the oil until it is smoking. Put in the chicken wings and fry for a couple of minutes until they are lightly browned. Remove them and set them aside. Season the slice of beef shin, fry it hard on both sides until well crusted then remove it and set aside. Now tip up the pan and spoon out any excess fat. Put in all the vegetables, seasoning and herbs, with the chicken wings, the beef and the water. Bring to the boil, skim off any scum that rises to the surface and simmer for 1½ hours on a very low heat, or even in the oven (275°F/140°C/gas mark 1), uncovered.

Lift out the piece of beef and put it on a plate (you could use it for rissoles or a beef hash). Strain the stock through a roomy colander into another pan and allow it to drip for 10 minutes or so. Discard the solids, then pass the strained stock through a fine sieve into a large clean stainless steel or enamelled pan. Allow it to settle for a few minutes and then remove any fat from the surface with several sheets of kitchen paper. Simmer the stock and reduce it gently, skimming off any more scum that may form. When the stock measures about 1.5 litres (this does not have to be dead accurate), take it off the heat and leave to cool.

In a roomy bowl, use your hands to mulch together the raw beetroots, port, egg whites and minced beef. Tip it into the stock and gently mix in. Put the pan over a moderate heat and return it to the merest simmer. During this stage, make sure that the mulched mixture does not stick to the bottom of the pan; feel around with a wooden spoon, perhaps, but do not disturb the beetroot/mince crust that forms on the surface. Simmer gently for 40 minutes. This is the clarification process: the egg whites and natural albumen in the meat are collecting all the impurities in the stock into themselves, while the meat, grated beetroot and port are flavouring it. As the stock gently blips through the crust it should be clear and ruby red. After the 40 minutes is up, make a hole in the crust with a spoon and lift some of it away. Now, using a ladle, pour the clear liquid that lies beneath through a muslin-lined sieve into a clean pan. Collect all you can, then discard the crust.

Now grate the cooked beetroot into the hot, clear beetroot-flavoured consommé, pour in the vinegar and gently stir it all together. Cover the pan and leave the mixture to infuse for 30 minutes.

Drain the soup through a fine sieve, into a clean bowl (keep the beetroot for a salad, perhaps, sharpened with a little red wine vinegar), and leave it to cool. Then put it into the fridge and allow to set. Spoon out the jellied

the continental restaurant 109

Borscht into chilled soup plates and decorate with a slurry of soured cream, a shake of paprika and some chives. Serve with buttered rye bread and a glass of iced vodka.

Makes about 35 stuffed vine leaves

You are never quite sure what goes into these plump, dark green bundles. Rice is always present – sometimes coloured and flavoured with saffron – and, if you are lucky, the finished product will offer a moist mouthful of perfectly seasoned minced lamb with a hint of fresh mint and cinnamon. The vine leaf – if you have your own vine you can use your own leaves – adds its own flavour to the dish and the essential slow cooking renders it so tender that it almost melts away as you bite.

Stuffed Vine Leaves are rewarding to make and our recipe will spoil you for those slimy, under-seasoned, tasteless roll-ups (usually served freezing cold straight from the fridge) with their tough, heavily veined covering, that are passed off as the real thing. The recipes, for both hot and cold vine leaves, come from the expert on such matters, Claudia Roden, who taught both of us to cook these and other Middle Eastern specialities, from her book, *A New Book of Middle Eastern Food*, which was originally published in 1968 as *A Book of Middle Eastern Food*. The beauty of these recipes is that once you've got the hang of the technique, you can vary them by adding other herbs, spices and fillings – and that's what we've done.

Hot Stuffed Vine Leaves

250 g preserved vine leaves (usually sold in flat plastic packets), drained
100 g long grain rice, washed in boiling water, then rinsed with cold and drained

200 g minced lamb
1 ripe, medium-sized tomato, skinned and chopped
4 spring onions, finely chopped
2 tbsp finely chopped flat-leaf parsley

stuffed vine
leaves

2 tbsp finely chopped mint leaves

½ tsp cinnamon

2 tbsp toasted pine kernels

1 garlic clove, crushed to a paste with a
    little salt

1 tbsp tomato concentrate

salt and pepper

juice of 2 lemons

150 ml water

2–4 plump garlic cloves, peeled and
    slivered

an optional pinch of saffron strands,
    softened in a little hot water

Spread out the vine leaves in a large bowl and pour boiling water over them, making sure that the water penetrates the layers. Leave them to soak for 20 minutes, then drain. Fresh vine leaves need only to be plunged in boiling water, a few at a time, until limp, then drained.

Place the rice in a large bowl with the lamb, tomato, spring onions, parsley, mint, cinnamon, pine kernels and garlic paste, and add the tomato concentrate. Season the mixture lightly with salt and generously with pepper. Mix thoroughly.

The assembly takes a little practice. Start with the vine leaf on a flat surface, smooth side down. Place a scoop of filling – not too much – in the centre, fold one side of the leaf to cover the filling, then fold in the sides to cover the ends of the filling and then carry on rolling forwards making sure the final join is underneath – if you have ever made spring rolls, it follows the same principle. Use damaged leaves to line a shallow earthen-ware dish and pack in the rolls tightly, in layers. Squeeze over the lemon juice and water, and tuck the slivers of garlic between the rolls. Cover the dish with foil, punch a few holes in the top to allow the steam to escape and bake in a low oven (300°F/150°C/gas mark 2) for 2 hours. Serve hot from the dish as they are, or with a fresh tomato sauce. If you are serving them cold, allow them to cool in the dish, then arrange them attractively on a larger platter.

Cold Stuffed Vine Leaves

250 g preserved vine leaves, drained

250 g long grain rice

2–3 tomatoes, chopped

1 bunch spring onions, finely chopped

2 tbsp coriander leaves, chopped

2 tbsp mint, chopped

2 tbsp currants

½ tsp – or more – dried chilli flakes

¼ level teaspoon ground cinnamon

¼ level teaspoon ground allspice

salt and black pepper

several tomatoes, sliced (optional)

2–4 garlic cloves, slivered

juice of 2 lemons

150 ml olive oil

150 ml water

a large pinch of saffron stamens or ½ tsp turmeric

Proceed exactly as for Hot Stuffed Vine Leaves but mix the olive oil with the water and saffron or turmeric.

hummus

Serves 4

Greece, Turkey, Lebanon and other Middle Eastern countries all have their version of this grainy, creamed paste. It first caught the imagination of the British public in the sixties and early seventies, when it seemed a daring choice on the mezze menu of those early kebab houses. These days, you find it everywhere (even on pub menus and in most supermarkets) but it is rare to find a version that lives up to expectations. Sometimes it is too sloppy, or it can be so thick it gums your mouth up, and there is nothing worse than Hummus that is either under-seasoned or has been made with chickpeas that haven't been cooked long enough.

Like most simple dishes made with a minimal number of ingredients, it is important to achieve the right balance – as when making mayonnaise, for instance. Take the garlic, for example: you need enough to give the dip a decent zing but it shouldn't overpower the other flavours. The consistency should be all at once thick and sloppy.

An authentic version of this now ubiquitous paste would be made with dried chickpeas but the following recipe uses tinned. They are just as good but it is vital that they are thoroughly rinsed. If you prefer to make the Hummus with dried chickpeas, soak them overnight before simmering in unsalted water for at least two hours. The flavour of the dish is improved by including a little of the cooking liquid when the chickpeas are puréed.

420 g can chickpeas, drained and rinsed   *about 100 ml olive oil*
juice of 1 small lemon   *salt*
1 large garlic clove, peeled and crushed   *Tabasco sauce*
1 tbsp tahini (sesame seed paste)   *½ tsp ground cumin*

Blend the chickpeas with the lemon juice, garlic, tahini and a little water to form a paste. Pour in the olive oil in a thin stream, as if you were making mayonnaise (adding more or less than the 100 ml stated, depending on how creamy you want the Hummus). Season it with salt, Tabasco and cumin. Spoon it into a bowl and serve with fingers of toasted pitta bread.

Serves 4 (as a snack)

taramasalata

The artificially pink Taramasalata encountered in supermarkets, corner shops and some Greek-Cypriot restaurants is a far cry from the real thing. Perhaps it is thought that the authentic pale, flesh-coloured (for want of a better description, but accurate) paste is unattractive to the British – but it is not to those who know how a true Taramasalata should look.

Originally, Greek Tarama (*salata* only means salad) was – and still is – made from dried, salted mullet roe, not smoked. We have to use smoked cod's roe here, as that is all that is available, which is naturally a deep orange-red colour from the curing and smoking process. Once the other ingredients have been added, this is when the tinge of pale pink begins to emerge. If you really insist on the Day-Glo look, add three tablespoons of cochineal.

juice of 1 large onion
50 g fresh white breadcrumbs
4 tbsp milk
100 g smoked cod's roe, skinned
2 small garlic cloves, peeled and crushed to
    a paste with salt

juice of 1 small lemon
plenty of freshly ground black pepper
75–100 ml virgin olive oil

To make the onion juice, work one chopped onion in the food processor, then tip it into a thin tea-towel or a scrap of muslin. Squeeze out the juice into a small bowl.

Soak the breadcrumbs in the milk and drain them in a sieve. Discard the drained milk and lightly squeeze out any excess from the bread. Put this in a food processor with the roe, garlic, lemon and onion juices and pepper. Process till smooth and then start to add the olive oil in a very fine stream, as if you were making mayonnaise. The desired consistency is stiffened and mousse-like.

Pile the Taramasalata into a bowl and serve with buttered toast or hot pitta bread.

Note: Cayenne pepper or dried chilli flakes can be substituted for the pepper to add a fiery note.

chicken kiev   *Serves 4*

Chicken Kiev – also known as Pollo Sorpresa in Italian trattorias – is one of the best-selling lines at Marks & Spencer, and was also their first pre-pared dish when they diversified into food. So why is it that something so clearly popular disappeared, almost without trace, from the tables of good restaurants?

There are very few dishes that are more ingenious, downright tasty, simple to prepare and texturally brilliant as this one. Perhaps, unwittingly, Marks & Spencer are to blame for its demise, due to overexposure. But why, these days, does this so often happen to a dish, when everybody loves it? Well, sadly, once again we come back to that ugly word 'fashion'.

Chicken Kiev – along with Prawn Cocktail, Beef Stroganoff and Trout with Almonds – has been deemed naff. Well, it's not. They are all good dishes. It is the people who see them as such who are naff.

For best results, it really is necessary to deep fry for perfect Chicken Kiev.

100 g softened butter	*2 tsp Pernod (optional)*
2 small garlic cloves, peeled and finely chopped	*salt and pepper*
2 tbsp freshly chopped parsley	———
1 dsp freshly chopped tarragon	*4 chicken breasts, skinned with their little wing bones still attached*
1 dsp snipped chives	*2 tbsp flour*
grated rind of 1 small lemon	*1 large egg, beaten*
juice of 1 small lemon	*4–5 tbsp fresh white breadcrumbs*
3 shakes Tabasco	*peanut or sunflower oil for frying*

Blend the first 10 ingredients together in a food processor and allow the mixture to firm up slightly in a cool place (not the fridge). Then form four rough sausage shapes with a spoon and place them on a plate in the fridge to solidify.

On the underside of the chicken breast you will find a small flap (it looks like a miniature chicken breast and is sometimes called a fillet). Remove this and place it between a folded sheet of greaseproof paper. Beat it gently with a rolling pin to flatten it – it will double in size – but don't bash the living daylights out of it or treacherous holes may form. Following the same formula, do the same to the larger part of the chicken breast. Lay all eight pieces on a flat tray.

Have the flour, egg and breadcrumbs in three separate shallow bowls (traditional flat soup plates would be ideal). Brush the insides – where the fillets were – of the large flattened breasts with egg and then sprinkle with the merest dusting of flour. Rub in with the tip of a finger and place a sausage of garlic and herb butter on each breast. Do the same egging and flouring to each of the little flattened fillets and lay over the butter, allowing the edges to flop down on either side. Press the two parts together, sealing the butter with the two pieces of chicken. Place on a cling-filmed tray and put in the freezer for 30 minutes to firm up.

Heat the deep fryer to around 310°F/160°C (for those without a thermometer, this is when a scrap of bread turns golden after a couple of minutes). Carefully remove the chicken from its tray and gently drag it through the flour, making sure that any crevices are well coated. Dip each piece into the egg, making sure that all surfaces are coated and, perhaps, pushing some of it into the crevices with the end of a pastry brush. Finally, coat the chicken with the breadcrumbs, pressing them in lightly with your fingertips, until it is thoroughly covered. Lower the parcels into the oil and fry for exactly 8 minutes. Lift them out, allow to drain for a few seconds and place onto kitchen paper. Serve with chips, naturally, some lemon quarters and bunches of watercress.

Note: Depending on the size of your fryer, you may have to cook only two at a time. If so, keep the first two warm in a low oven, placed upon a wire rack.

hungarian beef goulash   *Serves 6*

What exactly *is* a Hungarian Beef Goulash? The first thought is that it is probably red – you know, paprika, tomatoes, pimientoes, that sort of thing. Well, that's just about it, but what a fine combination of rich flavours develops as it gently simmers away. Goulash can also be made successfully with pork or veal, but whichever meat you decide on, long slow cooking is always the key. As with any braise, try to find cuts of meat that have good strata of fat and sinew, for it is from these that flavour and richness exude. The addition of a little bit of pepperoni sausage is certainly controversial but lends extra spice – chilli and paprika – and flavour.

salt and freshly milled pepper

1 kg tender top rump or veal shoulder, cut
    into 5 cm cubes

2 heaped tbsp flour

2 tbsp olive oil

50 g butter

150 g spicy pepperoni sausage, skinned
    and cut into dice

3 medium onions, peeled and thinly sliced

1 small can or jar of peeled and roasted
    peppers (Spanish brands are best)
    sliced into thickish strips

1 dsp Hungarian paprika ('noble sweet' is
    the best variety)

1 tsp caraway seeds, crushed

200 ml dry white wine

juice of 1 lemon

150 ml soured cream, thinned down with
    2 tbsp milk

1 dsp chives, freshly chopped

Pre-heat the oven to 275°F/140°C/gas mark 1.

Season the beef or veal and roll it in the flour. Melt the oil and butter in a large, heavy-bottomed, lidded cast-iron pot (Le Creuset would be ideal). Once the fats are foaming, put in the pepperoni and fry until it is crusted and brown. Remove to a plate and set aside. Now slip in the beef or veal, cooking only 6–7 pieces at a time so as not to overcrowd the pot. Colour it well on each side until it is a rich brown, then remove it to a plate and continue with the rest. Once all the meat has been coloured and set aside, add the onions and fry them gently until they are golden brown. Tip in the peppers and cook them with the onions for 5 minutes. Stir in the paprika and caraway seeds, stew for a few minutes, and then add the wine and lemon juice. Return the meat to the pot, give it a stir and bring it to a simmer. Put on the lid and cook in the oven for 1½ hours.

Take the pot out of the oven, check the seasoning and remove any excess fat from the surface with a few sheets of kitchen paper. Place over a low heat and while the Goulash is still bubbling gently, quickly spoon over the soured cream and sprinkle with the chives. Serve straight from the pot. Suitable accompaniments would be some big fluffy boiled potatoes or some buttered wide egg noodles, seasoned with nutmeg and garlic.

moussaka

Serves 4

Moussaka is the Greek version of Shepherd's Pie, made with sliced aubergines and a topping of béchamel sauce instead of mashed potato. As with Shepherd's Pie, it has been badly made for years but no one seems to notice or care.

It doesn't have to ooze oil (given back from badly cooked aubergines) or be virtually tasteless, and the béchamel shouldn't be cracked and dried, which usually happens after the Moussaka has been reheated several times. It should be a luxurious dish, a rich and well-flavoured 'layer-bake', and that creamy topping needs to be thick and generous so that it sets with a wobble.

3 medium aubergines, sliced	*For the béchamel sauce:*
salt	*550 ml milk*
200 ml pure olive oil	*1 small onion, peeled and chopped*
350 g onions, finely chopped	*1 bay leaf*
3 garlic cloves, finely chopped	*2 cloves*
½ tsp ground cinnamon	*salt*
1 heaped tbsp tomato purée	*50 g butter*
500 g minced lamb	*50 g flour*
200 ml red wine	*freshly grated nutmeg*
salt and pepper	*75 g feta cheese, grate*
flour	——
——	*3 tbsp chopped flat-leaf parsley*
	1 tsp dried oregano

Lay the aubergine slices on a tray in one layer and sprinkle lightly but evenly with salt. Then bring them together, place in a colander and leave to drain for 30–40 minutes.

Meanwhile, in a heavy-bottomed pan, heat 2–3 tablespoons of the olive oil. Fry the onions and garlic until they have softened and are just turning golden. Add the cinnamon and stir it around, then put in the tomato purée.

moussaka

Cook the mixture slowly, stirring well, until the tomato paste has lost most of its bright red colour. Tip in the lamb, break it up with a wooden spoon and stew gently for 10–15 minutes, stirring and turning the meat until it is well coloured. Add the wine and the seasoning. Give it a good stir and put it over a very low heat. Allow the sauce to braise gently for 40 minutes, stirring occasionally (use a heat-diffuser pad, if you have one).

In a large frying pan, heat 3–4 tablespoons of olive oil until it is good and hot. Pat dry the aubergine slices on kitchen paper. Flour them and fry a few at a time in the olive oil until they are golden on both sides. Continue doing this until all the aubergines are cooked, adding more oil as necessary.

To make the béchamel sauce, place the milk, onion, bay leaf, cloves and a pinch of salt in a saucepan. Simmer gently for a few minutes, then turn off the heat, cover the pan and leave the mixture to infuse for 10 minutes. Meanwhile, melt the butter and stir in the flour, mixing to make a roux. Cook very gently for a couple of minutes without allowing the roux to colour. Strain the milk into the roux, whisking vigorously as the sauce comes to a simmer. Leave it to cook over a very low heat, stirring every now and again, for about 15 minutes. Season generously with nutmeg, stir in the feta and cook for a few more minutes until the cheese has melted and the sauce is thick and creamy. Cover the pan to prevent a skin forming and keep it warm.

Pre-heat the oven to 375°F/190°C/gas mark 5.

Once the meat is cooked, stir in the herbs, then tip the mixture into a colander to drain off any excess fat, and leave it for a few minutes. Line the base of a deep, oval, ovenproof dish with slices of aubergine, season thoroughly with pepper and spoon over the drained meat. Cover with the remaining aubergines and pour over the béchamel sauce. Place the dish in the oven and bake for 25–30 minutes until the top is blistered and bubbling.

Note: If you prefer, allow the unbaked moussaka to get cold and use an egg slice to cut out individual square servings. Place on an oiled baking sheet and bake at a similar temperature for 20–25 minutes. The beauty of this method is that each portion becomes well crusted around its edges and on the surface, which is particularly nice.

Serves 4 as a snack

spanish omelette

One should be strict with the ingredients when contemplating a Spanish Omelette. Eggs, potatoes and onions are the trinity of the original, but chopped peppers, peas and other bits and bobs have also put in appearances. This is a shame, really, because they detract from the purity of the dish. 'Less is more' has never been more apt.

300 g potatoes, preferably a waxy variety

3 tablespoons olive oil

1 Spanish onion, peeled, halved and cut into small dice

4 large eggs

salt and pepper

Tabasco

Cook the unpeeled potatoes in plenty of salted water until tender to the point of a knife. Drain, and when they have cooled slightly, remove the skins and dice the flesh.

While the potatoes are cooking, take a 20 cm non-stick frying pan, heat the oil and fry the onion in it until pale golden. Season with salt and pepper. Add the potatoes to the pan with the onion and stir together for a couple of minutes.

Pre-heat an overhead grill. Whisk the eggs, season with salt and pepper and a few drops of Tabasco. Keeping the heat under the potatoes and onion moderate, pour the egg into the pan. Gingerly move the egg in, around and underneath the vegetables and allow to cook for about 45 seconds or until the base of the omelette is uniformly set. Remove the pan to the grill and cook the top of the omelette until puffed and golden.

Place an inverted plate over the pan and deftly turn it upside-down. Lift off the pan to reveal the beautifully burnished omelette. Eat it warm, preferably, or cold, serving the omelette cut in wedges like a cake. It is unconventional, but delicious, to spoon over soured cream mixed with chopped spring onions.

swedish meatballs

Serves 4

Meatballs in a creamy sauce, which is what Swedish Meatballs are, have been a feature of the menu at Anna Hegarty's North London Swedish restaurant for over twenty years. Unlike other versions of this once ubiquitous dish, Anna's meatballs are firm, small and meaty, made with a mixture of minced beef and pork. What makes them so special is the addition of cream-soaked breadcrumbs to the mixture, with a particularly fine gravy.

As is traditional in Sweden, the meatballs at Anna's Place are served with preserved lingonberries. These are small crimson berries that look and taste a bit like cranberries and offset this rich and satisfying dish with their sweet yet tart flavour. A top-quality cranberry sauce or relish would make a good alternative.

Made well, this is a handsome dish – in fact Anna's is so good that it is her recipe we give here. It goes without saying that the meatballs must be made with best quality minced meat, and should be accompanied by plain boiled potatoes.

1 onion, peeled and finely chopped	*For the cream gravy:*
50 g butter	*1 medium onion, peeled and chopped*
200 ml whipping cream	*1 medium carrot, peeled and chopped*
50 g white breadcrumbs	*2 small sticks celery, chopped*
200 g beef, minced	*275 ml chicken stock (see page 47)*
200 g pork, minced	*1 tbsp redcurrant jelly*
1 egg, beaten	*a generous pinch of allspice*
½ tsp allspice	*150 ml double cream*
salt and freshly ground white pepper	*salt and freshly ground white pepper*

Sauté the onion in half the butter. Tip it on to a plate and leave it to cool. Meanwhile, pour the cream over the breadcrumbs in a bowl and leave them to soak for a few minutes. Place the cooled onion in a mixing bowl with the meat, breadcrumbs and cream. Add the egg and allspice, and season with salt and pepper. Use your hands to mix everything together and form the mixture into walnut-sized balls. Fry them gently in the rest of the butter until golden; you will probably need to do this in batches, setting them aside when they are cooked.

To make the cream gravy, fry the onion, carrot and celery until tender. Transfer them to a saucepan, pour over the stock and simmer until the liquid has reduced by half. Strain it into a clean pan, stir in the redcurrant jelly and season with allspice, salt and pepper. When the jelly has dissolved, strain the stock into a pan that can also accommodate all the meatballs. Add the cream and continue cooking until the sauce is thick and nicely amalgamated. Check the seasoning, then stir in the meatballs and simmer for two minutes.

Serves 4

beef stroganoff

Most people think that Beef Stroganoff is as Russian as blinis and beluga, but the dish's name might just as well have been picked out of a Cossack's furry hat. Whether it was a Count Stroganoff or a Chef Stroganoff after whom the dish was named is now shrouded in the mists of time.

However, the dish has just about survived since its heyday in the sixties and seventies, and is still seen lurking about here and there. The large amount of cream used in it has, perhaps, been partly responsible for its near demise but, after the beef, it is *the* essential ingredient.

Some say that it should be a slow-cooked dish; others vouch for a quick stir-fry, keeping the strips of meat as pink as possible. Whoever is correct here should also be aware that the most important point of the dish is its relentless richness and bland, creamy texture. Rice, for us, has never seemed right with it (maddeningly, rice seemed to accompany all those wet, creamy dishes thirty years ago), and we would suggest either some floury boiled potatoes or a big bowl of noodles. Come to think of it, grilled polenta wouldn't be too bad either if, perhaps, a little controversial.

In the restaurant trade, fillet 'tails' were freely available from butchers, particularly around the time that Strog was the dish of the day. This is the tapered end of the whole fillet, and used to be cheaper, as well as ideal for the dish. Cajole your local butcher to be nostalgic for those days when people were actually *willing* to buy the bit that nobody really wanted.

3 tbsp cooking oil	350 g button mushrooms, sliced
salt and pepper	1 heaped tsp paprika
600 g fillet steak, preferably tail, trimmed and cut into thick slivers	400 ml soured cream
	juice of 1 lemon
50 g butter	1 dsp finely chopped dill
3 medium onions, peeled and thinly sliced	

Take a heavy-bottomed, preferably non-stick, frying pan and heat half the oil until it is smoking. Season the meat well and put half of it into the pan. Fry quickly, moving it around briskly until it is lightly browned. Lift it out with a slotted spoon and put it on to a plate. Heat the remaining oil until it is as hot as before and repeat the process with the other half of the beef. It is important that the beef remains rare at this stage.

Add 25 g of the butter to the pan and cook the onions slowly until they are golden and sticky. Tip them out of the pan on to a plate. Melt the remaining 25 g of butter and fry the mushrooms, with the paprika, until they are soft and the spice has cooked a little. Remove them from the pan and put them with the onions.

Spoon the soured cream into the frying pan and warm it through until it is liquid. Put the beef, onions and mushrooms back into the pan, bring the mixture to a simmer and stew it very gently for 10–15 minutes until creamy and unctuous. Stir in the lemon juice and dill.

Serves 2

wiener schnitzel

There seems to be some confusion when it comes to the garnish for a Wiener Schnitzel. Some are decorated simply with a green olive wrapped in an anchovy perched upon a slice of lemon. However, the true version is far more elaborate, using hard-boiled egg, capers, gherkins and parsley, all finely chopped and arranged alongside the meat.

*2 thin veal escalopes, weighing
    approximately 100 g each*
salt and pepper
flour
1 egg, beaten with a few drops of oil
fresh breadcrumbs
1 tbsp olive oil
25 g butter
————

For the garnish:
*1 small lemon, all skin and pith cut away
    and thinly sliced*
4 pimiento-stuffed green olives
4 anchovies
*1 hard-boiled egg, yolk sieved and white
    finely chopped*
*1 tbsp capers, drained, squeezed dry and
    chopped*
4 gherkins, sliced
1 level tbsp parsley, chopped

Beat the escalopes flat with a meat bat or cleaver, between a folded sheet of greaseproof paper. Season then dip the meat into the flour, then into the oily egg and finally dredge it lightly with the breadcrumbs. Heat the oil and butter in a large frying pan until frothing. Slip in the escalopes, turn down the heat a little, and fry for about 2 minutes on each side. Drain on kitchen paper and put them on two hot plates.

Choose the four slices of lemon that look best and put two on each escalope. Wrap each olive in an anchovy and centre it on a lemon slice. Now arrange the chopped garnishes in separate piles around the meat. Eat with buttered new potatoes.

Serves 4

coleslaw

Home-made Coleslaw is such a doddle to make that it is hard to understand why it remains the most popular of bought salads. You know the sort – cloyingly sweet and sour, wet and gluey, sloppy and slimy.

½ medium-sized hard, white cabbage, core removed and cut into wedges
2 medium carrots, peeled
1 tsp salt
2 tsp sugar
1 tbsp white wine vinegar

4 tbsp home-made mayonnaise (see page 24)
1 dsp Dijon mustard
1 heaped tbsp chopped chives
freshly ground white pepper

Using the finest shredding blade of a food processor, grate the cabbage, then the carrots and put them in a large bowl. Sprinkle over the salt, sugar and vinegar. Mix together thoroughly with your hands, then tip into a colander and leave to drain over the bowl for an hour.

Remove the colander from the bowl, pour away the juices and squeeze the cabbage and carrot gently to remove any more excess liquid. Put the mayonnaise and mustard into the bowl with the chives and stir, with a generous seasoning of white pepper. Add the cabbage and carrots and once more use your hands to mix it all together.

Serves 4

potato salad

It is quite extraordinary how often you find undercooked potato (one of the worst things it is possible to eat) in commercially made Potato Salads. But it doesn't stop there: claggy, sweet mayonnaise, coarsely prepared onions and a total lack of seasoning. Mass catering at its worst.

One of the important points to remember when making a good Potato

Salad is to dress the potatoes while they are still warm. Although it can be fine to use mayonnaise, its thickness smears rather than coats the potato. The following mustard-based dressing is looser and more manageable, and if you want the eggy quality of mayonnaise, put in some chopped hard-boiled egg, which actually tastes even better.

700 g waxy potatoes
4 sprigs mint
1 tbsp smooth Dijon mustard
2 tbsp red wine vinegar
salt and pepper

75 ml tbsp vegetable oil
2 tbsp olive oil
1 small bunch spring onions, trimmed and
    finely chopped or *1 bunch chives,*
    snipped

Boil the potatoes in well-salted water with the mint. Meanwhile, make the dressing by whisking together the mustard, vinegar and seasoning, then whisking in the oils. Drain the potatoes and, depending upon which variety you are using, peel them or not. If they are very small – the size of marbles – leave them as they are. If they are a little larger, slice them in half at their lengthiest cross-section. When they have cooled a little, dress the potatoes with the spring onions or chives in a large enough bowl to allow maximum movement for even distribution of the dressing. Eat the salad lukewarm.

rhum baba

Serves 8

An old hand on the sweet trolley, the Rhum Baba is almost as familiar as its neighbour, the Black Forest Gâteau. Gaudily decked out with glacé cherries, slivers of angelica and piped cream, this sorry Baba is often not much more than a small dry sponge cake.

The secret of a good Rhum Baba is to saturate it with booze and syrup. As it soaks in its alcoholic bath, the cake almost doubles in size. There is no need for superfluous decoration, as the Babas look inviting unadorned, languishing in their aromatic lotion. Eat them with very cold, loosely beaten and slightly sweetened cream, flavoured with fresh vanilla seeds.

the continental restaurant   129

rhum **baba**

3 tbsp lukewarm water
2 tsp dried yeast
225 g plain flour
½ tsp salt
3 eggs, lightly beaten
1 tbsp caster sugar
100 g butter, softened
extra butter for lining the moulds
——

For the syrup:
500 g caster sugar
1 litre water
100 ml rum
——

For the whipped cream (crème
  Chantilly):
150 ml whipping cream, very well chilled
150 ml double cream, very well chilled
40 g icing sugar
vanilla seeds scraped from half a split
  fresh vanilla pod

You will also need a roomy metal bowl which has been in the freezer for 15 minutes.

Pour the lukewarm water into a bowl, sprinkle over the yeast and leave it for a few minutes until it has dissolved. Sift the flour and salt into a mixing bowl, make a well in the middle and add the yeasty water, eggs and sugar. Mix everything together with your hands. Knead and pull up the dough with your fingers and slap it back, continuing for several minutes until you have a smooth, elastic dough. Cover the dough with flakes of the softened butter, then cover the entire bowl with a damp tea-towel. Stand the bowl in a warm place and leave it for about an hour: the dough will expand to almost double its size and encompass the butter. Knead the butter into the dough, continuing until it is smooth and glossy.

Meanwhile, butter eight indented ring, dariole or other small deep moulds and chill them in the freezer. Then repeat with another smear of butter. Pour in the mixture, until the moulds are three parts full, place them on a baking sheet, cover with a cloth and leave to prove in a warm place for about 15 minutes.

Bake the Babas in a hot oven (400°F/200°C/gas mark 6) for 15–20 minutes or until they are golden brown. Turn them out carefully on to a pastry rack and leave them to cool.

Meanwhile, dissolve the sugar in the water in a large saucepan and boil hard for a few minutes to make a clear syrup. Stir in most of the rum and add the Babas, a few at a time, turning them carefully to soak up as much syrup as possible; this takes a few minutes. Transfer the swollen Babas to a serving platter, sprinkle with the last of the rum and serve the remaining syrup separately in a small jug.

It is important that when you come to whip the cream everything is cold. This allows the least chance of the cream separating while it is beaten. Put all the ingredients in the ice-cold bowl from the freezer and whip the cream by hand with a balloon whisk, using fluid motions, until it is loosely thick and floppy, but just holding its shape. This will not take long and it is a pleasure to see the marked difference between hand-whisked and electrically beaten cream.

apple strudel

Serves 6

To make a really fine strudel, you have to make your own paste. Some cooks use ready-made sheets of filo pastry, but the sheets are too small and the result is never as good. It may seem a bore to put together, but it is actually quite good fun to make (there's a lot of kneading and throwing about involved to make the pastry elastic and pliable) and, once baked, the texture is uniquely crisp, yet yielding.

For the strudel dough:
250 g plain flour
a pinch of salt
1 large egg, beaten
125 ml tepid water
squeeze of lemon juice
————

For the filling:
50 g raisins, soaked in 3 tbsp Calvados
500 g Granny Smith apples, peeled, cored
  and thinly sliced
grated rind and juice of 1 large lemon
flour
100 g light soft brown sugar
1 tsp ground cinnamon
120 g unsalted butter, melted
icing sugar

Sift the flour and salt into the bowl of an electric mixer. Mix together the egg, water and lemon juice. Using a flat beater, turning slowly, pour in the mixture and allow it to come together to form doughy crumbs. Then, with your hands, press together the bits of dough to form a ball. You can also make the dough in a food processor, but it can put quite a strain on the motor.

Lightly flour a work surface and knead the dough energetically for up to 10 minutes, lifting and slapping it until it is very elastic, glossy and supple. Put it into a large plastic bag and leave it to rest, but not in the fridge.

To prepare the filling, drain the raisins in a sieve. Take a roomy bowl and mix the apples with the lemon juice and grated rind, the soaked raisins, brown sugar and cinnamon. Put it to one side.

Cover a table with an old sheet, dust it with flour and start to roll out the pastry. When you have got it as thin as you can with the rolling pin, leave it to rest for 20 minutes covered with a couple of damp tea-towels.

Remove the tea-towels and, with your hands, start to stretch the dough, pulling gently and carefully until it is as thin as can be; the action should be all at once deft and fluid, allowing the pastry to drape and flop over the backs of your hands – there may be a few holes but this will not affect the final result. You are aiming for a sheet of strudel paste that measures about 1 metre square.

Pre-heat the oven to 375°F/190°C/gas mark 5.

Brush the dough generously with the melted butter, which will not use it all up; once the filling is in place dribble most of the rest over the fruit, leaving a little behind for brushing over the wrapped strudel.

Now, strew the apple mixture evenly over the pastry and roll up the strudel with the aid of the sheet, allowing the filling to be wrapped up loosely rather than as a tight package. Carefully – you may need help here – place it on a well-buttered baking sheet, curling the strudel into a horseshoe shape so that it will fit, and brush it with the remaining butter. Dust it thickly with icing sugar, trying to get some round the sides as well, and bake it in the oven for about 40 minutes or until the surface, when tapped, feels like parchment and is also glossed by the melted sugar. Dust over a little extra sugar if you wish before serving the strudel in thick slices. Eat at room temperature.

cheesecake

Two sorts of Cheesecake are familiar to us: one is the Jewish cooked cheese-cake, with its 'clarty' texture (a descriptive northern English expression and precisely accurate here, meaning it sticks to the roof of your mouth) and strong vanilla flavour. The other is uncooked and mousse-like, made with beaten egg yolks, lemon and cream cheese, sometimes including sour cream, and set with gelatine. Both are particular in their own way, but it is the cooked variety that you will always find in the continental restaurant, often on display behind a glassed-in serving counter, ready to be hewn into dense, highly calorific slabs.

For the pastry:
200 g plain flour
a pinch of salt
125 g curd cheese
50 g caster sugar
cold water

——

For the filling:
500 g curd cheese
150 g caster sugar

*2 rounded tbsp potato flour (*fécule de
pommes de terre*)*
a pinch of salt
4 large eggs
*50 g sultanas, soaked in enough hot water
to cover, plus 1 tbsp rum (optional)*
grated rind of 1 lemon
freshly grated nutmeg
150 ml soured cream

First make the pastry. Sift the flour and salt into a mixing bowl then rub in the curd cheese and sugar until it resembles damp breadcrumbs. Incorporate enough water to bind the dough into a cohesive ball, then place it in a plastic bag and chill in the fridge for 30 minutes before using.

Pre-heat the oven to 350°F/180°C/gas mark 4. Roll out the pastry thinly, and use it to line a deep, buttered 25 cm loose-bottomed cake tin, cover it with a sheet of tin foil and scatter over it some pastry beans, rice or dried haricot beans. Bake for about 15–20 minutes, remove it from the oven and transfer the foil and beans to a tin for future use. Brush the inside of the case with a little beaten egg or spare egg white, which will form a seal and prevent any leaks. Put it back in the oven for a further 5 to 10 minutes until it is well cooked through and biscuit coloured, particularly the base.

To make the filling, beat together the curd cheese, sugar, potato flour and salt until they are well blended. Whisk in the eggs one at a time until the mixture has increased in volume and is thick and fluffy. Drain the sultanas and add them to the mixture with the grated lemon rind. Pour the filling into the pastry case, dust it with the nutmeg and return it to the oven to bake for 45–50 minutes or until just set. Then turn off the oven, leave the door ajar and allow the cake to cool in the waning heat. Make sure the cake is thoroughly cold then unmould it from the tin and spread the soured cream smoothly over the surface.

expresso bongo

'A little knock-drawer under the machine made of wood and lined with metal paper, conspicuously opened and closed for every cup, held the discarded coffee. The tiny black cups of caffeine-rich espresso which provided day-round pick-me-ups in Italy were less popular in Britain than the more mellow cappuccino. Cappuccino (the name came from the brown and cream habits of the Italian order of Capuchin friars) was the drink that defined coffee bar culture.'

Terri Colpi, *The Italian Factor*, 1991

According to *Slice of Life* by Christina Hardyment, by 1960 there were two thousand coffee bars nationwide, and five hundred in Greater London alone. The most famous of all these places, the Two I's, was a breeding ground for pop idols, launching the likes of Tommy Steele and Adam Faith. And it was here in 1959 that Cliff Richard filmed *Expresso Bongo*, confirming the arrival of the Gaggia and coffee-bar culture.

For the first time the young had somewhere to hang out. The counter was dominated by that hissing, spluttering machine, which kept the room (and its windows) reassuringly steamy – and, with the cigarette fug (everybody smoked then), the coffee bar became a teenage sanctuary.

Although food wasn't really the point of the coffee bar, these Italian joints in 'continental' Soho not only knew how to make good coffee but also how to fashion a decent salami roll or to serve an authentic continental pastry. Depending on their size, some bars also offered breakfast and a few 'foreign' dishes.

Typically, when it came to our version, we got it wrong.

The British equivalent was the greasy-spoon café or the sandwich bar. Here, if you were lucky, you could get an OK fry-up and a slice of factory-made apple pie buried in Bird's custard. On the counter, under a sweaty plastic dome, there was usually a pile of orange Scotch eggs and, under another cover, a plate of flabby pasties, pies and sausage rolls. Sometimes these unsavoury savouries were kept at a steady warm temperature in a heated cabinet for most of the day – sometimes, perhaps, for days on end.

It wouldn't seem that there could be much worth salvaging from this sorry lot. After all, once you know about *saucisson en brioche* or *pâté en croûte* – the French versions of our sausage roll and pork pie – which would you rather eat? But that is to do our culinary heritage a disservice, because, should you bother to cook a carefully made sausage roll, meat or pork pie, Cornish pasty or Scotch egg, it will come as a revelation to discover just how delicious these five old friends can be.

cornish pasty

Serves 4

For a dish that involves so few ingredients and is so common all over the United Kingdom, it is amazing how many 'correct' recipes there are for a Cornish Pasty. The *paasty*, as it is pronounced in Cornwall, was invented as a way for miners to take their lunch to work. The thick seam that runs over the top of their midday meal was originally the handle – and, as such, chucked away – and each man had his initials written with scraps of pastry in the corners of the pasty.

Aficionados (including Hettie Merrick, who wrote *The Pasty Book*, and her daughter, Anne Muller, who owns the Pasty Shop at the Lizard) reckon it is made with skirt or chuck beef, potatoes, swede (others say turnip), onion and that's it. Whether the ingredients are diced or sliced is also debatable but everyone agrees that they must go in raw and that seasoning is restricted to salt and pepper, preferably a mixture of black (for flavour) and white (for pungency).

For the pastry:
300 g block lard
450 g strong plain flour
a pinch of salt
ice-cold water to mix

——

For the filling:
200 g onion, coarsely chopped
200 g swede, peeled and diced

400 g flank or *skirt* or *chuck beef,*
   trimmed and diced
600 g floury potatoes, peeled and diced

——

extra butter
a little water
egg wash
salt and freshly ground black and white
   pepper

cornish
pasty

Place the lard in its wrapper in the freezer and leave for about an hour until it is hard.

Sift the flour and salt into a mixing bowl. Take the lard out of the freezer, peel back the paper, dip into the flour and grate it into the bowl, dipping back into the flour every now and again to make the grating easier. Now, mix the lard evenly into the flour by making sweeping scoops with a palette knife until it resembles heavy breadcrumbs. Stir in one tablespoon of water at a time until the dough clings together, and form it into a ball. Put it in a polythene bag and chill in the fridge for 30 minutes.

Pre-heat the oven to 400°F/200°C/gas mark 6.

Meanwhile, arrange the filling ingredients in four equal piles, keeping each one separate. Roll out the pastry and cut out four circles. Sprinkle onion and swede across the centre of the pasty in an oval, leaving a 2 cm border at each end. Season with salt and pepper, then cover the vegetables with the meat and half of the potato. Season again and add the remainder of the potato.

Moisten half the pastry border with a little water, bring up each side of the circle to enclose the filling, and press together to form a ridge. Crimp with your fingers to form what looks like the backbone of a stegosaurus.

Butter a flat baking sheet and sprinkle with water. Transfer the pasties to the baking sheet, prick in a few places on either side of the seam with a fork and paint them all over with the egg wash.

Bake for 15 minutes. Lower the temperature to 300°F/150°C/gas mark 2 and cook for a further 30–40 minutes.

Serve wrapped in a paper napkin: a *paasty* is *never* eaten with a knife and fork.

pork pie

'The characteristic note of pork pies from Melton Mowbray, the great pie centre of England,' writes Jane Grigson in *English Food*, 'is the anchovy essence. It makes an excellent piquancy without the least fishiness.'

There is something about the combination of textures and flavours of a good Pork Pie that is hard to beat. The crisp, crumbly yet chewy pastry with a damp inner lining is imbued with meat juices along with an intensely savoury thin layer of golden jelly. This surrounds a well-seasoned, unctuous meaty filling. It is especially good when daubed with a smear of bright yellow English mustard.

No one has written about raised pie making with more authority and clarity than Jane Grigson and we give here (modified for metric ingredients) her excellent and explicit recipe from *English Food* (1974).

We think you will agree that, although quite a lot of time is needed to make the real McCoy, it isn't difficult and the rewards are immense and quite different from the usual fatty, bland lump of white and pink meat that shrinks from its thick, dull pastry cladding (always too much pastry and not enough filling) and rubbery jelly.

For the jellied stock:
bones from the meat used to make the
  filling
2 pig's trotters, or 1 veal knuckle
1 large carrot, sliced
1 medium onion, stuck with 3 cloves
bouquet garni
12 peppercorns
2.3–2.8 litres water

———

For the pork pie filling:
900 g boned shoulder of pork or *spareribs,*
  with approximately ¼ fat to ¾ lean
  meat

225 g thinly cut unsmoked bacon
1 tsp chopped sage
½ tsp each cinnamon, nutmeg, allspice
1 tsp anchovy essence
salt and freshly ground black pepper

———

For the hot-water crust:
200 ml water
175 g lard
450 g plain flour
½ tsp salt
1 egg (optional)

'To make the stock, put all ingredients into a pan and simmer for 3–4 hours steadily (cover the pan). Strain off the stock into a clean pan and boil down until you have about 400 ml of stock. Season with salt, and add more pepper if you like. This liquid will set to a firm jelly, and is much better than the stock plus gelatine recommended in some pie recipes.

'To make the pie filling, chop some of the best bits of pork into 0.5 cm dice. Mince the rest finely with two or three rashers of the bacon (the bacon cure improves the colour of the pie on account of the saltpetre: without it the filling would look rather grey when the pie is cut). Add the seasonings. Fry a small amount and taste to see if adjustments are needed. Mix in the diced meat. Line the base of the pastry with the remaining bacon, and fill with the pork mixture. You will always get a better texture if the meat is finely chopped rather than minced.

'To make the hot-water crust pastry, bring water and lard to the boil, then tip it quickly into the middle of the flour and salt, mixing everything rapidly together to a dough with a wooden spoon or electric beater. Add the egg if you like; it gives extra colour and richness, but is not essential – some people use a scant tablespoon of icing sugar instead which increases the crispness of the pastry. Leave the dough until it can be handled without too much discomfort, but do not allow it to cool. Cut off about a quarter for the lid, and put the rest into a hinged raised pie mould, or a cake tin with a removable base. Quickly and lightly push the pastry up the sides of the tin, being careful to leave no cracks. If the pastry collapses down into a dismal heap, it is a little too hot, so wait and try again.

'Many butchers making their own pies used wooden pie moulds and "raised" the dough round them. Jam jars can be used instead, but they need to be well-floured, or you will find it difficult to remove the jar without spoiling the raised pastry. Before putting the filling in, a band of brown paper was tied round the pies to help them keep their shape, and this remained in place during baking. Unless you are very skilful with your hands, and have plenty of time, the first method is much quicker and more successful – particularly if you invest in one of the attractively-decorated hinged pie moulds.

'Having raised the crust, make the jellied stock and choose a filling from the recipes below. Pack the filling into the pastry, roll out the lid and fix it in place with beaten egg. Make a central hole and decorate the pie with leaves and roses made from the trimming (sweet pies are not decorated in English cookery, but the meat ones often end up looking very decorative). Brush it over with beaten egg, and put into the oven at 400°F/200°C/gas mark 6, for half an hour to firm the pastry and give it a little colour. Then lower the heat to 325°F/170°C/gas mark 3, and leave for 1 hour (small pies) to 2 hours (large pork and chicken pies) so that the meat can cook. Keep an eye on the lid and protect it with brown paper if it colours too quickly.

'Remove the pie from the oven, and take it out of the mould (or untie the brown paper bands). Brush the sides with beaten egg and return to the oven for 10 minutes to colour them. When they look appetisingly brown, take them out and pour in jellied stock through the central hole using a tiny kitchen funnel or a cone of cardboard. This stock will fill the gaps left by the shrinking meat: it is important to have it nicely flavoured.

'Leave the pies for 24 hours before eating, or even longer.'

meat pie   *Serves 4*

The success of a good savoury Meat Pie relies heavily on all the ingredients being cooked together within the pastry. Juices from both meat and onions run into the crust as it cooks, producing that lovely soggy-yet-crisp texture beloved of all meat-pie aficionados. The addition of a little chopped potato adds a lovely flavour and soaks up the juices.

For the pastry:
175 g dripping or lard, very cold from the
    fridge, cut into small pieces
350 g plain flour
salt
4–6 tbsp cold water

For the filling:
550 g stewing steak – make sure it has bits
    of fat and sinew in it – cut into small
    dice
350 g onion, chopped
275 g potato, peeled and diced

salt and plenty of freshly ground white
pepper
1 level tbsp plain flour

175 ml water
a little milk
1 small egg, beaten

You will need a loose-bottomed, lightly buttered pastry tin, measuring 3 cm deep by 20 cm wide, and a flat oven tray, which is put into the oven to heat up so that the base of the pie cooks through evenly.

Pre-heat the oven to 400°F/200°C/gas mark 6, and put the baking tray on the middle shelf.

To make the pastry, rub together the fat, flour and salt until it resembles coarse breadcrumbs. Quickly mix in the water and work together until a coherent mass. Knead the dough lightly and put it into a plastic bag. Leave to rest in the fridge until the filling has been prepared.

Put all except the last three filling ingredients into a roomy bowl and, with your hands, mix together well. Cut off about a third of the pastry. Roll the larger piece into a circle about 3 mm thick – it should not be too thin. Line the tin, leaving the overhang intact. Roll out the rest of the pastry for the lid and set it aside. Pile the filling in right to the top (it will go in, don't worry) and carefully pour in the water, which should *just* reach the surface. Brush the edge of the overhanging pastry with water and put on the lid. Press the edges together at the rim of the tin, then slice off the excess pastry all in one go with a knife.

Brush the surface of the pie with egg wash, then decorate it as the fancy takes you and further press the edges together with the tines of a fork. Make two generous incisions in the centre of the pie and place it in the oven. Cook for 25 minutes, and then turn down the temperature to 325°F/170°C/gas mark 3. Bake for a further 1½ hours, checking from time to time that the pastry is not browning too much. If it is, turn down the oven a little more. What makes this sort of pie so special is a long, slow cook, with all the elements combining as one. To be truly authentic, douse with a little malt vinegar before eating.

sausage rolls

Makes 15 large sausage rolls

'Oh, I'm sure *she*'s got a light hand with pastry,' said Sister Dew eagerly. 'I hope I get a chance to taste one of her sausage rolls . . .'

'I hope they're all right,' said Ianthe. 'It's quite a long time since I made any.'

– Barbara Pym, *An Unsuitable Attachment*

No one makes Sausage Rolls now or, if they do, they cheat a little and use ready-made pastry – and why not? It can be very good – or bought sausage-meat, embellished with onion and herbs, or both. Home-made Sausage Rolls are worth the effort, even if you do cheat because hot and puffy from the oven they are always going to be far superior to the leathery, often repeatedly reheated, meanly filled versions that get passed off as the real thing.

For the pastry:
225 g strong plain flour
a pinch of salt
225 g cold butter, cut into small pieces
juice of ½ a lemon
150 ml ice-cold water

For the sausagemeat:
400 g lean belly pork, skinned and boned
300 g lean pork shoulder
150 g rindless streaky bacon
100 g pork fat

grated rind of 1 lemon
1 rounded tsp black pepper, freshly ground
1 level tsp salt
1 level tbsp chopped thyme leaves
2 heaped tbsp chopped parsley
8–10 sage leaves, chopped
2 tbsp syrup, from a jar of stem ginger

For glazing:
2 egg yolks, beaten with a dribble of water
    and a pinch of salt

Sift the flour and salt together into a bowl and add the butter. Loosely mix, but don't rub the two together in the normal way of pastry-making. Mix the lemon juice with the ice-cold water and pour it into the mixture. With a metal spoon, gently mix it all together until you have formed a cohesive

sausage rolls

mass. Turn the pastry on to a cool surface and shape it into a thick rectangle, measuring about 35 cm × 20 cm. Fold a third of the rectangle over towards the centre and fold the remaining third over that. Lightly press together and rest the pastry in the fridge for 10 minutes.

Return the pastry to the same position on the work surface and turn it through 90 degrees. Roll it out to the same dimensions as before, fold and rest again in the same way. Repeat this turning, rolling, folding and resting process three more times. Put the pastry in a polythene bag and leave it in the fridge for several hours or overnight.

To make the sausagemeat, mince together the three meats and fat twice, then mix them with all the other ingredients in a large bowl, mulching everything together with your hands – or put it in the bowl of a Kenwood mixer using the K-beater and work until it is nicely amalgamated. If you don't have a mincer you can use a food processor, but beware of over-processing which tears the meat and can make the mixture pasty.

Pre-heat the oven to 400°F/200°C/gas mark 6. To assemble the sausage rolls, divide the sausagemeat into 15 sausage shapes approximately 10 cm long × 2.5 cm thick. Roll the pastry into four or five long thin strips, approximately 10 cm wide. Using one strip at a time, brush the surface with the beaten egg yolk. Place one piece of sausagemeat about 3 cm in from the front of the sheet of pastry and roll over until the join is underneath. Cut across the strip of pastry just beyond the rolled sausage and press together. Continue in this mode until all the sausagemeat and pastry is used up. The sausage rolls are now ready for baking.

Place them on a greased baking sheet (making sure the join is underneath), brush with more beaten egg yolk and make four or five small diagonal slashes through the surface of each sausage roll. Bake for 15 minutes, then turn down the temperature to 350°F/180°C/gas mark 4 and continue baking for another 15 minutes.

scotch egg

Quite why Scotch Eggs are so called remains a mystery to us: no particularly Scottish ingredients are involved (not even whisky) and our researches revealed no trace of a Scottish heritage.

Most people have never eaten a home-made Scotch Egg and if they had they would never bother with the nasty versions which give this ubiquitous snack such a bad name. You know the sort of thing, the breadcrumbed coating is a funny orange colour and is all at once stodgy and dry and devoid of flavour. The 'sausagemeat' overcoat is always several sizes too big for the egg and the egg is rubbery hard with a sinister grey ring round a powdery yolk.

Like so many of the dishes in this book, you have only to make a Scotch Egg properly to discover why they became popular in the first place. What they *should* be is freshly made. Just imagine biting into a crisply coated, well-seasoned sausagemeat shell that gives, for once, on to a freshly cooked, free-range egg, its yolk still with a hint of softness. Yum.

10 medium free-range eggs

——

For the sausagemeat:
200 g lean belly pork, skinned and boned
150 g lean pork shoulder meat
75 g rindless streaky bacon
50 g pork fat
grated rind of ½ a lemon
1 rounded tsp freshly ground black pepper
½ level tsp salt

½ level tbsp chopped thyme leaves
1 heaped tbsp chopped parsley
6 sage leaves, chopped

——

flour for dusting
2 eggs, beaten
250 g fresh breadcrumbs made with stale
 bread
oil for deep frying

Put the eggs in a saucepan of cold water, bring to the boil and cook for 4 minutes. Refresh under cold running water for 3 minutes and then peel carefully.

To make the sausagemeat, mince together the three meats and the fat twice, and mix them with all the other ingredients in a large bowl, mulching everything together with your hands – or put it in the bowl of a Kenwood mixer, use the K-beater and work until it is nicely amalgamated.

Lay out in advance everything you need to assemble the Scotch eggs: flour in one shallow bowl, egg in another and breadcrumbs in another. Roll the hard-boiled eggs in the flour, shaking off any excess and set aside. Dust a work surface with flour and pick off a 50 g piece of sausagemeat. Flatten it with your hand and work it into an approximately 10 cm oval. Paint the surface with beaten egg and place a hard-boiled egg in the middle. Bring up the sides of the sausagemeat to encase the egg, making sure there are no gaps. Dip it first in the flour, then the egg and finally the breadcrumbs, and set it aside on a plate while you continue with the other eggs.

Bring the oil in the deep fryer up to 310°F/160°C (for those without a deep fryer or thermometer, this is when a scrap of bread turns golden after a couple of minutes) and lower the eggs into the oil. Depending on the size of your fryer, you will have to do this in several batches; the Scotch eggs should be completely immersed and not crowded in the pan. Cook for 8 minutes until evenly crisp and pale golden. Drain on kitchen paper and eat warm or cold. Delicious with piccalilli.

the sixties bistro

'This was the time when Chelsea was first becoming what would now be called "trendy" with a curious social mixture of people doing odd things.

'It was in the midst of this that Nick [Clarke] had first conceived the idea of running a workman's transport café and Ifield Road was almost perfect for him.'

Gregory Houston Bowden, talking about Nick's Diner,
British Gastronomy, 1975

As we approach the millennium, when restaurants and continental cafés are two-a-penny in every city centre and most rural towns, it is hard to imagine the impact that the arrival of a clutch of idiosyncratic restaurants with strangely plain names such as The Spot, The Casserole, Gaslight and 19 Mossop Street, had on already bohemian Chelsea.

But in the Swinging Sixties just as hairdressing was being turned on its head, as it were, with the appearance of unisex salons with trendy names like Smile and Scissors, and clothes shops suddenly metamorphosed into boutiques, the restaurant scene underwent an overnight renaissance. What all these places had in common was that they were opened and run by enthusiastic young people showing a healthy disrespect for tradition, and in the case of restaurants, many owners were new to the catering business.

These were places that could not be pigeon-holed in the way that restaurants always had been – the hotel restaurant, the 'French' restaurant, Lyons Corner House – and were the first real stirrings of our new-found restaurant culture. They were not exactly French – many modelled themselves on the mythical Left Bank bistro – and although closer in spirit to the mood of the trattorias springing up in fashionable parts of London, these new places most certainly couldn't be classified in the same way as the continental restaurant (see chapter four).

Their menus were exciting in a way that was quite unknown – it was very daring, for example, to sit opposite a 'date' and nibble corn off a cob, knowing that you were smearing butter all over your face. There were odd things to eat, like frog's legs and mussels, which had to be picked up with fingers (hands-on food in restaurants then was more than unusual, it wasn't 'nice') and many dishes were made with what seemed like unnatural amounts of garlic (*zut alors!*) and almost all the main dishes were cooked with wine.

Nick Clarke, an old Etonian with no particular training in catering, was typical of this new breed of restaurateur and his famous Nick's Diner, on the edge of Chelsea, was only one of a growing number of pioneering places that offered a new way of eating out. For the first time, going to a restaurant was regarded as something one might do as a matter of course – if you could get a table – and not something to save for a special occasion.

The food was comparatively inexpensive and for the young professionals who flocked to these places the menus, with dishes such as tomato salad, French onion soup, chili con carne and chocolate mousse, offered exactly the sort of food they aspired to cook for their dinner parties. Many of the customers, and staff too, were friends of the *patron* and this led to a new informality that broke down all barriers between server and served and changed the balance between customer and staff for ever. And there were no dress codes: the chaps were just as likely to wear their jeans (neatly pressed with a crease, and a cravat replacing the tie) as a suit, and, thanks to Biba and Mary Quant, the gulf between day and evening dress was beginning to blur.

The décor, too, was noticeably different: many went the French bistro route with red gingham tablecloths, candles (dripping down an old Mateus Rosé bottle) and red paper napkins and some showed signs of eccentricity in the detailing – olive-green paper napkins and matching candles, perhaps, or waiters dressed in flowered or vividly coloured shirts with huge collars. Other restaurants went for the farmhouse look (stripped pine tables and a kitchen dresser) or were decked out like a private dining room.

Another toff who cut a dash on the Chelsea restaurant scene in the sixties was Alexander Plunkett-Green, Mary Quant's husband. Like Nick Clarke he named his restaurant after himself – Alexander's – and the following review, which appeared in *The Good Food Guide*, *circa* 1961–62, is so evocative we produce it here in full:

This restaurant is now established, successful and fairly expensive. It is on the corner of Markham Square; you eat by candlelight, in front of a blazing log fire in winter, and get served by professional (red-shirted) waiters. It opens for lunch (12.30–2.30 p.m.) and dinner and stays open till pretty late (from 7.30; last orders at 11.15 (10.30 on Sundays)) but will remain open till 1 a.m., or later, for lingerers). The menu offers all the usual unusual dishes from avocado pears, dolmades and scampi at one end of the menu, zabaglione and lemon sorbet at the other. Both chefs are Italian but the main dishes are impartially Italian or French and cost between 8/6 [less than 50p] and 14/6 [around 75p], without vegetables. Fully licensed; adequate wine list, not over-priced. No reply to our inquiries received from the restaurant.

Incidentally, the telephone number was KNIghtsbridge 4604.

celeriac remoulade   *Serves 4*

Available in every small-town *charcuterie* in France, Celeriac Remoulade is the staple of the cold lunch and is as French as Coleslaw is American. No self-respecting *femme de maison* would dream of making it at home in France when she can get a small plastic carton of it from the end of the *rue*. However, in Britain, there is every reason for pushing a lump of celeriac through the blade of the Magimix, as most of us have one of those but do not, sadly, have the little *charcuterie* on the *coin*.

½ small to medium celeriac, peeled
juice of ½ a small lemon
a little salt and some freshly ground white
*   pepper*
3 tbsp good quality mayonnaise, preferably
*   home made*

2 tsp smooth Dijon mustard
1 tbsp double cream
1 rounded tbsp coarsely chopped flat-leaf
*   parsley*

Finely grate the celeriac, place it in a bowl and thoroughly mix in the lemon juice and seasonings with your hands. Leave for 30 minutes: this will soften

the sixties bistro   153

the celeriac and also keep it white. Add the other four ingredients and mix well.

Very good served with sliced ham, or, even better, with prosciutto.

eggs florentine

Serves 4

Along with chicken and tarragon, avocado with prawns and sausage and mash, spinach with eggs is a perfect combination. Whether the Florentines are entirely responsible for the recipe is a moot point, but let us graciously give them the benefit of the doubt. The use of a good béchamel in the dish would certainly suggest Italian, but we have yet to discover why spinach has always been synonymous with Florence.

For the sauce:
200 ml milk
2 cloves
1 small onion, peeled and finely chopped
1 bay leaf
salt and pepper
40 g butter
25 g plain flour
75 ml double cream

50 g butter
450 g fresh spinach, picked over,
*   thoroughly washed and dried*
salt, pepper and freshly grated nutmeg
4 eggs
vinegar
50 g Parmesan, freshly grated

Pre-heat the oven to 425°F/220°C/gas mark 7.

To make the sauce, heat together the milk, cloves, onion, bay leaf and seasoning. Remove the pan from the heat, cover and leave it to infuse for 15 minutes or longer. Now, melt the butter in a heavy-based saucepan, and stir in the flour to make a roux. Strain the milk into the roux and whisk thoroughly. Bring to a simmer, gently, over a low heat for a good 10 minutes. Strain again and adjust the seasoning, stir in the cream and keep it warm.

Heat the 50 g butter in a large shallow pan until it is just turning nut-brown. Put in the spinach, season with salt, pepper and nutmeg and stir-fry until it is limp and just cooked. Drain in a colander, pressing gently to extract excess moisture. Keep it warm.

Poach the eggs in water, with a splash of vinegar. Leave them a little undercooked. Meanwhile, divide the spinach between four shallow, individual white dishes (those ones with 'ears' are perfect), leaving a hollow in the middle for the eggs. Crack an egg into each hollow, pour over some of the sauce and bake in the oven for 4–5 minutes. Finish off under a hot grill so that the sauce blisters somewhat. Then sprinkle each serving with Parmesan and eat without delay.

escargots à la bourguignonne

Serves 4

Along with garlic bread and garlic mushrooms, snails in garlic butter served in their shell on special indented dishes epitomize the sixties bistro menu. They positively reeked of garlic, their molten buttery juices weeping out of the shell just begging to be soaked up with – if you were lucky – some decent French bread. Some people chose them out of bravado not caring to dwell too long on what they actually were, while others liked their chewy texture and enjoyed the business of holding them with their special tongs and plucking the gastropod from its spiral shell.

This was the dish that sorted the men, as it were, from the boys; and when women chose snails (often chalked up on the blackboard as a chef's special, almost as if it was too risqué to make it on to the main menu), well, that was likely to be greeted with congratulations all round (this happened to LB in a bistro in Hampstead, around 1968). An adventurous choice indeed. Sadly, those snails were often dry, rubbery and tasteless, the harsh garlic butter covering up a multitude of sins. This is how to make them properly at home using ready-cooked, canned snails, which are sold with their ready-washed shells in a separate package.

For the snail butter:	*1½ tsp salt*
450 g unsalted butter, softened	*½ tsp freshly ground black pepper*
50 g garlic, as fresh as possible, peeled and	*¼ tsp cayenne*
finely chopped	*5 drops Tabasco*
75 g flat-leaf parsley, leaves only	———
25 g dry breadcrumbs	*48 snails*
2 tbsp Pernod	*48 snail shells*

You will also need 4 traditional snail dishes, with their little indentations, or you could, at a pinch, use an oven tray filled with sea salt and balance the shells in it. However, should any butter flow out — and it does, it does — the salt will soak it up, which, frankly, misses the point, doesn't it?

First make the snail butter. Put the butter and garlic in an electric mixer or food-processor and beat together. Blanch half the parsley briefly in boiling water. Drain it, refresh under cold running water and squeeze it dry. Chop this and the remaining parsley as finely as possible. Add to the butter with the remaining ingredients and beat everything together until it is thoroughly blended. The butter should be very green.

Pre-heat the oven to 450°F/230°C/gas mark 8.

An important point *not* to forget when putting the butter in the shells, is to push in a small amount (about ½ tsp) before you insert the snail. This helps to prevent the snail meat scorching, it being close to the base of the shell as it becomes very hot. So do this first, then push in the snail – pointed part uppermost and quite far down into the shell – and pack the rest of the butter over the top making a good seal.

Place the snails on four snail dishes, making sure that the apertures of the shells are as horizontal as possible. Bake at the top of the oven for 15–20 minutes, or until the snails are bubbling furiously. Serve immediately, so they are still frothing when they reach the table. Crusty bread is essential.

french onion soup

Serves 6–8

The amount of onions – enormous – is the key to a good onion soup, whether it is this one or one made with cream and puréed. The length of time for which they are cooked, sweated, stewed and eventually caramelized is also terribly important to the making of a French Onion Soup. Patience is all. A beady eye is also needed or the onions will soon catch and scorch as they flop down into the bottom of the pan. Some cowboy cooks add a pinch of sugar to aid browning; this should never be necessary, as onions have a high sugar content and will exude their own sweetness as they sweat.

For the family table, it is marvellous to serve the soup in the heavy pot it has been cooked in. Finishing in the oven, with *croûtes* and much cheese, enables the whole bubbling mass to blister and burnish evenly, allowing dribbles of soup and crusted, melting cheese to erupt over the edge of the pot in the most authentic manner.

100 g butter

2 kg large onions, peeled, halved and very finely sliced

——

For the *croûtes*:

1 small day-old baguette

1 garlic clove, peeled

50 g melted butter

150 g grated Gruyère cheese

——

1 tbsp flour

1.5 l hot beef stock: see the recipe for meat glaze (pages 26–7) and use the stock as it is before reduction

approximately 150 ml dry white wine or dry cider

3 tbsp cognac

salt and pepper

a little extra grated Gruyère

Melt 75 g of the butter in a large, heavy-bottomed, lidded pan (a good-looking Le Creuset would be the thing to use here as this is what the soup will be presented in, and the pan should be of such a size that the soup comes almost to the brim). Tip in the onions, cover, and sweat them very gently, stirring every now and again for 15 minutes. Remove the lid, turn up the heat slightly, and cook for at least 45 minutes, stirring regularly until the onions are tender and a deep golden brown.

Meanwhile, make the *croûtes*. Pre-heat the oven to 425°F/220°C/gas mark 7. Rub the outside of the baguette with the garlic until it has all been used. Cut into approximately 16 slices and lay them on a buttered baking sheet. Drizzle over the melted butter, strew with the grated cheese, covering the slices evenly, and bake for about 15 minutes until all is a mass of golden bubbles. Take them out and leave them to cool, when the cheese will have hardened and the bread will be crisp. Break up and separate the slices. Put them on one side.

In a small pan, melt the remaining 25 g of the butter. Add the flour and make a roux. Pour in two ladles of the hot stock and whisk until it has thickened. Pour back into the pan of hot stock, whisk again and keep it hot. When the onions are ready, add the wine or cider and allow it to reduce and evaporate. Pour the thickened hot stock into the pan with the onions, stirring constantly. Bring it to a simmer and cook for a further 15 minutes. Stir in the cognac and check the seasoning.

If you have one of those ovens with a grill inside it then heat this to its fullest. If not, turn up the oven to full whack; putting the heavy pot under a standard overhead grill could be a bit dicey. Cover the surface of the soup with the *croûtes*, strew over the extra cheese and bake until the top is, once more, bubbling and blistered.

Serves 4

garlic mushrooms

The heady scent of grilled red peppers that drifts out of restaurant kitchen windows today is the equivalent of the inexorable waft of garlic that licked the hem of the mini-skirt in the sixties. Garlic was it! Garlic was God! Garlic was good!

This was when Terence Conran opened Habitat and sold garlic presses

garlic mushrooms

by the dozen. Elizabeth David had her shop in Pimlico and didn't – she loathed them. Robert Carrier served *Carré d'Agneau à la Provençal* with its garlic and parsley crust, and L'Escargot Bienvenue in Soho sent out dish after dish of bubbling, garlic-laden *Escargots à la Bourguignonne*. But it was mushrooms that took the lion's share. Mushrooms cooked in garlic butter were king of the sixties bistro.

The following recipe is one of the best ways of cooking garlic mushrooms. This recipe uses flat black mushrooms, as they really do have the best flavour. Serve it as a first course or, alternatively, as a vegetable to go with grilled steak or lamb cutlets.

20 flat black mushrooms, stalks removed

olive oil

2 small lemons, zest removed and chopped,
*   and juice squeezed*

salt and pepper

100 g fresh breadcrumbs

1 large bunch flat-leaf parsley, leaves only

4 garlic cloves, peeled and chopped

100 g butter, melted

Pre-heat the oven to 400°F/200°C/gas mark 6.

Put the mushrooms on a roasting tray, gills uppermost, drizzle each with a little olive oil, pour over the lemon juice and season. Bake for 30 minutes until well cooked through. Remove them from the oven and leave them to cool in the tray.

Meanwhile, place the breadcrumbs in a food processor, then add the parsley, garlic and lemon rind. Process until well blended; the crumbs will turn a lovely green colour, but don't overwork the mixture or it will become pasty. Carefully spoon some over each mushroom and then gently press in the mixture with your fingers. Spoon the butter evenly over each mushroom. Turn up the oven to 450°F/230°C/gas mark 8 and return the mushrooms to the top shelf of the oven. Bake for 10 minutes until the crumbs are starting to brown. If necessary finish them off under the grill. Serve immediately.

garlic bread

Serves 2–4

Anyone who says that they don't really like garlic bread must be lying. It is surely one of the most simple gastronomic pleasures and one that thankfully hasn't gone away. Supermarkets sell it ready to cook, unpretentious country restaurants and good pubs wrap it in silver foil and send it out with a bowl of soup, and LB's boys wolf it down like pizza. When you think about it, it's actually a lot nicer than most pizza.

100 g butter, softened

3 plump garlic cloves, very finely chopped

2 tbsp finely chopped flat-leaf parsley

1 small baguette

Pre-heat the oven to 400°F/200°C/gas mark 6.

Mix the butter with the garlic and stir in the parsley. Using a sharp knife, make diagonal incisions about 3 cm apart, as if you were slicing the loaf but without cutting right through. Take a sheet of silver foil large enough to parcel the loaf and place it in the middle. Spread the garlic butter between the slices using a small knife, close up the parcel and bake for 10 minutes. To achieve a crusted top, open the foil and bake for a further 5 minutes.

moules marinière

Serves 2

This was an exciting dish for any true *bon viveur*. The sight of a steaming pile of little mussels brought to the table would bring forth whoops of delight. After all, this quayside speciality of Brittany had usually only been encountered on continental holidays. Why we in Britain, with our love of cockles, whelks and oysters, have never been famous for cooking mussels is a mystery – and something we should be ashamed of.

Reckon on a good pig-out if you're contemplating this, the greatest and simplest of all mussel dishes. Allow a kilo of mussels per person, make a whole meal of them with some decent bread – and take your time. The quality of wine here is important: it does not cook for very long, so the alcohol and flavour will not dissipate much. Use a reasonable white wine and drink the same.

75 g butter

2 medium onions, peeled and finely chopped

½ bottle Muscadet, or similar

2 kg mussels, cleaned, discarding any that
   are open

4 tbsp freshly chopped flat-leaf parsley

plenty of freshly ground black pepper

Take a very large lidded pan. Heat the butter and fry the onions in it until they are softened and transparent. Pour in the wine and allow it to come to the boil. Tip in the mussels, put on the lid and, holding the handle in both hands, shake the pan around a bit. Put it over a high heat and cook for 3 minutes. Lift off the lid, have a look to see if the mussels are opening – it doesn't take long – and give them another shake, trying to bring the already opened mussels on the bottom to the top. Replace the pan on the heat, put on the lid and continue to cook for a few more minutes. Have another look and give another shake. When it seems that most of the shells are open, toss in the parsley, grind in lots of pepper, shake and stir everything around for the last time and tip the lot into a large hot bowl or eat them straight from the pan. It goes without saying that you may just need a little bread here.

   Note: Don't eat any mussels which haven't opened.

Serves 4

salade niçoise

We prefer not to include the ubiquitous tuna in a Salade Niçoise. There is nothing wrong with tuna, but if the anchovies you use (and these *are* an absolutely essential ingredient) are of the very best quality – Spanish ones are particularly good – then it's better to up the quantity and forgo the tuna.

The innermost leaves of floppy, silky round lettuces is the salad to use here, although purists insist that 'salad' as such is not an important ingredient. Frilly ones such as silly lollo rosso are right out and frisée and lamb's lettuce – the latter two being winter salad anyway – seem out of place, considering that the very look of a colourful Salade Niçoise yells sunshine.

However, a few leaves of peppery rocket can be nice, some mildly aniseed-flavoured sprigs of chervil (used, for once, as itself and not minutely placed as a pretty garnish) and a few torn leaves of basil will add the essential scent of the Riviera. As for the main ingredients, these are finally a matter for you. Some say that all the ingredients should be raw, whereas others, us included, insist on a few little cooked potatoes and some green beans. Garlic, on the other hand, is an essential component, as are olives, olive oil, eggs and tomatoes. Two ingredients, however, that are seldom seen but are delicious inclusions are tiny broad beans and similarly infantile artichoke hearts.

For the dressing:
1 tbsp red wine vinegar
salt and pepper
2 garlic cloves, peeled and chopped
75–100 ml Provençal extra virgin olive
   oil – deeply fruity

⸻

4 large eggs, as fresh as possible
the inner leaves of 2 round lettuces, washed
chervil sprigs, flat-leaf parsley, a few torn
   basil leaves, rocket, etc.
1 heart of celery, just the tender inner
   stalks, sliced into strips
4 ripe tomatoes, skinned and quartered
a large handful of green beans, topped and
   tailed, boiled in well-salted water,
   refreshed and drained

broad beans, shelled, about 4 tbsp, given the
   same treatment as the green beans
8 small artichoke hearts (fine-quality
   bottled ones can be very good),
   quartered
12 small new potatoes, scraped, boiled and
   then cut in half: keep warm in their
   water until ready for use
16 small black olives, the tiny Niçoise are
   best
1 heaped tbsp capers, drained and lightly
   squeezed dry
6 small spring onions, trimmed and thinly
   sliced
20 anchovies, fat, pink, and preferably
   packed in olive oil

the sixties bistro 163

Make the dressing by whisking together the vinegar, seasoning and garlic in a bowl. Continue whisking, adding the oil in a thin stream until it is amalgamated, and put it to one side. Boil the eggs for exactly 5 minutes, in fast-boiling water. Drain and refresh them under a cold running tap for 3 minutes. Peel them carefully (the yolks will be runny) and cut them into quarters. In a large, shallow terracotta or white dish, arrange the lettuce leaves in a single layer. Disperse the other ingredients in a random fashion and spoon over the dressing. Serve immediately.

pâté maison

Pâté Maison once covered a multitude of sins. Granted, some of them might have been home-made (the familiar plastic round dishes containing some sort of pink paste, supposedly hailing from the 'Ardennes', had not quite reached these shores by then), but possibly the ingredients were . . . how shall we put it? . . . suspiciously sourced.

A pâté or terrine is not just a hotch-potch of ingredients and it is something that takes time and trouble to prepare well. Sure, there are simple examples such as the smooth duck liver pâté (see page 166) from Paul Merrony's book, *The New French Cooking in Australia* (it's a sure sign of global cuisine when you want to use a recipe from a gifted Australian chef to locate a good pâté, even though he did work in Paris for four years), but, even so, the techniques and care involved will always need vigilant monitoring.

When tackling something such as the rough pork pâté or country terrine (*terrine de campagne*) given below, the proportions of fat and lean, offal (liver, usually) and bacon, seasoning and alcohol, if any, should be understood and respected if a coherent result is to be achieved. And if not, then the memories of a crumbling, tasteless wedge of grey matter perched upon a leathery lettuce leaf will return to haunt one and all.

Pâté maison 1: Traditional country terrine   *Serves 8–10*

This is one of the simplest terrines to make. It only requires some coarse mincing and thorough mixing. The resultant texture of the terrine is firm and densely meaty, ideal to serve with a perky chutney or onion marmalade.

450 g onions, peeled and coarsely chopped
75 g butter
450 g belly pork, skinned and any little bones removed
350 g rindless streaky bacon
450 g pig's liver
175 g pork back fat
50 ml cognac
50 ml port or *sherry*

4 garlic cloves, peeled, crushed and finely chopped
1 small bunch flat-leaf parsley, leaves only, coarsely chopped
1 egg
1 flat tbsp herbes de Provence
½ tsp ground allspice
1 tsp freshly ground white pepper
salt

Pre-heat the oven to 300°F/150°C/gas mark 2.

Gently fry the onions in the butter until golden brown, which will take about 20 minutes, and tip them on to a plate to cool. Don't wash the frying pan yet.

Put the belly pork, bacon, liver and back fat through the largest hole of the mincer (if you want a finer texture, put it through twice) and then into the bowl of the mixer with the cooled onions. Pour the cognac and port or sherry into the onion pan and heat slowly. Whisk together to lift off any caramelized bits of onion and then ignite the liquid with a match. Once the flames have subsided, remove the pan from the heat and allow it to cool. Add the rest of the ingredients, including the cooled alcohols, but not the salt. Mix slowly but thoroughly with the flat blade of a mixer until well combined, or by hand in a large bowl.

At this point it is a good idea to take a spoonful of the mixture and fry it in a scrap of butter until cooked through; allow it to cool, then eat some. It is important to let the little taster cool, as this, naturally, will be the temperature at which the terrine is to be served. Now decide on the amount of salt you need to add.

Once the mixture is correctly seasoned, pour it into a 1 litre capacity terrine mould. Then, dip your hand in warm water and smooth the surface to give a slightly domed appearance. Put on the lid, or cover the dish with foil, and place it in a deep roasting tin. Fill the tin with hot water until it reaches three-quarters of the way up the side of the dish. Put it in the oven for 1 hour, then check to see how it is coming along by inserting a thin skewer right through the deepest part of the terrine. Leave it there and count to ten. Pull it out and test it with your tongue. The skewer needs to be hot – warm is not enough – and the juices should be clear and rosy. Replace the dish in the oven, but without the lid. This will allow the surface of the terrine to brown a little. Cook for another 10 minutes and check again. The approximate time for a terrine such as this to cook is around 1½ hours, but this can vary, depending on your oven. Once you feel that the terrine is cooked remove it from the water and replace the lid or foil. Leave it to cool at kitchen temperature, then put it in the fridge and hold it there for two days at least before eating, thus allowing the flavours to develop and mature. It will keep for several days.

Pâté maison 2: Paul Merrony's smooth duck liver pâté   *Serves 4*

350 g duck livers, cleaned

75 ml double cream

100 g unsalted butter at room temperature,
    cut into 1 cm cubes

75 ml port

1 tsp salt

½ level tsp white pepper, freshly ground

⅓ tsp ground quatre-épices *(see*
    page 44)

75 g melted butter

Bring a large pan of salted water to the boil and poach the livers for 2 minutes. Drain and liquidize them with the cream while they are still warm. Stir the butter into the puréed livers until it is completely absorbed. Pass the mixture through a fine sieve into a clean bowl.

Bring the port to the boil, ignite it with a match, allow it to cool, then whisk it into the butter and liver mixture. Season with the salt, pepper and *quatre-épices*. Pour the pâté into a small shallow oval dish and place it in the fridge to cool for 30 minutes. Take it out and carefully spoon over the melted butter to seal the pâté. Return it to the fridge and eat it within 48 hours.

To serve, take a dessert spoon, dip it into hot water and scoop the pâté on to individual plates. Serve with hot crisp toast.

cheese fondue

Serves 4

To quote Emily Green in an article published in the *Independent* in 1996 on the touchy subject of 'fashionable food', she so correctly observed that:

. . . it should be admitted that retro-cuisine *is* here, if not exactly new. In more civilized countries, it is known as tradition. Imagine, if you will, Chinese re-discovering the egg noodle, or the people of Marseille opening their morning paper to read: 'Bouillabaisse is back.' Would the rich industrialists of Turin ever need to be told, 'Risotto has returned'? Paella will never need reviving in Spain. Fondue never went out in Switzerland, Germany and Alsace, where it marries the best of local cheese and wine into a dish that suits the climate.

Fondue is not about playing at table cookery. The reason for the burner under the pot is for practical reasons: it prevents the cheese mixture from stiffening up, which it does quite swiftly if left to cool. Purists would probably insist that no extraneous thickening is necessary to fashion a true *fondue Suisse*. However, the merest suggestion of arrowroot, that cure-all thickener, ensures that this most voluptuous cheesy mass is safe from curdle and spoil.

450 ml Gruyère cheese, grated

450 ml white wine (something fruity such as an Alsace variety)

1 garlic clove, peeled and mashed to a paste with a pinch of salt

1 rounded tsp arrowroot

2–3 tbsp kirsch

25 g butter, softened

1 small or half a large baguette, cut into large chunks – approximately 3 cm cubes

Pre-heat the oven to 400°F/200°C/gas mark 6.

Put the cheese, wine and garlic into a heavy-bottomed pot and place on a very low heat (alternatively, use a double boiler if you feel timid; or, if you take the first option, a heat-diffuser pad can be useful). Stir constantly as

the sixties bistro   167

cheese fondue

the cheese melts, until it is thick. Mix the arrowroot with the kirsch and stir it in: this will bind the mixture together. Finally, stir in the butter. Keep the fondue warm over a bowl of barely simmering water while you put the bread cubes on a rack in the oven. Bake them for 15 minutes until they are golden and crusted. Pour the fondue into the traditional pan (if you still have one tucked at the back of the kitchen cupboard), set it on its burner, place it in the centre of the dining table and give each participant their two-pronged fork. Dunk the bread into the fondue and yodel.

boeuf à la bourguignonne

Serves 4

French food shops and market traders (unlike most English ones) are often as knowledgeable as their customers about what a purchase is to be used for. Cuts of meat and displays of fish are promoted using those familiar black and red plastic labels, which indicate not the name of the cut of meat or type of fish necessarily but how they are to be prepared. Hence, instructions might suggest '*blanquette*' (as for veal stew), or '*bouillabaisse*' and '*soupe*' (as for the Marseille fish stew and soup) and, particularly in Burgundy, simply 'Bourguignonne' for its own dish of braised beef cooked in red wine of the region.

Incidentally, having been shocked to see some quite disgusting-looking red mullet in a British supermarket recently, it moved us to wonder what would be the French translation for 'Isn't it about time these were chucked in the bin?'

Choose a sinewy-looking piece of meat for Boeuf à la Bourguignonne, and ask your butcher to cut it into large pieces weighing in at around 150 g a piece. A true Boeuf à la Bourguignonne is not about little 0.5 cm cubes of meat stewed in Hirondelle.

the sixties bistro 169

1 bottle well-flavoured red Burgundy

1 dsp redcurrant jelly

1 large carrot, peeled and chopped

1 small onion, peeled and chopped

2 celery ribs, chopped

8 garlic cloves, peeled and bruised with the
      back of a knife

3 sprigs thyme

2 bay leaves

½ beef stock cube

_____

salt and freshly milled pepper

1 kg well-hung sinewy beef – chuck,
      shoulder or shin, perhaps, cut into
      large pieces, allowing about 3–4 per
      serving

1 heaped tbsp flour

2 tbsp olive oil

50 g butter

100 g streaky bacon or pancetta, in one
      piece, cut into 1 cm pieces

24 button onions, peeled (place in a bowl of
      hot water first; they are then easier to
      peel)

20 button mushrooms

1 pig's trotter, split lengthways by the
      butcher

75 ml cognac

juice of ½ a lemon

1 heaped tbsp chopped parsley

Put the first nine ingredients in a non-reactive (stainless steel or enamelled) pan and bring to the boil. Ignite the wine with a match and allow the flames to subside. Turn down the heat and simmer for about 30 minutes until the wine has reduced by almost half. Strain it into a bowl through a fine sieve and reserve.

Season the beef and roll it in the flour. Melt the oil and butter in a large heavy-bottomed, lidded cast-iron pot (Le Creuset would be ideal). Once the fats are foaming, put in the bacon or pancetta and fry until it is crusted and brown. Remove it to a plate and reserve. Now slip in the beef, cooking only 4–5 pieces at a time, so as not to overcrowd the pot. Colour it well on both sides until it is a rich brown, remove it to a plate and continue with the rest. Once all the beef is coloured, add the button onions and fry gently until they are golden brown. Remove them to a plate and reserve. Treat the mushrooms in the same manner.

Put the two halves of the pig's trotter into the pan, cut side down, and fry gently until well burnished. Repeat on the other side. Now, leaving the trotter in the pot, tip out everything else but the merest amount of fat, and then return the beef, together with the onions and mushrooms.

Pre-heat the oven to 275°F/140°C/gas mark 1.

Turn up the heat under the pot and pour in the cognac. Ignite it with a match, then pour over the reserved and reduced wine. Gently bring it to a simmer and skim off the scum as it forms on the surface. At this stage there may not look as if there is enough liquid in the pot. Worry not, as juices will come out of the beef and trotters, as well as a certain amount from the vegetables. Place the pot in the oven, cover it and braise for 2 hours.

Remove the trotter from the pot and put it on a plate (to nibble at later perhaps, with a splash of wine vinegar) or discard it. Check the seasoning, add the lemon juice and remove any excess fat from the surface with a few sheets of kitchen paper. Sprinkle with the parsley and serve straight from the pot with some plainly boiled potatoes.

coq au vin

Serves 4

Linked inextricably with Boeuf à la Bourguignonne, as the quintessential sixties stew. Some of them weren't half bad, come to think of it, but then it would have to be a complete moron who managed to cock up a Coq au Vin.

Even if the dish is almost thrown together, the result will still be palatable, if not exactly good-looking.

Traditionally, Coq au Vin is made with an older bird and the cooking time is considerably longer, resulting in a deeply flavoured rich stew. A split pig's trotter or two might have been included to add extra richness, and the blood from the fowl would have been introduced towards the end of the cooking time to thicken the juices as with jugged hare.

In the following recipe, however, the bird is young, cooked for much less time, but still tasting good and winy, comforting, and as memorable as ever. As with the preceding recipe and, incidentally, Boeuf à la Bourguignonne, Coq au Vin tastes infinitely better reheated the next day. This also allows for any fat that has collected on the surface to be easily removed, as it will have solidified in the fridge.

1 bottle full-bodied, decent quality red wine

3–4 sprigs fresh thyme

2 bay leaves

1 dsp redcurrant jelly

1 small onion, peeled and stuck with 2 cloves

2 celery ribs, chopped

1 carrot, peeled and chopped

4 garlic cloves, peeled and bruised

an extremely good chicken, weighing about 2 kg maximum

salt and pepper

1 tbsp flour

25 g butter

1 tbsp olive oil

75 g piece of pancetta, cut into thick strips or cubes

20 button onions, peeled

20 button mushrooms

3 tbsp cognac

Put the first eight ingredients into a stainless steel or enamelled pot and bring it to the boil. Reduce the wine by half over a medium flame, then strain it through a fine sieve and reserve.

Joint the chicken into four parts, that is, two legs – which comprise drumstick and thigh – and two breasts, including the wings, all of which must be cut away from the carcass. Remove the skin and cut the thigh pieces from the drumsticks. Season all the pieces well and roll them in the flour. Heat the butter and olive oil in a heavy-bottomed, lidded pan and sauté the chicken until it is golden brown. Remove it to a plate and fry the pancetta in the same fat until it is crisp. Put this with the chicken. Now tip the onions and mushrooms into the pot and stew them until well coloured – about 10 minutes. Put back the chicken and bacon and turn up the heat. Pour over the cognac, set it alight, allow the flames to die down then pour in the reduced wine. Shake the pan about a bit, allow everything to settle down, cover and set it over a very low heat. Simmer at a mere blip for about an hour. Plain boiled potatoes are a fine accompaniment.

carbonnade of beef

Serves 4

It was interesting to discover that neither of us knew about the inclusion of bread in a carbonnade. We knew that it is cooked in ale with onions and braised ever so slowly, resulting in a rich brown stew with deep, earthy flavours, but the bread thing was a revelation thanks to our very own Constance Spry (Connie to her admirers).

The slices of bread are dripped with fat from the surface of the casserole, spread with mustard, laid on the surface of the stew and finally baked in the oven for the last few minutes until crusted and richly browned. How sad, then, that this clearly wonderful finish to the dish never made it to the candle-lit table of the sixties bistro. Well, if it did, we never had any of it. The following recipe comes from *The Constance Spry Cookery Book* (1956).

1 or 2 tbsp dripping

750 g braising beef, cut into large squares

300 g onions, peeled, halved and thinly sliced

15 g flour

1 garlic clove, crushed with a little salt

275 ml hot water

275 ml brown ale

bouquet garni, made by bundling together with cotton 1 clove peeled garlic, parsley stalks, 1 bay leaf, ½ an onion stuck with a few cloves and a few sprigs of thyme

salt and freshly ground pepper

a pinch of nutmeg

a pinch of sugar

a dash of vinegar (optional)

4–5 squares bread, 0.5 cm thick and about 5 cm square, with crust removed, or *slices of baguette with the crust left on*

Dijon mustard

Heat the dripping in a flameproof stew-pan, put in the meat and colour it quickly on both sides. Add the onions and allow them to brown well. Pour off a little of the fat, sift in the flour over the beef and throw in the garlic. Mix the hot water with the beer and pour it onto the beef, drop in the bouquet garni, and season with salt, pepper, nutmeg, sugar and vinegar.

the sixties bistro   173

Cover and cook gently in the oven (300°F/150°C/gas mark 2) for about 1½ hours. Fifteen minutes before serving, skim from the gravy any surface fat and pour it on to the squares of bread. Spread these thickly with a good French mustard and place on top of the meat, pushing it down below the surface to ensure that it is soaked with gravy. It will float again to the top. Leave the lid off and put the pot back in the oven for another 15–20 minutes or until the bread is a good brown.

Serves 2

steak au poivre

This is the absolutely traditional Steak au Poivre: no cream and no silly pink peppercorns. Irritatingly, one sees more and more of these foul-tasting scarlet berries (they are not peppercorns at all) making their frankly pathetic little presence felt in more and more daft dishes. Cream can sometimes earn its place in this dish, especially when it is used in conjunction with green peppercorns – and these are fine, being simply underripe black or white ones, and warmly aromatic.

This recipe is simple, but needs care and attention to get the pepper to act properly and also in the making of the sauce. The result, however, is one of the finest ways to cook steak. The combination of both black and white peppercorns produces an agreeable contrast of heat and gives the pepper flavour an added dimension.

1 tbsp white peppercorns	*1 tbsp olive oil*
1 tbsp black peppercorns	*50 g butter, plus a little more if necessary*
2 × 175 g thick rump steaks	*2 tbsp cognac*
a little salt	*1 tbsp meat glaze (optional: see page 26)*

Coarsely crush the peppercorns in a coffee grinder and put them in a sieve. Shake out all the excess powder (this is very important as it will make the steaks too hot). Press the pepper into both sides of the steaks and push it in well with your fingers. Sprinkle on a little salt now; don't do it before the pepper, as then the peppercorns tend to fall off.

Heat the oil in a heavy-bottomed frying pan until it is smoking. Put in the steaks and leave them untouched for a couple of minutes, then turn down the heat a little. Cook for a further 3 minutes or so, then carefully turn them over. Turn up the heat again and repeat on the other side. Add the butter and allow it to foam. Baste the steaks with the butter over a gentle heat until the butter has browned slightly. Remove the steaks and keep warm in a low oven with the door ajar. Add the cognac and allow it to seethe. What you want now is for the cognac and the buttery juices to amalgamate and form a sauce – the addition of a little meat glaze helps here. The idea is to form an emulsion, so the use of a whisk will also help. Add more butter, too, if necessary. Check the sauce for salt and pour it over the steaks.

chili con carne   *Serves 4–5*

'In spite of repeated warnings this recipe seems to have caused more trouble than all the others put together, in a writing career spanning over 20 years!'

– Robert Carrier in *The Best of Robert Carrier.*

A memorable recipe for Chili con Carne came from *Great Dishes of the World* by Robert Carrier. One would suspect that many people came a cropper with this one, not realizing (as he explained in later books) that his instruction for four tablespoons of powdered chili referred to Mexican chili powder, a relatively mild one blended with other seasonings including oregano, garlic and cumin, and not powdered chilies. Of course, you only made the mistake once, but the memory lingered on your tongue for some time.

The recipe itself, however, is really good, and has excellent flavour and texture. This is partly because the meat is hand chopped into small cubes and fried in bacon fat. Another excellent recipe for chili is included in Jeremiah Tower's *New American Classics.* Here, the meat is coarsely minced but uses equal quantities of beef and pork; flavours are pointed up with chopped whole lemon and lime, plus a little cider vinegar and peeled, deseeded and diced tomatoes. These authentic chilies are not just your slurry of mince with a few beans floating around: our recipe is much influenced by both. Incidentally, chili is best if cooked the day before and the beans are cooked separately.

Note: Authentic Chili con Carne (*chili* means spice, *carne* means meat) never has red kidney beans mixed in; they are usually eaten separately. But if you want to put some in (previously cooked, naturally), add them at the end.

2 tbsp olive oil

75 g pancetta, cut into dice

1 large Spanish onion, finely chopped

4 garlic cloves, finely chopped

225 g lean belly pork, trimmed and cut into 1 cm cubes

700 g lean beef, trimmed and cut into 1 cm cubes

3 tbsp Mexican chili powder or mild chili powder (Schwartz do a good one but check the ingredients on the label to make sure)

1 tsp powdered cumin

1 tbsp flour

2 bay leaves

salt

1 small lemon, seeded and chopped

1 tsp dried oregano

2 tbsp tomato paste

450 ml beef stock, see the recipe for meat glaze (see page 26) and use the stock as is, before reduction

300 ml red wine

Take a large flameproof casserole, heat the olive oil in it and gently cook the pancetta until it is crisp and brown and releasing most of its fat. Then add the onions and garlic, and cook for a few minutes until they are slightly golden. Remove the contents of the pan to a bowl with a slotted spoon and keep warm. Put the meat in the casserole and brown it all over. Add the chili powder and cumin and, stirring constantly, cook over a gentle heat for a further 2 minutes. Then add the flour and cook for a further minute. Now add the bay leaves, salt, lemon, oregano, tomato paste, beef stock and red wine. Bring it to a simmer over a gentle heat and cook uncovered for about 2 hours until the sauce is thick and most of the liquid has reduced. Taste to see if it needs more salt.

Allow it to cool to room temperature and leave it in the fridge overnight. Dishes such as this one are infinitely better eaten the next day, when the flavours have matured and mellowed.

The following day spoon off any excess oil that has set on the surface of the chili, reheat it gently and serve with or without beans, the choice is yours. Boiled potatoes would be good.

trout with almonds *Serves 2*

The secret of a good trout with almonds involves more than the usual casual fling of flaked nuts over a soggy fish that has been cooked in a mingy amount of butter.

The preferred article here is whole almonds, which are then hand-chopped into slices. This may sound an impossible task but the secret is to blanch them briefly in boiling water. This softens them and they can then be easily sliced into slivers – about three per nut. It is also important to dry the prepared almonds before cooking them in copious amounts of butter, once the trout have been fried.

Finding a wild river trout these days is about as easy as not coming across sun-dried tomatoes on the menu of yet another fashionable restaurant. But at least make sure that your fish is slimy and firm, bright of eye and red of gill. Only then will this simplest of fish dishes perform as it should.

2 rainbow trout, approximately 300 g each, gutted, tails and fins trimmed but heads left on
salt and pepper
flour

75 g butter
75 g whole blanched almonds
1 tbsp finely chopped parsley
juice of ½ a lemon

Season the fish inside and out with salt and pepper, then dredge them in flour, shaking off any excess. Take a frying pan large enough to hold the fish comfortably, heat 50 g of the butter in it until it is frothing and about to turn

trout with **almonds**

nutty. Slip in the fish, turn down the heat to low and cook for 6–8 minutes on each side, checking inside that the fish has turned opaque.

Meanwhile, place the almonds in a small pan and cover them with water. Bring it to the boil and simmer for 2 minutes. Drain and use a sharp knife to slice the nuts lengthways. Pat dry the sliced almonds with kitchen paper.

Remove the fish from the pan to a warm serving dish. Now put the almonds in the pan with the final 25 g butter. Toss around as the butter froths up but keep going until the nuts are browned, taking care not to let them burn – this takes 3–4 minutes. Add the parsley and lemon juice – stand back, it will splutter – and spoon the nuts and butter over the fish.

petits pois à la française *Serves 4*

Not many bistros produced this, but when they did it was often made with tinned peas. Now, curiously, the dish actually turns out better with tinned rather than frozen ones, and you would be surprised to hear how many people love the taste of tinned peas, and that includes us (French ones are usually the finest).

When made with fresh peas, however, the dish comes into its own. Gently stewed, using plenty of butter, this becomes quite luxurious and is possibly best eaten all on its own, allowing the subtlety of its preparation to shine through.

Traditionally Petits Pois à la Française is eaten with triangles of fried bread. If you like that idea, serve the peas in a small bowl and eat with a spoon.

2 Little Gem lettuce, outer leaves removed, shredded

100 g butter, in pieces

1 kg fresh peas in the pod

12 bulbous spring onions, trimmed to 4 cm above the bulb

2 tbsp parsley, chopped

¼ tsp salt

½ tsp sugar

25 g extra butter

Place the lettuce in a colander, rinse it under cold running water and shake it dry. Melt 25 g of the butter in a heavy-bottomed pan with a well-fitting lid. Remove it from the heat and make a nest in the bottom with the shredded lettuce. Add the shelled peas and mix in the spring onions, parsley, salt, sugar, the remains of the diced butter and 4 tablespoons of water. Cover the pan tightly and stew for about 30 minutes until the peas and onions are tender and the liquid has nearly disappeared. After then if it hasn't evaporated, cook the peas uncovered, shaking the pan constantly, for a couple of minutes until it has. Taste and season with extra salt if necessary, then gently stir in the 25 g of extra butter and serve.

Serves 6

ratatouille

Although Ratatouille is often regarded as the essence of Provençal cookery, it languishes in a somewhat tarnished reputation. Chopped aubergine, pepper, courgette, tomato, onion and garlic, chucked together in inferior olive oil, do not constitute a good ratatouille.

To bring out all the flavour of the vegetables, care should be taken to colour them properly, which should be carried out in individual stages; this is not a browning process as such, just a seasoned gilding. Torn-up leaves of fresh basil and a judicious sprinkling of crushed coriander seeds (most effectively done in a pepper grinder to obtain maximum aroma) should be stirred in just before serving and when the heat of the Ratatouille is on the wane.

6 tablespoons olive oil

1 large onion, peeled, quartered and thinly sliced

4 garlic cloves, very finely chopped

1 large red pepper, quartered lengthways, deseeded and finely sliced

1 medium aubergine, quartered lengthways and finely sliced

3 medium courgettes, finely sliced

8 ripe tomatoes, peeled and cut into 8 pieces

salt and pepper

1 bay leaf
3 sprigs of fresh thyme

12 basil leaves, torn
1 level tsp coriander seeds, crushed

Pre-heat the oven to 325°F/170°C/gas mark 3.

Heat half the olive oil in a large frying pan and sweat the onions, adding the garlic after a couple of minutes. Add the red pepper and allow it to wilt slightly. Remove everything from the pan to a large, roomy mixing bowl.

Meanwhile, place the aubergine in a bowl and sprinkle over it half the remaining olive oil. Use your hands to smear the slices thoroughly, then put them in the pan, fry quickly and briefly until coloured then transfer to the bowl along with the other vegetables. Using the last of the olive oil, repeat the smearing business with the courgettes, cook in the same way as the aubergines and add them to the other vegetables. Finally, give the tomatoes a quick fry so that they collapse slightly, and add them to the bowl.

Season generously with salt and pepper and, using your hands, mix everything carefully together. Then put it into a shallow earthenware baking dish. Lay the bay leaf and thyme over the top and cover with a lid or foil. Bake for 40–45 minutes. Remove the Ratatouille from the oven, stir in the basil and the coriander seeds, cover once more and allow to stand for 15 minutes before serving, or eat cold.

green salad

Serves 4

Why is it that a simply dressed Green Salad is so difficult to find? It has always been the most elusive of culinary standards.

One of the most obvious downfalls is not being able to leave well alone. How often do you find unrequested sliced cucumber, cress and green pepper attendant upon the lettuce leaves? Even when you specify that it should be green, there is often a quartered tomato and strips of red pepper lurking. Why? *Why?*

Is there a sort of nervous twitch with some larder chefs, where their hands just cannot resist flinging in something else – something to make it

the sixties bistro   181

better? Something to 'jazz it up'? Something to make it *not what was ordered*? It really is tiresome, and reminds one of the bolshy American in *Fawlty Towers* who wants a Waldorf salad and just can't get it: '*Celery. Apples. Walnuts. In mayonnaise,*' he demands, with exasperation.

So, look here. A Green Salad is *lettuce leaves*. Washed. Dressed. Tossed. Simple as that. And, incidentally, why not use simple round lettuces, old-fashioned floppy ones? Do be generous, however, and, at the same time, ruthless with the removal of tough and often bruised outer leaves. Allow a whole lettuce per person; they are still the cheapest lettuce one can buy.

Here's a nice dressing:

1 tbsp tarragon vinegar	*½ tsp caster sugar*
2 tbsp tepid water	*75 ml virgin olive oil*
salt and pepper	*125 ml sunflower oil*
1 level tsp mustard powder	

Put the vinegar, 1 tablespoon of the water, seasoning, mustard and sugar into a mixing bowl. Whisk together and add the oils, one after the other, in a thin stream, continuing until the dressing has homogenized. Add the remaining water to thin the dressing a little and pour it into a screw-top jar. When you are ready to use, shake well. It makes quite a lot and will keep for a couple of weeks in the fridge.

When dressing the lettuce leaves, use your hands, ensuring that each leaf is coated but not drenched: there should not be a great pool of dressing left in the bowl.

Serves 4

tomato salad

As with a green salad, a fine Tomato Salad should be a simple affair; assuming, of course, that the tomatoes in question are worth using for a salad in the first place. What, pray, is this obsession we have with 'tomatoes for slicing'? In other words, tomatoes that are half green or speed-ripened in controlled conditions and which are, therefore, tasteless, hard, unyielding and dull.

What you really need is the sort of tomato found in Provence: slightly misshapen, a deep sweet red and bursting with sunny flavour. A fruit such as this requires nothing more than a slick of good olive oil, salt and pepper. However, you rarely see a tomato like this outside that province; presumably – and scandalously – because it simply does not take to the rigours of travel quite so economically as the grossly unready and underripe specimen. When you consider that we import live, green-lipped mussels (quite foul) all the way from New Zealand, might it not just be possible to transport a few trays of decent ripe tomatoes from the south of France?

Another way of dressing tomatoes is with cream. A London Italian restaurant called Montpeliano used to serve – and perhaps still does – a delicious version of this. It is all at once luscious, cooling and colourful; perfect for a hot summer's day.

*4 large, ripe, very red tomatoes, skinned
    and cored
1½ tbsp red wine vinegar
salt and pepper*

*200 ml double cream
a few shakes of Tabasco (optional)
4 spring onions, trimmed of most of the
    green part and finely sliced*

Slice the tomatoes thinly and lay them out on a large flat dish. Whisk together the vinegar and seasoning, then pour in the cream, continuing to whisk until frothy and slightly thickened (the vinegar will naturally help this to happen). Add the Tabasco and carefully spoon the dressing over the tomatoes. Sprinkle with the onions and allow the salad to sit for 20 minutes or so before serving.

lemon meringue pie

Serves 4–5

Anything piled up with soft sweet meringue just asks to be eaten, especially by children and those with an over-sweet tooth. In fact, Lemon Meringue Pie, even though it is partly made with something acidic, can often be so unbearably sugary that you can almost feel your teeth disintegrating at each and every mouthful.

Meringue desserts such as this are originally an American import, along with such sicklies as Angel Cake and Devil's Food Cake, Lemon Chiffon and Pumpkin (particularly unpleasant) Pie, and the often virulent, worryingly green Key Lime Pie. And, in essence, the last is simply a Lemon Meringue Pie made with limes.

We have adapted many recipes for the following Lemon Meringue Pie, so that it leaves a fresh lemon taste in the mouth rather than an avalanche of saccharine.

For the pastry:
225 g plain flour
50 g icing sugar
a pinch of salt
125 g butter, cut into cubes
2 eggs, beaten

For the lemon filling:
5 large eggs
3 lemons
200 g caster sugar
100 ml double cream

To make the pastry, sift the flour, sugar and salt together in a large mixing bowl and quickly rub in the butter with your fingertips until it resembles coarse breadcrumbs. Add the eggs, stirring with a fork until the mixture clings together. Form the dough into a ball and transfer it to a floured surface. Knead it gently until it is smooth and homogeneous. Wrap the ball in cling-film or place it in a plastic bag and chill in the fridge for at least 30 minutes before rolling.

To pre-cook the pastry shell, heat the oven to 350°F/180°C/gas mark 4. Roll out the pastry to line a 20 cm loose-bottomed tart tin. Bake it blind (see pages 223–4) for about 25 minutes until pale biscuit in colour, but thoroughly cooked through. Allow to cool.

To make the lemon filling, separate two of the whites from the five eggs, put them in a bowl and set aside. Place the three whole eggs and two yolks into the bowl of a food processor. Add the zest of two of the lemons and the juice of all three. Tip in 125 g of the sugar, process until smooth, add the cream and pour the mixture into a bowl. After several minutes skim off any froth. Then pour it into the pre-baked pastry case, bake for 20–25 minutes until just set and leave it to cool.

Note: If the edges of the pastry look as if they are colouring too much, cover the case with a dome of foil.

Beat the egg whites to a firm snow, tip in the remaining 75 g of sugar and continue beating until the meringue is glossy and thick. Pile it into the pastry case on top of the lemon filling and gently press down with the back of a wet tablespoon until the surface looks a bit like rumpled sheets. Dust with a little extra caster sugar and return the pie to the oven for 15–20 minutes until the meringue is a pale coffee colour and crusted.

Serves 4–5

profiteroles

Making choux paste is not as difficult as you might think – it is certainly easier than puff pastry, for instance. And the chemistry of it is something to be admired as you watch the little mounds of shiny dough puff and swell as they bake to golden crispness.

It seems a shame that the ones on a mediocre sixties sweet trolley were so often packed into a glass bowl, buried in a chocolate sauce of dubious pedigree and cack-handedly spooned out in a messy great pile on to the waiting plate. The meagrely cream-filled interiors could not help but burst forth, thereby spoiling the look of the thing and turning what should have been something special into the proverbial dog's dinner.

To do them justice, profiteroles should never have been consigned to the trolley in the first place: they should be assembled about half an hour before you wish to eat them, which allows the choux paste to remain crisp and the filling cold. But, most important of all, the chocolate sauce can be poured over while it is still piping hot – especially good if you have decided to fill the profiteroles with ice-cream.

For the choux paste:

200 ml water

70 g butter

90 g plain flour

3 medium eggs

egg wash, made with 1 egg yolk and a
    splash of milk

———

For a traditional chocolate pastry
    cream filling:

1 egg, separated

1 egg yolk

50 g caster sugar

30 g plain flour

300 ml full cream milk

75 g bitter-sweet chocolate, broken into
    pieces

———

For the chocolate sauce:

200 g bitter-sweet chocolate, broken into
    pieces

300 ml water

100 g caster sugar

First make the choux paste. Put the water and butter in a large, thick-based pan and bring it to the boil. Once the water and butter have seethed together, take it from the heat and tip in the flour – all in one go. Take a wooden spoon – or, even better, a stiff metal whisk – and beat furiously until the mixture amalgamates and comes away from the sides of the pan. Cool it slightly, then add the eggs one at a time, beating well between each addition (you may find that an electric beater aids this process). Once all three eggs have been incorporated, and the mixture is very thick and glossy, fit a piping bag with a plain 1 cm nozzle and fill with the choux paste.

Generously butter a baking sheet and chill it in the fridge for 20 minutes – this will stop the choux paste slipping about when it's piped. Pipe walnut-sized mounds on to the baking sheet, spaced about 2.5 cm apart. Gently brush the tops with a little egg wash, then very slightly flatten the balls to round off their shape. Bake in a hot oven (400°F/200°C/gas mark 6) for about 20 minutes or until they are golden and puffy.

Using a small, sharp knife, make a horizontal cut in each puff to release the steam, then allow them to cool.

To make the chocolate pastry cream, place the egg yolks and sugar in a mixing bowl and cream them together until they are pale and fluffy. Add the flour with just enough milk to make a smooth paste, and transfer the mixture to a medium-sized saucepan. Place the chocolate in a small pan with the remaining milk and simmer very gently, stirring until the chocolate has melted and the two have amalgamated. Place the egg mixture pan over a low heat and pour in the chocolate cream. Bring it slowly to the boil, making sure that the mixture is entirely smooth before letting it boil; if lumps form as it thickens, remove the pan from the heat and beat the chocolate cream with a wooden spoon until it is smooth – if it becomes too stiff, add a little more milk. Once it is boiling, remove the pan from the heat and set aside.

Whip the egg white until it is stiff. Pour a little of the boiling chocolate cream into a bowl, fold in the egg white and tip this back into the chocolate cream pan. Stir carefully over a very, very low heat for about 3 minutes to set the egg white. Turn the mixture into a bowl to cool.

To make the chocolate sauce, place the pieces of chocolate in a pan with the water and melt over a low heat. When nicely smooth, add the sugar and continue to cook gently until it has dissolved. Now bring to the boil and simmer for 10–15 minutes until the sauce is rich and syrupy with a good coating consistency.

Half an hour before serving fill the profiteroles with the chocolate cream. Place three or more in individual pudding bowls and serve the hot chocolate sauce separately in a jug, so that everyone can pour on as much (or as little!) as they like.

Serves 5–6

crème caramel

Beware the Crème Caramel that sports lots of little holes. Holes were quite common in sixties Crème Caramel, mainly because it was thought to be a doddle to make (which it isn't) and, possibly, many thought that they were supposed to be there.

Holes mean overcooked custard, where the water in the bain-marie has been allowed to boil, causing the egg and milk mixture to cook too hastily. This may also be compounded by a rubbery texture, almost separated

crème caramel

eggy curds and a tell-tale brown skin that lurks underneath after it is turned out.

Gentle, gentle cooking is paramount for a fine Crème Caramel, along with careful mixing. The use of a whisk should not be energetic, as the need for air bubbles is, for once, not an issue here. Also, the eggs and milk should be allowed to settle before the mixture is poured into the dish, with any resultant surface froth having been previously seen off with a large spoon.

500 ml full-cream milk　　　　　　　*2 whole eggs*
1 vanilla pod, split lengthways　　　*4 egg yolks*
220 g caster sugar

Scald the milk with the vanilla pod, cover and leave to infuse while you make the caramel. To do this, put 120 g of the sugar in a heavy-based saucepan or copper pan, add enough water to just cover it, bring it slowly to a simmer and cook to a rich golden caramel. Pour it into an ovenproof dish (with a capacity of about 1 litre), making sure that the base of the dish is completely covered, and put it on one side.

Place the eggs and egg yolks in a bowl, with the remaining sugar. Whisk lightly and strain over the infused milk. Mix together but try not to allow it to become frothy. Let the mixture rest for 15 minutes and skim the surface. Pre-heat the oven to 300°F/150°C/gas mark 2.

When the caramel has set, gently pour on the milk mixture. Place the dish in a bain-marie, making sure that the water comes at least two-thirds of the way up the sides of the dish. Cook for 1½–2 hours, checking from time to time to see whether the custard is set. When you think that it's not quite cooked – the centre still looks a little runny – take it out but leave it in the bain-marie for anything up to 30 minutes, by which time it should have set. Then remove it from the bain-marie and chill it in the fridge for at least 6 hours.

To turn it out, run a small thin knife around the edge of the dish, place a plate over the top and carefully invert it.

Note: You can also make Crème Caramel in ramekins or dariole moulds.

chocolate mousse

Serves 4

One of the great desserts and universally adored by one and all. It is an elementary procedure that simply involves chocolate and eggs, plus a scrap of butter to help it set. And if you always have a stock of good chocolate in the cupboard, you will never be without a quickly made dessert – assuming, of course, that eggs and butter are always in the fridge. Use this recipe for the mousse part of the Chocolate Roulade on pages 243–4.

200 g best quality, bitter-sweet chocolate   *1½ tbsp rum*

3 tbsp strong espresso coffee   *3 large eggs, separated*

25 g butter

Break the chocolate into pieces and put it into a bowl with the coffee and butter. Suspend the bowl over – that is, not in contact with – a pan of just simmering water and allow the ingredients to melt, stirring occasionally until they are amalgamated. Then remove the bowl from the pan and stir in the rum. While the chocolate mixture is still relatively hot, stir in the egg yolks one by one, mixing in well between each addition (the yolks must 'cook' slightly). Beat the egg whites to a firm snow. Take 2 tablespoons of egg white, and gently stir them into the chocolate; this slackens the mixture somewhat. Then fold in the rest with a metal spoon until there are no streaks or pockets of egg white. Pour into traditional pots (bulbous little white porcelain chaps) filling them almost to the brim, cover with a small sheet of cling-film and chill in the fridge, for at least 6 hours or overnight.

Two of the nicest ways to serve the mousse are either with some very cold pouring cream spooned over the surface (as each spoonful is eaten, the cream fills the new hole), or a float of Grand Marnier or Cointreau.

the tratt era

'In London with a beautiful hungry girl one must show her to Mario at The Terrazza. We sat in the ground floor front under the plastic grapes and Mario brought us Campari-sodas and told Jean how much he hated me. To do this he practically had to gnaw her ear off. Jean liked it.'

Len Deighton, *The Ipcress File*, 1962

In 1961 Mario Cassandro and Franco Lagattolla hired Enzo Apicella to redesign the Terrazza, their successful Italian restaurant in Romilly Street, Soho. Out went the mural of Mount Vesuvius, the fake vine with its real grapes, the hanging garlic and candle-lit dark corners. A bold new look took its place: white walls, ceramic tiles, curved archways leading from one room to the next, and spotlights epitomized what came to be known as the 'trat', or, to give it its full name, the trattoria.

Already fashionable, the Terrazza became *the* place to be seen, and its famous customers – Michael Caine, Sean Connery, Jean Shrimpton and other glamorous sixties people – were photographed coming and going. People flocked to Mario and Franco's bustling establishment, eager to be part of the Terrazza set. And it zinged with life.

Almost immediately, other Mario and Franco trats popped up in fashionable parts of London – and fashionable they certainly were. Kensington had the Trattoo, this time designed by Sean Kenny (who also did Peter Cook's infamous Establishment Club), which became a favourite of Spike Milligan and Peter Sellers. The Tiberio opened in Mayfair's Queen Street and, legend has it, Sammy Davis Jnr and Frank Sinatra were such regular visitors that dishes were named after them. The concept even spread as far afield as Leeds and Manchester.

No one had ever seen an Italian restaurant like this, and before long clones appeared all over London with names such as Da Carlo, Leonardo, Siena, and I Paparazzi. Apicella, who also designed the legendary Pizza Express chain, opened his own temple of style, Meridiana, in South Kensington.

With the new look came a cleaning up of the old-style Italian menu. Grissini, the crisp breadstick, which, for many of us, is the first memory of the trat, became a status symbol on the restaurant table. People took them home, for there is nothing more satisfying than ripping open the flimsy cellophane packet, shaking out a couple of sticks (rather like a soft pack of Lucky Strike) and then ploughing its rough end into cool butter. Cush, cush, cush, go the teeth.

And *antipasti*: hitherto a sad display of wilted squid rings, curling salami, congealed potato salad and crusty old bean and tuna mix, it became something to get excited about and was wheeled across the tiled floor on its smart new trolley looking fresh and appetizing.

Italian specialities were revitalized: Fegato alla Veneziana (calves' liver in the Venetian style, thinly slivered with onions), Saltimbocca alla Romana (thin slices of veal, sage and prosciutto fried in butter and finished with wine), and Scaloppini alla Marsala or Limone, were, for once, freshly made with care and became really quite good. *Dolci* were taken seriously too: Zabaglione was light and frothy and oozed Marsala, and a decent Fresh Fruit Salad (Macedonia di Frutta!) was something worth having.

Needless to say, it wasn't long before the whole Italian restaurant scene in London became confused and standards started to slip. By the end of the seventies, people were beginning to talk about the Trat Trap. Many of London's old-established family-run Italian restaurants who had tried to go new-Trat had missed the point and betrayed theirs. They too had their giant-pepper-grinder-wielding, occasionally singing, always smooth-talking Lothario waiters and they hung on to the hanging Chianti bottles and the ladderback chairs, which was the style of the old-look trattoria.

Their menus too lost their way. Veal, usually offered cooked in a dozen different ways, came to be hit and miss. Heavy sauces, often based on a floury, badly cooked béchamel, and mixed with tired old mushrooms or plastic ham, could be claggy in the extreme. Pasta was always overcooked and never home made and stale rolls sat untouched on side plates from midday to midnight.

There was also a definite borrowing from the continental repertoire, with dishes such as Pollo alla Sorpresa (chicken Kiev), Veal Cordon Bleu, Crespelle di Frutta di Mare (seafood pancake) and those factory made desserts – always a *bloody* cheesecake – decorated with what looked like shaving cream, loaded onto the ever-present trolley. And, of course, Black Forest Gâteau.

Menu language became a joke, at times plain silly. Zuppa Inglese, for example, which loosely means English trifle, was translated on one particular menu as 'Trifle Bamboo'! And 'Costata Michelangelo – T-bone steak, seasoned, brushed with olive oil, grilled'. Perhaps it had something to do with the brush strokes . . .

Cheese, if you were lucky, was either freezing cold or a sweaty Dolcelatte, Gorgonzola Torta, perhaps Provolone, or Taleggio. Certainly never a hunk of Parmigiano Reggiano. Most of us assumed that *that* was made ready grated, and only used for sprinkling – on almost everything.

By the mid-eighties the trattoria had had its day but now, as we approach the millennium, it is the pleasure of passionate home-grown cooks, such as Rowley Leigh, Alastair Little, Rose Gray and Ruthie Rogers, to cook great Italian dishes, rustic, home made and simple. The reason they are breathing new life into Italian food is because they are cooking it properly, and with care. *That* is the basic difference between then and now.

In the sixties, in Soho, where trattoria cooking was born, there was already a thriving Italian community supporting wonderful continental grocers, bakers and butchers. Some of this produce, of course, found its way into the restaurant kitchens and on to the menus. But not enough of it. Furthermore, we, the customers, didn't know our *penne* from our *pollo* and lapped up whatever was put in front of us, as long as it was served by a flirty waiter who looked like Marcello Mastroianni.

Perhaps there is a strong element of nostalgia going on here. What would pin-striped, drunk-too-much-Valpolicella man have made of olive-oil-soaked foccacia or ciabatta *circa* 1970? Are there still those who prefer the buttered breadstick to the oily tear of a 'new' breed of bread?

Fashion in food is relatively new and seems to be creating a class of quasi-sophisticated Euro-eaters who will brainlessly bin bruschetta for yet another silly new bread. Why should a dish of green tagliatelle in a cream sauce be any less attractive than a warm bean salad with balsamic vinegar and a slick of extra virgin? In our greedy search to discover new ingredients and novel interpretations we are in danger of throwing out the béchamel with the borlottis.

Serves 6

minestrone

Although it is a depressing thought, it was no bad thing that a bowl of poor – often packet or tinned – Minestrone was the norm in so-called Italian restaurants, because to have tipped in generous amounts of freshly grated Parmesan would have been an insult to the cheese. But, of course, that is mere fantasy as the (so-called) Parmesan used to come in little green tubs with a shaker, smelt of old socks and matched the quality of the soup to a tee.

It was possibly not until Mario and Franco opened their first trattoria that a decent bowl of thick, home-made Minestrone, with a bowl of freshly grated, real Parmesan, was tasted for the first time. It must have been quite a shock to those who had never eaten the real thing, which was often encountered only on Italian holidays.

According to season, almost any vegetable can be added to Minestrone – peas, beans, spinach, leeks and courgettes to name just a few. In Italy, it is often served lukewarm. The following recipe is based on the one from Elizabeth David's epic work, *Italian Food* (third edition, 1987). You need to start 24 hours in advance.

100 g dried haricot beans

2 carrots, peeled and diced

1 small turnip, diced

2 small potatoes, peeled, diced and rinsed

1 rib of celery, peeled and chopped

½ a small cabbage, cored and shredded

2 onions, finely sliced

olive oil

2 garlic cloves, chopped

2 rashers bacon, chopped

2 tbsp herbs, made up either of one or a
    mixture of marjoram, thyme, basil
4 tomatoes, peeled and chopped
1 small glass red wine
50 g broken-up macaroni or *spaghetti* or
    small pasta shapes

1.75 litres hot water
2 tbsp Parmesan
extra Parmesan
salt and pepper

'Put the haricot beans to soak overnight. Next day prepare all the vegetables, and melt the sliced onions in the oil, adding two cloves of garlic, the bacon cut into pieces, the herbs and the chopped tomatoes. Pour in the red wine, let it bubble a minute or two, then add the drained haricot beans; cover them with 1.75 litres of hot water and let them boil steadily for two hours. Now put in the carrots and about 15 minutes later the turnip and potatoes. Ten minutes before serving, add the celery, the cabbage cut into strips and the pasta. See that the soup is properly seasoned, stir in two tablespoons of grated Parmesan, and serve more Parmesan separately.'

pasta alla carbonara   *Serves 4*

Some culinary authorities proclaim that Pasta alla Carbonara is particularly Roman in origin. As most capital cities seem to have enough of a hard time embracing a local dish for themselves (due to a desire to please all visitors and make at least some of them feel at home), it would be churlish to dispute this claim.

Along with Spaghetti all'Alfredo (named after a Roman restaurateur, the sauce contains cream, butter, much black pepper and grated nutmeg), Spaghetti alla Carbonara used to be one of those table-side preparations with the pasta having been already cooked, and then tossed with cream, bacon, egg yolk and Parmesan. Interestingly, Marcella Hazan adds garlic and white wine to her recipe for Carbonara and omits the cream. She also uses whole eggs rather than just yolks. Whose is authentic? We shall probably never know.

One of the finest examples of Carbonara that we have both enjoyed has been at London's River Café. Rose Gray and Ruthie Rogers cook some of the best Italian food we have ever eaten and the following recipe comes from their book, *The River Café Cook Book*. *Penne* is the pasta they use, and to great effect, but the same weight of spaghetti can obviously be substituted if you wish.

200 g pancetta, cut into matchsticks
1 tbsp olive oil
freshly ground black pepper
6 egg yolks

120 ml double cream
sea salt
150 g Parmesan, freshly grated
250 g penne rigate

In a large pan, fry the pancetta slowly in the olive oil, so that it releases its own fat before coming crisp. Grind over it some black pepper.

Beat the egg yolks with the cream and season with salt and pepper. Add half the Parmesan.

Meanwhile, cook the *penne* in a generous amount of boiling salted water, then drain thoroughly. Combine immediately with the hot pancetta and the oil, then pour in the cream mixture. Stir to coat each pasta piece; the heat from the pasta will cook the egg slightly. Finally, add the remaining Parmesan and serve.

Note: The River Café suggests that this recipe will feed six. It just depends on how hungry you are.

spaghetti bolognese

Serves 4–5

Why this became the great student stand-by is a mystery. Carbonara (see pages 197–8) would have been (a) cheaper, (b) easier to prepare, and (c) possibly less difficult to turn into a complete disaster.

Spag Bol, as it affectionately became known, was also one of those stand-by dishes churned out by bright young things who bought chicken bricks

from Habitat and who were also quite taken with those tall glass storage jars in which to keep tall spaghetti. The mince was purchased, onions chopped, tins of tomatoes opened, garlic crushed in the garlic press, and heat applied. Well, you just boiled it all up for an hour, didn't you? Oh, and perhaps a big pinch of oregano too – especially if you had just seen Glenda Jackson buy some from the Italian deli in Soho in *A Touch of Class*, for the spag bol she was making for George Segal's supper.

It's not a boil-up. It's a pot of stewed meat, a *ragù*, cooked very, very slowly and thoughtfully seasoned.

For the *ragù*:

2 medium onions, peeled and finely chopped

75 g butter (the Bolognese don't use much olive oil)

1 large carrot, peeled and finely diced

3 flat black mushrooms, finely chopped

3 celery stalks, peeled and finely chopped

2 garlic cloves, peeled and chopped

300 g beef, minced

100 g chicken livers, chopped and the green bits removed

350 ml dry white wine

freshly grated nutmeg

salt and pepper

200 ml passata (fresh pure pasteurized tomato pulp, sieved, sold in cartons)

300 ml whipping cream

2 tbsp freshly chopped flat-leaf parsley leaves

———

500 g spaghetti, cooked according to the packet instructions

In a heavy-bottomed cast-iron cooking pot, fry the onions in the butter until they are soft. Add the carrot, mushrooms, celery and garlic and fry for a few more minutes until all are pale golden. Add the minced beef in small amounts, turn up the heat a little and fry carefully, breaking up the meat with a wooden spoon as you go. Tip in the chicken livers, stir them around for a moment and introduce the wine a little at a time with the heat turned up full. Allow it to bubble away to almost nothing, and to be absorbed, before adding more. Once all the wine is in, season with nutmeg and salt and pepper and pour in the passata. Stirring constantly, bring the *ragù* to a simmer and turn down the heat to the lowest possible (use a heat-diffuser pad if you have one). Let the *ragù* merely blip occasionally, for 1–1½ hours, stirring from time to time. Pour in half the cream now, stir, and continue to cook for a further 30 minutes. Pour in the rest of the cream and simmer for a final 30 minutes. Check the seasoning, stir in the parsley and serve over spaghetti – although in Bologna it is thought more traditional to use *linguine* or *tagliatelle*. Suit yourself.

Note: The *ragù* should cling to the strands of pasta rather than be slopped on top like a cow pat.

lasagne al forno
Serves 6

There are still those who think that lasagne is the name of the dish that involves layers of mince, sheets of pasta and cheese sauce but, in fact, the word refers only to the pasta (the same misconception occurs with paella, which is the name of the wide two-handled cooking pan, and terrine, the pot in which a coarse pâté is cooked).

In Liguria, northern Italy, the home of pesto, one of the most common preparations is Lasagne al Pesto where thin sheets of lasagne are cooked, liberally coated with that celebrated bright green paste and folded over each other. Incidentally, this is sometimes also called Mandilli de Saea al Pesto Genovese, which translates as 'silk handkerchiefs' due, no doubt, to the extreme thinness of the pasta.

As with all recipes in this book, but particularly the more familiar ones, making a true Lasagne al Forno should be a pleasure; for once, one that you can be proud of doing properly.

For the *ragù*:

2 tbsp olive oil

125 g rindless streaky bacon, chopped

1 large onion, finely chopped

2 garlic cloves, finely chopped

3 medium carrots, peeled and finely
    chopped

2 celery ribs, peeled and chopped

500 g best quality beef, minced

200 g chicken livers, picked over and finely
    chopped

400 g can chopped tomatoes

1 tbsp tomato purée

2 glasses red wine (approximately 300 ml)

salt and black pepper

2 tbsp chopped basil

2 tbsp chopped flat-leaf parsley

———

For the béchamel sauce:

1 medium onion, finely chopped

2 cloves

1 bay leaf

8 black peppercorns

1 tsp salt

500 ml milk

50 g butter

50 g flour

150 ml double cream

———

9 sheets dried egg lasagne

large knob of butter

freshly grated nutmeg

2 tbsp freshly grated Parmesan cheese

To make the *ragù*, heat the oil in a spacious, heavy-bottomed pan and gently fry the bacon. Add the onion and let it brown slightly before adding the garlic, carrots and celery. Cook, stirring all the time, until the vegetables are beginning to soften, then add the beef. Stir the contents of the pan until the meat is evenly browned and then add the livers. When they have started to firm up, add the tomatoes, tomato purée and wine. Season with salt and pepper and add the herbs. Simmer very gently for approximately 1 hour, stirring occasionally (use a heat-diffuser pad if you have one) until the sauce is richly flavoured and almost all of the liquid has been absorbed.

Meanwhile, make the béchamel. Place the onion, cloves, bay leaf, peppercorns, salt and milk in a pan. Bring it to the boil and simmer for 5 minutes, then remove the pan from the heat, cover and leave it for 15 minutes. Melt the butter in a separate pan and stir in the flour to make a roux. Strain the milk into the roux and whisk thoroughly. Simmer for 10 minutes, then add the cream. Put it to one side.

Cook the lasagne until it is tender (eating a bit is always the best way to check it) in plenty of boiling salted water with a splash of olive oil, taking care that the sheets don't stick together. Drain, then dry them on a tea-towel.

Choose a fairly deep, wide earthenware or porcelain dish and butter it well. Assemble the dish by making layers, first with pasta, then *ragù* and then béchamel, continuing in this style until everything is used up but finishing with a thick layer of béchamel. Dust the top with nutmeg, then cover it with a generous coating of Parmesan. Bake in a hot oven (400°F/200°C/gas mark 6) for 35 minutes until bubbling and blistered.

Note: If you prefer, allow the lasagne to get cold and use an egg slice to cut out individual square servings. Place on an oiled baking sheet and reheat at a similar temperature for 20–25 minutes. The beauty of this method is that each portion becomes well crusted around its edges and on the surface, which is particularly nice.

calamari fritti
Serves 4, as a first course

Maybe Calamari is more synonymous with Greek holidays than something from the tratt-era. However, whether you first ate it in Crete or Lesbos with your Lothario, you most certainly would have seen it on Mario and Franco's menu.

Deep-fried squid is clad in either breadcrumbs or batter. Both are equally enjoyable, as long as the fat you use to fry in is clean, hot and fresh, and the squid is super-fresh, neatly sliced into rings and properly floured, egged and breadcrumbed/battered.

The frying time is about 2 minutes. Squid is one of those funny cephalopods, where very quick cooking in small pieces or long slow braising, perhaps as stuffed whole tubes, is the right thing to do. Anything in between is a disaster. You might as well eat a bicycle inner tube.

For the batter:
200 g plain flour
*50 g potato flour (*fécule de pommes de terre*)*
275 ml light beer
1 egg yolk
25 ml sunflower oil
225 ml milk
salt and pepper

500 g squid, cleaned, sliced into thin rings, with tentacles – cut in half if large
salt
flour
a handful of parsley sprigs, washed and well dried
cayenne pepper
1 lemon, cut into quarters

calamari fritti

First make the batter by putting all the ingredients in the blender and blending until smooth. Pass it through a sieve and leave it for 1 hour before using. Incidentally, when using this batter to fry fish, always flour the fish before coating it with the batter.

Season the squid with salt and roll it in flour. Heat a deep-fryer until the temperature reaches 375°F/190°C (for those without a deep-fryer or thermometer, this is when a scrap of bread turns golden after a couple of seconds). Dip a few squid rings – about 5–6 at a time – in the batter and fry for 2–3 minutes in the oil. Drain, shake off any excess oil, place on kitchen paper and keep it warm in a low oven, uncovered and still on the paper. Do the rest in similar batches, finishing with the tentacles, which will take a little longer. Drop the sprigs of parsley into the oil for a few seconds – be careful of the sputtering – then drain, sprinkle with salt, and tip onto kitchen paper.

To serve, pile the squid on a big serving dish, dust it with cayenne and arrange the lemon quarters around it. Fling over the crisp little clusters of parsley and eat without delay.

fegato alla veneziana *Serves 4*

One of the best examples of this dish is cooked at Bibendum in London. Although SH has a vested interest (well, why not?), the restaurant is proud to have based it upon the one served at Harry's Bar in Venice, where dishes are not only regional and rigorously authentic, but also easy to replicate – if only because they are simple, their ingredients stand out as first rate and they are beautifully cooked.

In this instance, the onions are carefully stewed, the thinly sliced liver cut into small squares the size of postage stamps, and the two combined together in a frenzy of last-minute frying. Vinegar and parsley bring the flavours together, and there you have it. There was most definitely a brown stew of liver and onions around during the sixties and seventies, but heaven knows what it was meant to be.

3 mild Spanish onions, peeled and very
thinly sliced

3 tbsp light olive oil (pure, not virgin)

salt and pepper

40 g butter

8 exceptionally thin slices of calves' liver,
cut into small squares

1 tbsp chopped parsley

2 tbsp red wine vinegar

Fry the onions in the oil until they are completely cooked through and soft. They may take on a little colour during this time but it doesn't matter; the most important thing is that they cook slowly – which can take up to 30 minutes. Season with salt and pepper.

In a roomy and not-too-thick frying pan, heat the butter until foaming. Season the calves' liver with salt and pepper, and briefly toss it in the butter for about 20 seconds. Drain in a colander. Put the cooked onions into the liver pan and similarly toss briefly until they are golden brown, and in parts slightly scorched. Return the liver to the pan with the parsley, and finally stir in the vinegar. Serve without delay and not without mashed potatoes.

Note: The final cooking of this dish – that is, after the initial cooking of the onions – should not take more than about 1 minute.

Serves 4

osso bucco

This great braise of veal shins ranks as one of the finest dishes in the world. However, there is much controversy as to how the sauce should be finished. Sauce, that is, if an intense juice – almost a smear – may be regarded as such.

The Italians have a way of cooking a dish such as this that loosely translates as 'wet roasting'. An oven is rarely used, as many families did not have one, so any slow cooking was carried out over the heat. Whole joints of veal are possibly the most common vehicle for this preparation, although pork, meatballs (*polpette*) and smaller pieces of meat perform well too.

Marcella Hazan, in her *Second Classic Italian Cookbook*, refers to wet roasting as *in bianco*: 'Unlike the classic Milanese recipe for *ossobuco*, these veal shins are cooked without vegetables or tomatoes. This is why they are called *in bianco*, a term universally used in Italian cooking for juices or sauces that are not tinged with tomato and are therefore "white" . . . They cook at a slow heat entirely on top of the stove, until they are tender enough to be cut with a fork.'

Serve wet polenta with Osso Bucco or, if you prefer, mashed potatoes. It is only when cooking the Milanese version that saffron risotto is considered the correct accompaniment.

75 g butter
4 tbsp olive oil
900 g–1.25 kg veal shin, cut into 8 small
    pieces or *4 large ones*
salt and pepper
flour

1 bottle decent, dry white wine – you may
    not need all of it, so make it good
    enough to drink
juice of 1 lemon
2 sprigs rosemary or *sage* or *marjoram –*
    please yourself

Take a wide but deep pan of a size that will hold the pieces of meat in a single layer and in it heat the butter and oil until they are starting to froth. Season the veal pieces with salt and pepper, dip lightly in the flour and shake off the excess. Put them into the pan and fry on both sides until each surface is crusted and golden brown. Now pour in a glass of wine, allow to bubble up and turn down the heat. Cover the pan and simmer so gently that the liquid merely trembles. Once the wine has reduced somewhat, turn the meat over and add a little more wine, with the lemon juice and your chosen herb. Cover and braise for a further 30 minutes. Check occasionally that the liquid has not evaporated too much. If it has, add some more wine. The total cooking time should not be much longer than 1–1½ hours, and the juices syrupy.

If you wish to add a little extra seasoning at the end, sprinkle over some finely chopped parsley and lemon rind, or you could stir it into the juices just before serving. If you add some garlic too, you will produce the classic 'gremolada' seasoning.

Serves 4

saltimbocca

Saltimbocca – literally 'jump into the mouth' – is the ideal supper for four, and takes no time at all to prepare. Use very large, very thin escalopes of veal, because you are going to fold them over, enclosing the essential thin slice of prosciutto and sage leaves within.

pepper

8 veal escalopes, beaten very thin between
    greaseproof paper

16 sage leaves

8 paper-thin slices prosciutto

75 g butter

flour for coating

salt

1 small glass dry white wine

a generous splash of Marsala

4 lemon wedges

Grind pepper over one side of the veal escalopes. Place one sage leaf on each escalope and cover with a slice of prosciutto so that it fits as neatly as possible to the shape of the escalope. Fold it in half, put back in the grease-proof paper and lightly beat to sandwich it together. Melt the butter in a large frying pan until it is about to turn nut-brown. Quickly dip the saltimboccas in the flour and fry briefly on either side until golden brown; about 2 minutes a side – do this in two batches if necessary to avoid overcrowding – and keep them warm in a low oven.

    While the fat is still hot, throw in the remaining sage leaves and let them sizzle for a few moments until they are crisp. Lift out onto absorbent paper, sprinkle with salt and put them on top of the veal in the oven. Tip out most of the fat and pour in the wine and Marsala. Allow to bubble and reduce until it forms a light, syrupy gravy. Spoon this over the veal, and serve immediately with the lemon wedges.

saltimbocca

Serves 2

zucchini fritters

Soggy and greasy are epithets synonymous with fried zucchini. But how rare it is to find a wonderful rustling mass of them: crisp and salty, dry yet sweet and moist within and wonderfully savoury.

At Harry Cipriani in New York City (related to Harry's Bar in Venice), they put a plate of them on the table when you (finally) sit down – surely one of the best appetizers there is. Here, tiny zucchini are sliced into discs the thickness and size of a penny piece, piled up on a paper napkin in a tremulous tower. Eat them quickly, accompanied by a very dry Martini, the likes of which cannot be bettered when mixed by a Harry's bartender.

2 tsp salt

4 medium-sized zucchini (courgettes),
    thinly sliced on the diagonal

1 egg white, loosely beaten to a sloppy froth

flour

peanut or *sunflower oil for frying*

freshly ground pepper

Sprinkle the salt over the zucchini and put them into a colander to drain for 30 minutes. Rinse briefly and dry thoroughly in a tea-towel.

Heat a deep-fryer to 375°F/190°C (for those without a deep-fryer or thermometer, this is when a scrap of bread turns golden after a couple of seconds). Stir the zucchini with the egg white, drain in the same colander for a moment, roll through the flour and shake off the excess. Drop the zucchini into the hot oil a few at a time. Drain on kitchen paper and keep warm while you do the rest. Grind over the pepper and serve immediately.

Serves 4 # oranges in caramel

A trolley terror if ever there was one. This could be anything from an insipid collection of badly trimmed slices (pith included, of course) languishing in a sickly sweet syrup or, even worse, crunchy sliced oranges with sugar, where the crystals have not yet had a chance to dissolve.

Although the dish is a simple one, and we believe more Spanish in origin than Italian, Oranges in Caramel is a most refreshing end to a meal. If you take the trouble to peel the fruit carefully and make a proper caramel, the result is a revelation. And a good slosh of Cointreau or Grand Marnier would not go amiss either.

8 medium-sized sweet oranges, if possible seedless
225 g caster sugar

150 ml cold water and 150 ml very hot water
8 cocktail sticks

Peel the rind, without the pith, from four of the oranges and cut it into thin julienne strips. Blanch it in a small pan of boiling water, then tip it into a colander, rinse with cold water, drain and set aside.

Peel all the oranges to the flesh, working over a plate to catch the juice. Slice the oranges round their circumference and reassemble with two cocktail sticks through the centre to keep them in position. Place the oranges in a serving bowl with the juice from the plate.

Put the sugar and cold water in a medium-sized saucepan over a low flame and bring slowly to a simmer, shaking the pan as the sugar dissolves. Raise the heat and boil rapidly, swirling the liquid occasionally to dissolve any crystals that form, until the syrup turns a rich amber colour – watch carefully at this stage. Remove the pan from the heat, cover your hand with a tea-towel and stand well back. There will be a lot of spluttering as, very quickly, you pour in the hot water *carefully*. Once the spluttering has subsided, stir the caramel with a wooden spoon until it is thoroughly blended. If it turns lumpy, return the pan to the heat. Add the orange zest to the syrup, cook for a few more minutes, then pour the caramel over the oranges. Place in the fridge to chill.

Serves 4

zabaglione

We are huge fans of Riva restaurant in Barnes, in south-west London, named after Andrea Riva, its owner. It is the consummate neighbourhood place and the bulk of its clientele really do live just around the corner. We have been going there regularly since it opened, five years ago now, and an outing usually lasts about the same time measured in hours – sometimes extended way beyond that, once the grappa bottles appear.

Andrea's chef, Francesco Zanchetta, makes the finest Zabaglione: just warm from the pot, well whisked, yet with body, and generously liquored with heady Marsala. Things are never done by halves when you eat at Riva . . . Here are two recipes from the restaurant.

Zabaglione al Vin Santo con Panettone

4 egg yolks
80 g caster sugar
80 g Vin Santo

Optional additions:
4 slices panettone
4 scoops chocolate ice cream

Place the egg yolks, sugar and Vin Santo in a copper or stainless-steel bowl and put it over a pan of gently simmering water. Beat the mixture with a whisk, increasing the speed and circular motion as it becomes paler, light and fluffy. The zabaglione is ready when, lifting the whisk from the bowl, the mixture peaks and floats a little before melting in again with the bulk of it.

To serve, arrange the slices of *panettone* on warm plates and place a scoop of ice cream on top of each one. Pour over the Zabaglione and eat at once. Alternatively, pour the Zabaglione into glasses and serve with boudoir biscuits.

Crema di Zabaglione alle Fragole

12 fresh strawberries

4 egg yolks

4 tbsp granulated sugar

4 tbsp grappa

4 tbsp dry white wine

rind of 1 lemon, finely shredded into
    whiskers

1 tbsp icing sugar, sifted

Wash and cut the strawberries into quarters and divide them between 4 large ramekins. Prepare a Zabaglione by placing the egg yolks, sugar, grappa, white wine and lemon whiskers into a copper or stainless-steel bowl and proceed as in the preceding recipe. Pour it over the strawberries, dust with a little sifted icing sugar and glaze under a very hot grill. Serve at once.

Note: Both versions can also be served cold, by cooling over a cold bain-marie (or pan of chilled water and some ice cubes) and adding 400 ml of whipped cream.

chez gourmet

'Do not be afraid of simplicity. If you have a cold chicken for supper, why cover it with a tasteless white sauce which makes it look like a pretentious dish on the buffet table at some fancy dress ball?'

Marcel Boulestin, *Simple French Cooking for English Homes*, 1923

Chez Gourmet was born around the end of the 1950s with such notable enthusiasts as George Perry-Smith (the Hole in the Wall, Bath), Kenneth Bell (the Elizabeth, Oxford), Walter Baxter (the Chanterelle, London) and Francis Coulson (Sharrow Bay Hotel, Ullswater). Of this quartet, Coulson remains, perhaps, the most cherished of all and, in 1997, with his partner Brian Sack, will have notched up a staggering forty-eight years in the business.

The common denominator between these pioneers is that all four started out as highly gifted amateurs. This is a phrase chosen with care and is in no way derogatory: on the contrary, it is a description that illustrates a type of restaurateur who would shun the limelight (not that such a thing existed then); the genuine host, the diffident cook with an enquiring mind, the individual who loves food.

There were others too, tucked-away places such as the Miners' Arms at Priddy, Somerset, Au Rendezvous des Gourmets, way down in Truro, the Walnut Tree Inn 'in the brackeny parish' (*The Good Food Guide*, around 1971) of Llandewi Skirrid near Abergavenny, the Horn of Plenty at Gulworthy, Devon, the Fox and Goose in the tiny Suffolk village of Fressingfield, the Box Tree below the moor in Ilkley, Yorkshire, and, although it did not open its doors until the mid-1970s, the Carved Angel in Dartmouth – but more of that one later. Then, of course, there was the Howard Arms at Ilmington, near Stratford-upon-Avon, where the remarkable Jimmy Last bred his own ducklings and reared them on bread soaked in milk and brandy. People came from miles around to eat his roast duck and reservations were at a premium as he declined to feed more than eight people at a sitting.

Further afield there was Myrtle Allen at Ballymaloe in County Cork, and also, in Scotland, Keith Knight: he was first noticed at the Royal Hotel in Comrie, Perthshire, before moving nearer Edinburgh to Houston Hall, at Uphall, where he made his name and put together one of the most astonishing wine lists in the land.

You only have to look up old editions of the *Good Food Guide* to see what was going on in those heady pre-breathalyser days when country restaurants were always busy with an inquisitive clientele who had travelled from far and wide with the sole intention of searching out good food. More is the pity that this isn't so much the case today. All restaurants, country places especially, depend on a regular clientele. In the sixties and seventies some of that clientele would make weekly (sometimes twice weekly) visits to these out-of-the-way places.

So, what is the difference between those fabled establishments and their successors today? Well, sure, the breathalyser cannot have helped, but of all those legendary restaurants, only Myrtle Allen's Ballymaloe, Joyce Molyneux's Carved Angel, Francis Coulson and Brian Sack's Sharrow Bay and Franco and Ann Taruschio's Walnut Tree have sustained a continued success in the sticks. Could it be, perhaps, largely because their enthusiasm and generous hospitality has never waned? Which, coupled with an incredibly loyal clientele, created a very special relationship.

It goes without saying that there are now more restaurants in the United Kingdom than ever there were then, but it is in the capital and in a few provincial county towns where glitzy restaurants – and they are growing in size almost daily – attract the galloping gourmets of today. But there is also another far more interesting trend: many innovative chefs, disillusioned by the bustling city restaurant but who know only too well the pitfalls of the quiet country restaurant, have spotted the potential of taking over a rural pub and developing its restaurant as well as providing an inventive bar menu. In fact, the British countryside is now peppered with pubs such as these, which are doing a healthy trade at both lunch and dinner. However, the traditional country restaurant – albeit often serving excellent fare – finds its lunch trade so nearly non-existent that it rarely opens during the day.

The difference between the cooking of the fifties, sixties and seventies and the nineties is, without question, also markedly different. Everyone is aware of the influence of Asian flavours these days, along with a welter of olive oils, sun-dried tomatoes, endless variations on the pesto theme and mad ingredients in mashed potato (of which some are, frankly, bonkers). Many dishes are thrown-together composites and show anything but a true feeling for cookery.

Joyce Molyneux, of the Carved Angel in Dartmouth, who started her cooking career with George Perry-Smith at the Hole in the Wall, is possibly the most important link between then and now. The dishes that you might enjoy at the Angel are so perfectly judged and so generously offered that there is a real sense of 'being fed'. For instance, the finest lobster bisque is presented in a tureen and left on the table. Similarly, roast chicken may also be served in this way, carved and jointed for all to see and cuts to be chosen.

It is the dishes in this chapter that have, perhaps, given us the most pleasure to cook. They seem like old friends: Cold Salmon Mousse, a good Gazpacho (more often seen these days as sauce gazpacho that might dress some convoluted shellfish composition rather than being drunk from a bowl), Quiche Lorraine, Champignons à la Grecque, Leeks Vinaigrette and a properly made Blanquette de Veau. In fact, it was precisely these dishes that prompted us – about five years ago now – to think about writing this book in the first place. Or have we said this before?

champignons à la grecque

Serves 6

You would have to be unlucky indeed to eat a poor example of Champignons à la Grecque. After all, the dish is simple to prepare and uses few ingredients that might cause problems. Even ones bought from the most ordinary French charcuterie are usually pretty good, even though sometimes they might be relatively high on the tomato purée content, with the sauce coming out really quite orange in colour.

The following recipe is the elementary one: mushrooms, herbs, olive oil, white wine, lemon and the all important crushed coriander seed, with the addition of some chopped fresh tomatoes for added fragrance and sweetness. This is one of the nicest of summer dishes.

700 g very clean, tiny button mushrooms	*juice of 1 large lemon*
75 ml virgin olive oil	*salt and pepper*
275 ml dry white wine	——
2 bay leaves	*4 ripe tomatoes, peeled, de-seeded and finely*
4 sprigs thyme	*chopped*
2 tsp coriander seeds, lightly crushed	*2 tbsp chopped flat-leaf parsley*

Put all the ingredients except the tomatoes and parsley into a large non-reactive or stainless-steel pan and bring gently to the boil. Allow to stew, covered, on an extremely low heat for 30 minutes, stirring occasionally. Stir in the chopped tomatoes and cool it thoroughly before adding the parsley. Serve in a handsome white dish, for the best effect, and eat with good bread and best butter.

Serves 6

gazpacho

One of the most refreshing cold soups, this hardly seems to be made as such these days. That dressing or 'sauce' mentioned in the introduction to this chapter of the book, by the way, is actually nothing new. In the hot town of Cordoba in southern Spain, there is a dish known as Salmorejo Cordobes or Gazpacho Cream. And there is an Andalusian *tapas* bar in Madrid where this cream is served spread on toasted slices of country bread. It is quite the most wonderful snack.

With the following soup recipe, Gazpacho can be made and served in a moment – assuming you have all the ingredients to hand – because the final amount of water asked for in this recipe is ice. Once that is stirred in and allowed to melt, the soup is already very cold and ready to eat.

For the soup:

75 ml red wine vinegar or sherry vinegar

300 ml water

1 cucumber, peeled and chopped

1 small red pepper, cored, de-seeded and
    chopped

1 small green pepper, cored, de-seeded and
    chopped

450 g very ripe tomatoes, skinned and
    chopped

150 ml passata (fresh pure pasteurized
    tomato pulp, sieved, sold in cartons)

2 garlic cloves, peeled and crushed

1 small onion, peeled and chopped

several good shakes of Tabasco

3 mint sprigs, leaves only

1 tbsp tomato ketchup

salt and pepper

400 g ice

200 ml virgin olive oil

——————

For the garnish:

1 heaped tbsp each finely chopped green
    and red peppers

1 heaped tbsp finely chopped peeled
    cucumber, seeds removed

1 heaped tbsp finely chopped red onion

2 tomatoes, peeled, de-seeded and finely
    chopped

small croutons, made from 2 or 3 slices
    white bread, cubed and fried in olive
    oil until crisp

8 mint leaves, chopped

Purée all the soup ingredients together, except half the olive oil. Pass through a coarse sieve, pressing well down on the vegetables, and stir in the other half of the olive oil. Pour the Gazpacho into chilled soup plates or bowls, distribute the garnishing bits between them, drop in an ice cube and serve with a chilled glass of fino sherry.

leeks vinaigrette

Serves 4

Of all vegetable dishes, this is one of the finest, a true French classic of brasserie and bourgeois restaurant. Any dish of vegetables dressed with a mustardy vinaigrette, be it beans, potatoes, artichokes or leeks, is a testament to how vegetables can shine.

The dressing is based on one of those rich creamy ones seen over and

leeks
vinaigrette

over again in traditional Lyonnaise and Parisian dishes. When used with rich gelatinous meats such as *tête de veau* and *jarret de porc* (pork knuckle), the dressing is equally at home with both the boiled potatoes (which should always accompany this type of dish) and the meat – the mustard, vinegar and oil lubricating each component as well as sharpening them.

*16 leeks, about thumb thickness, trimmed
    and washed, leaving about 2 cm green*
2 tbsp smooth Dijon mustard
4 tbsp tepid water
2 tbsp red wine vinegar

salt and pepper
*275–325 ml peanut oil or other flavourless
    oil*
2 large hard-boiled eggs
1 tbsp chives, snipped

Put the leeks into fast-boiling, well-salted water and cook until they are tender. Drain, and allow them to cool naturally. In a blender, process the mustard, water, vinegar, salt and pepper. With the motor running, pour in the oil in a thin stream until it homogenizes. If you think it is too thick, thin it with a little more water. The ideal consistency should be like thin salad cream.

Slice the leeks lengthways, cut side uppermost, drizzle with the dressing, grate over the hard-boiled eggs and sprinkle with chives.

lobster bisque

Serves 4

One of the finest Lobster Bisques we ever tasted was on a visit to the Carved Angel restaurant in Dartmouth (see page 217). The flavour in the soup was the very essence of lobster: sweet and deep, rich and fragrant, and lifted by a whisper of cognac – not, as is often the case, bullied by a big slug and thought to be clever and extravagant. All this does is ruin the soup.

You can make the soup with left-over shells saved after you have eaten cold lobster for a summer lunch. However, if you do this, keep a whole one back so that you can add some chunks of lobster meat to the finished soup.

1 × 500 g boiled lobster, plus any extra
    shells
75 g butter
1 carrot, diced
1 medium onion, chopped
2 garlic cloves, peeled and chopped
50 ml cognac
150 ml dry white wine

400 g can chopped tomatoes
bouquet garni, made with parsley, thyme
    and a bay leaf
400 ml chicken stock (see page 47)
1 tbsp long grain rice
100 ml whipping cream
salt and cayenne pepper

Remove the cooked lobster meat from the shell and set it aside. Chop the shells with a heavy knife. Take a heavy-bottomed pan, heat the butter and gently fry the shells until they are burnished. Add the vegetables and garlic, stirring them around until they brown and begin to soften. Pour in 25 ml of the cognac and ignite it. Once the flames have subsided, add the wine and tomatoes, simmer for 10 minutes, then add the bouquet garni and the stock. Bring it to the boil and simmer for 30 minutes.

Remove the claw shells and bouquet garni from the pan. Tip everything else into a food processor or blender and process until the motor runs easily. Then strain the mixture through a sieve into a clean pan, pressing down well on the solids to extract all the flavour. Reheat the mixture with the rice and cream and simmer it for 10 minutes or so until the rice is not just cooked but overcooked (it is only used for thickening), and liquidize once more. Pass the soup through a fine sieve into a clean pan and season it with salt and cayenne pepper. Chop the lobster meat and stir it into the soup with the rest of the cognac. Heat through and serve very hot.

Serves 6

quiche lorraine

The finest quiche is still the one from Alsace-Lorraine. The matchless flavours result from the exactness of ingredients in Quiche Lorraine, which should not therefore be tampered with. The problem arises from the controversy over what is the correct combination.

In *An Omelette and a Glass of Wine*, Elizabeth David writes mischievously:

Not so long ago it was quiche Lorraine. You could hardly go out to a cocktail party without somebody tipping you off about the delicious quiche they made in the penthouse restaurant of the new block at the far end of Finchley Road. At the dinner-table grave discussions would arise as to the proper ingredients of a quiche and the desirability of putting cheese into the filling.

This was first published as 'Your Perfected Hostess' in *Punch* in 1961. Having tried both, with and without cheese (and if it is to be with, then it must be Gruyère), we have to agree with ED: definitely no cheese.

For the pastry:

100 g plain flour

50 g butter, cut into cubes

a pinch of salt

1–2 tbsp iced water

1 egg yolk

a little beaten egg or *spare egg white*

For the filling:

8–10 thin rashers of rindless, smoked streaky bacon (Italian pancetta is superb for this), cut into slivers

4 egg yolks

3 whole eggs

500 ml double cream

½ bunch chives, finely chopped (optional)

little salt and much pepper

freshly grated nutmeg

To make the pastry, blend together the flour, butter and salt in a food processor until it resembles coarse breadcrumbs and tip it into a large, roomy bowl. Gently mix in the water and egg yolk with cool hands or a knife, until the pastry is well amalgamated. Put it into a plastic bag and chill it in the fridge for at least 1 hour before rolling.

Pre-heat the oven to 350°F/180°C/gas mark 4.

Roll out the pastry as thinly as possible and use it to line a greased 20 cm wide × 4 cm deep tart tin and bake blind. This is achieved by lining the uncooked pastry case with a sheet of tin foil and filling it with some dried haricot beans, for instance. It is then baked for 15–20 minutes, removed from the oven, and the foil and beans transferred to a tin for future use. Brush the inside of the pastry case with a little beaten egg or spare egg white, which will form a seal and prevent any leaks. Put it back into the oven for a further 5–10 minutes until it is well cooked through, particularly the base.

Turn down the oven to 325°F/170°C/gas mark 3.

In a dry non-stick frying pan lightly fry the bacon until it is beginning to crisp and some of the fat has run out. Drain it on kitchen paper and spread it out evenly over the base of the cooked tart case. Whisk the egg yolks and whole eggs, stir in the cream, and chives if using, and season with salt, pepper and nutmeg. Pour the custard into the case and cook for 30–40 minutes until set.

salmon mousse with cucumber salad

Serves 6

Of the many books that we used for research, *The Good Food Guide Dinner Party Book* has been one of the most useful. Our own copies were already well splattered and scuffed from years of use. Recipes such as Cold Curried Apple Soup from the Hat and Feather in Knutsford, Cheshire (where SH once worked in his teens), Cherry and Almond Tart from the legendary Box Tree at Ilkley, Yorkshire, Scallop and Artichoke Soup from Lacy's in London (it was originally Margaret Costa's recipe from the remarkable *Four Seasons Cookery Book*, and her husband was Bill Lacy). And there was the famous Prawn Cocktail from Jimmy Last, which included cucumber, melon and pineapple (!) in the list of ingredients and was surprisingly good.

The recipe for the Salmon Mousse originates from the Crusoe Hotel, Lower Largo, Fife, in Scotland, where the chef was one J. A. Crawford Horne. The dish is actually called Salmon Pâté, and includes cucumber in the mixture. We have adapted this fresh, summery-tasting dish, by taking out the cucumber and serving it as a refreshingly tart salad alongside. The salmon has also been flaked a little more, making for a smoother texture.

½ a medium-sized onion

225 g salmon, cooked and finely flaked

4 egg yolks

150 ml double cream

150 ml béchamel (see page 50)

salt and pepper

Pre-heat the oven to 325°F/170°C/gas mark 3.

Grate the onion finely and mix it into the salmon. Beat the egg yolks, stir the cream into them, then stir the mixture into the béchamel. Season the sauce and combine it with the salmon. Butter a mould or a round pie dish, fill it with the mixture and cover it with foil. Place it in a deep oven tray and pour in enough water to come half-way up the outside of the dish. Cook for 40 minutes or until it is firm to the touch. Take the mousse out of the oven and leave it to cool. When it is cold, turn it out on to a plate and serve with cucumber salad.

Cucumber Salad

salt

1 cucumber, peeled and thinly sliced

2 tbsp white wine vinegar

pepper

½ tbsp caster sugar

First, lightly salt the cucumber slices (use only the amount you would require if you were seasoning them to eat) and put them to drain in a colander for 30 minutes. Then wrap in a tea-towel and squeeze out any excess moisture. Place in a bowl and mix thoroughly with the vinegar, pepper and sugar. Leave the salad to marinate until it is required.

beef wellington

Serves 4

It has been called Boeuf en Chemise, Fillet in Shirtsleeves, Boeuf en Croûte, Fillet Steak in a Crust, and, of course, good old Beef Wellington. Did the Duke of Wellington ever eat fillet of beef cooked in pastry? Did he

chez gourmet   225

enjoy it if he did? Do we care? It was probably a French idea in the first place so it might have been nicked anyway. Perhaps it was cooked in a Wellington boot.

The whole point of cooking meat in pastry is to keep in the juices. Originally, ideas for this type of baking used sheets of clay (think chicken brick and tandoori oven) as cladding, which would bake to a biscuit. It was then rapped with a hammer, shattering the clay shell. Within, all would be moist and savoury thanks to the hermetic seal.

Of course, if the pastry is good and thin, buttery and rich, nothing is nicer than a meat-soaked crust. Brioche is one of the best to use here, although puff pastry is more traditional. However, the pastry recipe we give is similar to that used for Cornish Pasties (see pages 138–40) but substitutes butter for the lard. And the way this 'quick flaky pastry' is made – by grating very cold butter – is a tip from *Delia Smith's Complete Cookery Course*. Done properly and with care, Beef Wellington remains one of the most endearing dishes on the dinner-party circuit. And none the worse for that. Rather a slab of this than lukewarm *filet mignon*, sitting on a potato *rösti*, bedecked with five different wild mushrooms, and with thyme *jus* – or even '*jus* thyme', as it is described in some circles.

For the pastry:
250 g plain flour
a pinch of salt
200 g block butter, chilled in the freezer
ice-cold water to mix

——

For the duxelles:
150 g shallots, peeled and diced
50 g butter
250 g flat black mushrooms, chopped
150 ml dry white wine
salt and pepper

1 heaped tbsp chopped parsley
——
700 g trimmed beef fillet
1 tbsp cooking oil
salt and pepper
1 small egg, beaten
——

For the sauce:
use the same as for Tournedos Rossini,
*   but make double the quantity (see*
*   pages 43–6)*

Place the piece of butter in its wrapper in the freezer and leave for about an hour until hard.

Sift the flour and salt into a mixing bowl. Remove the butter from the freezer, peel back the paper, dip it into the flour and grate it into the bowl, dipping back into the flour every now and again to make the grating easier. Now, mix the butter evenly into the flour by making sweeping scoops with a palette knife until it resembles heavy breadcrumbs. Stir in 1 tablespoon of water at a time until the dough clings together, then use your hands to form it into a ball. Place the dough in a plastic bag and chill it in the fridge for 30 minutes.

To make the duxelles, fry the shallots in the butter until softened and a little golden. Add the mushrooms and continue cooking until they have collapsed and are sticky. Pour in the white wine, season, and reduce fiercely until all the wine has evaporated and the mixture is almost dry. Transfer it to a food processor, together with the parsley, and work until you have a coarse purée. Tip it on to a plate and let it cool.

Heat the oil in a roomy frying pan until it is smoking, put in the beef and colour well until it is crusted on all surfaces, including the ends. Season liberally and leave it to cool.

Pre-heat the oven to 375°F/190°C/gas mark 5 and put in a flat baking sheet.

Roll out the pastry to a rectangle 0.25 cm thick and brush all over with egg wash, particularly at the edges. Spread with the duxelles to within 3 cm of the edge. Place the beef at one end of the pastry, on top of part of the duxelles, and carefully roll up, making sure that the final join is underneath. Gather together the ends, trim off any excess and decorate with the tines of a fork, which will also seal the package.

Brush all over with egg wash, decorate with a suitable pattern – crisscrossing with the point of a knife, for example – and sprinkle with a little Maldon sea salt. Put the Beef Wellington onto a greased baking sheet and place it in the oven on the pre-heated baking sheet. Bake for 35–40 minutes until it is golden and shining, then remove it to a carving board. Leave it to rest for 5 minutes before cutting it into thick slices. Hand the sauce separately in a warmed gravy boat.

Serves 4

blanquette de veau

When David Scott-Bradbury ran a restaurant in the mid-seventies called Toad Hall in Battersea, London, he may have called this Gallic classic Veal in a Blanket. It would have sat neatly alongside other wacky dishes such as Cock in a Frock (chicken in cream sauce), Smacked Mack (smoked mackerel pâté), and Wharfedale Street Special (a rough chicken pâté – heaven knows why). There was no menu as such: these dishes were recited by Mr Scott-Bradbury on bended knee.

David is one of those rare people who made the restaurant business so much fun, for the punters *and* the staff. His wit and way with people at Toad Hall could shift and shimmy with a wink and a glance. Duchesses were given the same treatment as estate agents, pretties of both sexes were made to feel either very special or as though they had egg on their faces and both young and old could be made to feel precisely the opposite when teased by David. Oh, and the food was also very good – and astonishingly cheap to boot.

700 g lean veal shoulder, well trimmed and cut into 3 cm pieces

water

2 small carrots, peeled and cut into chunks

2 ribs celery, washed and sliced

2 bay leaves

3 sprigs fresh thyme

3 tbsp dry vermouth

3 strips pith-less lemon rind

salt

20 button onions, peeled (drop into boiling water for 30 seconds, drain and cool; they will be much easier to peel)

20 button mushrooms

40 g butter

40 g flour

2 large egg yolks

100 ml double cream

a squeeze of lemon juice

freshly ground white pepper

a little parsley or *chives, chopped*

Put the veal in a flameproof pot and cover it with water. Bring it to a simmer and drain, discarding the water. Rinse it briefly under cold running water

and return it to the cleaned pot. Cover it again with fresh water, put in the carrots, celery, bay leaves, thyme, vermouth, lemon rind and salt, and simmer very gently, with the lid on, for 40 minutes or until the veal is tender. Then lift out the pieces of meat and keep them warm on a covered dish, or in a very low oven, or in a steamer turned down low.

Strain the veal cooking liquor and discard the vegetables, herbs and lemon rind. Return the stock to the pan, allow it to settle and lift off any grease with kitchen paper. Add the onions and mushrooms and simmer, covered, until they are tender. Lift them out with a slotted spoon and also keep warm. Now measure the stock: you will need 700 ml. If there is more than this, reduce the liquid; if less, add a little water.

Melt the butter in a small pan, add the flour and cook gently without colouring, then add to the stock. Whisk them together and bring the sauce to a simmer, skimming off any scum that rises along the way. Allow it to cook for 20 minutes until syrupy and well flavoured. Check the seasoning.

Beat together the egg yolks and cream and, off the heat, whisk the mixture into the thickened stock. Put it back on to a very low heat and continue to whisk gently until the sauce has thickened again, but do not allow it to boil. Add a squeeze of lemon juice and some white pepper and keep it warm. Mix the veal, button onions and mushrooms in a hot serving dish and pour over the sauce, stirring everything gently together. Sprinkle with the parsley or chives and serve directly, with buttered new potatoes.

Serves 4

duck à l'orange

Possibly the best example of a dish that 'just isn't done any more, dear!'. The fact that it isn't – which is unfortunately true – can be put down to three observations: it had been over-done (not overcooked); it was badly prepared (mostly through boredom); and, most particularly, in the early eighties there was a massive influx of singular duck-breast portions, heralding the onset of 'nouvelle cuisine'. We embraced these neat cuts with much enthusiasm. Everybody was using them. Well, when you think about it, the portion control was second to none, and the cooking was simple: just grill, rest and slice; grill, rest and slice; grill, rest and slice. It sounds like a Jane Fonda exercise class. Of course, there were those who didn't rest: the result was a bouncy little horror marked by the grill, raw in the middle, with a layer of uncooked fat. Mmmmm!

Now, there is nothing wrong with a duck breast *per se*. It's just that their constant presence and availability caused everyone to forget how to *roast* duck. In fact, we are inclined to wonder how many young chefs today have the first idea about roasting in general. It is not necessarily an easy thing to get right, but surely it should be an essential part of the repertoire of every cook.

Last year, a new London restaurant sported Duck à l'Orange on its menu, placing the dish's name within inverted commas. Perhaps this was to signal that Duck à l'Orange is a classic and needs a sign of recognition to single it out. But it could have meant something quite different. Different to the extent that the duck breast was cooked separately from the leg (the latter the style of a French *confit*) with the breast having that aforementioned curious bouncy texture, and accompanied by a sauce that was nothing more than thin, watery, orange-flavoured gravy. Perhaps its rather unusual preparation was the real reason for drawing attention to it.

The Chinese method of pouring boiling water over a duck is the best way to achieve crisp skin. First, puncture the skin many times with a thin skewer or a small, very sharp knife. These punctures open up on contact with the boiling water and allow the subcutaneous layer of fat beneath to seep out. The bird should then be hung up to dry out.

If you have an electric fan, hang the duck directly in the flow of air. Try to do this by an open window and leave it for a few hours or preferably overnight. If you don't have a fan, then just hang it in a cool, airy place. The fan method, however, works best. The end result of all this carry-on produces parchment-like skin without the usual flabby fat but with beautifully moist meat.

1 duck, weighing between 1.5 and 2 kg,
    dressed weight, but with giblets
salt and pepper
3 sprigs thyme
1 onion, peeled and cut into quarters
1 orange, cut into 6 wedges

————

For the orange sauce:
a smear of duck fat (or butter)
4 rashers streaky bacon, chopped
the duck neck bone, coarsely chopped
the duck gizzard, cleaned (ask your
    butcher) and coarsely chopped
the duck wing tips, chopped
1 onion, peeled and chopped

1 carrot, peeled and chopped
2 ribs celery, chopped
1 tbsp cognac
2 tbsp Grand Marnier
150 ml Madeira
150 ml well-flavoured chicken stock (see
    page 47)
juice of 4 oranges
1 dsp rindless marmalade
1 heaped tsp arrowroot, slaked with a little
    water
juice of ½ a lemon
zest of 2 oranges, cut into thin strips
watercress

Prepare the duck as described in the introduction to the recipe.

Pre-heat the oven to 425°F/220°C/gas mark 7.

Rub salt all over the duck and sprinkle some inside the cavity as well, and add some pepper, thyme, onion and the orange wedges. Sit the duck on a wire rack in a roomy roasting tin, and put in the oven. Roast for 20 minutes, then turn down the temperature to 350°F/180°C/gas mark 4. Cook the duck for a further hour until crisp and the juices run when you pierce the thigh with a skewer. This is one of those rare instances when basting is not required, as the more fat that runs off the duck, the better.

While the duck is cooking, make the sauce. Heat the butter or duck fat in a heavy-bottomed saucepan and fry the bacon until crisp and brown. Add the duck neck bone, gizzard and wing tips and cook until they are well coloured; ditto the vegetables. Pour off any excess fat, add the cognac, Grand Marnier and Madeira, bring to the boil and reduce until syrupy. Pour in the chicken stock, orange juice and marmalade, simmer for 30 minutes then strain it through a fine sieve into a clean pan. Allow it to settle and lift off any fat that is floating on the surface with some kitchen paper. Reduce by about one-third, or until the sauce is richly flavoured. Whisk in the arrowroot and bring the sauce back to a simmer, until it is clear and slightly thickened. Stir in the lemon juice, turn off the heat and keep warm.

When the duck is cooked, remove from the oven and allow to rest for 15 minutes or so before carving. Plunge the strips of orange zest into a small pan of boiling water. Bring back to the boil, drain the zest into a sieve and run it under cold water until it has been thoroughly rinsed (this removes any trace of bitterness and also sets the colour). Then stir it into the sauce and serve in a heated gravy boat. Carve the duck, lay the slices on a serving dish and decorate with sprightly bunches of watercress. Lovely.

rognons sautés turbigo   *Serves 2*

After exhaustive and fruitless research we have come to the conclusion that this dish was named after a road. It must be a classic French recipe, possibly even Parisian. There is, you see, this filthy great road that runs through the *Troisième*, and it's called Turbigo. Street Kidneys is a particularly good dish to eat for a late weekend breakfast.

40 g butter
salt and pepper
6 fresh lamb's kidneys, skinned and cored
8 mini chipolata sausages
12 button onions, peeled (drop into boiling
*   water for 1 minute, drain and refresh:*
*   this makes them easier to peel)*
12 button mushrooms
1 tsp tomato purée

1 rounded tsp flour
2 tbsp medium-dry sherry
75 ml dry white wine
1 dsp meat glaze (see pages 26–7)
2 small bay leaves
6 triangles sliced white bread, fried in oil
*   and butter until crisp*
1 tbsp chopped parsley

Melt the butter in a heavy-bottomed frying pan until it is foaming, season the kidneys and chipolatas and fry them briefly on both sides until sealed and lightly coloured. Remove them and put into a sieve suspended over a bowl. In the remaining fat, gently fry the onions and mushrooms cooked through and golden. Stir in the tomato purée and flour and cook for a minute or two. Then add the sherry, white wine, meat glaze and bay leaves.

Now look under the sieve where the kidneys and sausages have been resting: there should be some juices. Add these to the pan and allow the whole lot to simmer gently for 10 minutes. Return the kidneys and sausages to this sauce and heat through for 5 minutes or so. Check for seasoning and tip into a heated serving dish. Dip the fried-bread triangles into the parsley and arrange around the dish. Serve with fried leftover boiled potatoes. Or, as a supper dish, with buttery mashed potatoes.

seafood pancake

Serves 4

Sometimes, pancakes are not worth filling. This is said in rather the same way as, 'Why bother to wrap all that lovely red fruit in slices of bread when making a summer pudding?' There is just something about it that works well. Perhaps it is the comfort of a curiously pleasing pappy texture, wrapped around something unctuous and rich.

However, the filling must be worthy of its wrapper. A Seafood Pancake should not be a vehicle for left-over scraps of shellfish and a rubbery bit of monkfish. It should be a whole outing into the realms of precisely prepared morsels, tentatively cooked and nicely sauced. Any seafood may be used, apart from oily fish such as salmon and herring. And, for once, don't try to make the pancakes too thin.

For the pancake batter:
100 g plain flour
a pinch of salt
1 egg
1 egg yolk
275 ml milk
50 g butter, melted

a little more melted butter for greasing the frying pan

———

For the seafood filling:
50 g butter
2 medium onions, peeled and finely chopped
1 × 500 g cooked lobster

400 g cooked shell-on prawns (these have
usually been frozen, but the quality is
fine): buy the size that will give you
20–25 prawns per half-kilo
4 tomatoes, peeled and chopped
3 tbsp cognac
½ bottle dry white wine or dry cider
1.5 kg fresh mussels, cleaned and de-
bearded

500 ml whipping cream
1 level tbsp chopped fresh tarragon
cayenne pepper
juice of ½ a lemon
4 large raw scallops, trimmed of the small,
attached hard muscle and cut into
chunks, but leaving the pink roe whole
2 tbsp freshly grated Parmesan

First make the pancake batter. Simply put all the ingredients in a blender
and blend well. Then pour it through a sieve into a jug and allow it to stand
for at least 30 minutes. Take a 15 cm frying pan, melt a small amount of
butter in it and allow it to sizzle. Pour in enough batter to cover the base of
the pan. The first pancake is often a bit of a mess; if so, chuck it out and start
afresh.

You should not need to use too much extra butter in the pan as you cook
the pancakes, just a trace now and again as the pan becomes dry (the melted
butter in the mix usually adds sufficient lubrication). Make the pancakes a
little thicker than normal, flipping them over in the usual way with a palette
knife, and as each is cooked lay it on a dry tea-towel. The latter should yield
rather more than eight pancakes, which is all you will need (eat the others
with lemon juice and sugar on another day). Put the pancakes to one side
while you make the filling.

In a spacious saucepan, melt the butter and fry the onions until they are
pale golden. Meanwhile, peel off the shells and remove the heads of the
lobster and the prawns and put the shells to one side. Cut the lobster tail
into slices and put it on a plate with the prawns.

Add the tomatoes to the onions and stew until soft. Pour in the cognac
and the white wine or cider and reduce by half. Now tip in the mussels and
put a lid on. Cook for a couple of minutes, shaking the pan a little, and drain
in a colander with another pan underneath to collect all the winey juices.
When the mussels have cooled (discard any that have not opened at all),

chez gourmet   235

shell them and put them on the same plate as the lobster and prawns. Return the mussel/wine liquor to the cleaned original pan.

Roughly chop the lobster and prawn shells with a heavy knife and add them to the liquor. Simmer, uncovered, for 40 minutes, removing any scum that may form with a large spoon or ladle. Strain once again through a colander into a pan and then through a very fine sieve.

What you now have is an intensely flavoured fish stock. This needs to be reduced to a quarter of its original volume or less, until it is syrupy. Remove any scum that forms during the reduction.

Pour in the cream, bring it to the boil and simmer very gently until the sauce is unctuous and the consistency of custard. Check the seasoning (the mussel juices should provide enough salt) and add the tarragon and a pinch of cayenne pepper. Stir in the lemon juice. Remove 8 tablespoons of the sauce into a small bowl and set it aside.

To the remaining sauce, add the cooked shellfish, the raw scallops and their roes – which take very little time to cook through – and simmer for 3–4 minutes. Tip this creamy seafood mixture into a shallow dish, allow it to cool and put into the fridge for 1 hour. (This makes the filling easier to handle before you put it into the pancakes.)

Pre-heat the oven to 400°F/200°C/gas mark 6.

Lay out the pancakes and divide the filling between them with a spoon, making a thick line of it down the middle of each. To roll up, fold over one side (about one-third of the pancake) to cover the mixture. Then tuck each end over the ends of the line of filling and finally roll up to meet the other side. Lay the 8 pancakes in a lightly buttered rectangular baking dish. Warm the reserved sauce, spoon it over and leave them at kitchen temperature for 30 minutes.

Note: If you feel that there is not enough sauce to cover the pancakes, mix a little double cream into it.

Sprinkle the Parmesan over the pancakes and bake in the top of the oven for 25–30 minutes until glazed and bubbling. Serve with a crisp green salad, lightly dressed with olive oil and lemon.

sirloin steak with red wine sauce

Serves 4

Also known as Entrecôte Marchand de Vin, or 'wine merchant's steak'. Not surprisingly, the use of good red wine is quite important, and much of it is needed if the sauce is to be noteworthy. Incidentally, there is also a steak dish known as Entrecôte à la Vigneronne, or 'vine-grower's steak'. This one uses chopped snails and garlic in the sauce as well as the wine. And very delicious it is too.

Sometimes, Entrecôte Marchand de Vin is confused with Entrecôte à la Bordelaise, which is also a steak or piece of beef cooked with a red wine sauce. And, strictly speaking, the wine in question should hail from Bordeaux. Nevertheless, the important difference between the two preparations is the several thick slices of fondant bone marrow that lie across the surface of the Bordeaux beef. Maddeningly, the sauce is identical, so add the bone marrow if you can get some, and change the name. Isn't French cooking super?

½ bottle full-bodied red wine
4 small shallots, peeled and finely chopped
3 sprigs fresh thyme
2 small bay leaves
1 tsp redcurrant jelly
1–2 tbsp meat glaze (see pages 26–7)
4 × 200 g thick sirloin steaks

50 g softened butter, mixed with ¼ tsp flour
a squeeze of lemon juice
1 rounded tbsp parsley, chopped
salt and pepper
olive oil

Put the wine, shallots, thyme, bay leaves and redcurrant jelly in a stainless-steel or enamelled saucepan and bring it to the boil. Ignite the liquid with a match, allow the flames to subside and reduce by two-thirds. Lift out the thyme and bay leaves and add the meat glaze. Keep warm.

Grill the steaks as described on page 10, and after allowing them to rest, tip off any collected juices from the meat into the waiting sauce.

Warm the sauce over a low heat and whisk in the butter, a teaspoon at a time, until it becomes thickened and glossy. Allow to simmer very gently for 2 minutes and add the lemon juice. Stir in the parsley and pour the sauce over the steaks.

If you wish to embellish with the bone marrow, in the Bordelaise style, ask your butcher for three beef marrow bones. Ask him if he might very kindly saw them through into 5 cm pieces. When you get home, soak them in cold water to get rid of any excess blood; this will also soften the marrow. To remove the marrow from the bone, simply push it through the bone with your finger; it should plop out. Slice it into thickish circles and warm through briefly in barely simmering salted water, until wobbly and jelly-like. *Do not have the water too hot, or the marrow will melt away to nothing.* Lift out with a slotted spoon and lay over the steak.

gratin dauphinois

Serves 4–6

Perfect eaten with the previous dish and just as agreeable when served with roast lamb where the combination of potatoes, garlic and cream with the sweetness of the lamb is possibly the closest one can get to pure gastronomy. Even when cold, it is pretty good.

The 'gratin' became almost synonymous with the style of restaurant to which we refer in the introduction to this chapter. Great bubbling dishes of it would be offered to one and all and served at the table by waitresses with strong arms. It was a joy to behold, watching huge spoonfuls of it lifted out, dripping with reduced, starchy cream. It was so much better than those mimsy little dishes of it that are sometimes seen now – made even worse when it has been cut out into neat little towers and reheated. The whole point of the dish is lost in a trice.

600 ml whipping cream
1 bay leaf
salt and freshly ground black pepper

1.5 kg potatoes, peeled and very thinly sliced but not rinsed
2 garlic cloves, finely chopped

1 tsp freshly grated nutmeg
knob of butter

Place the cream in a large saucepan – later it will also hold the potatoes – with the bay leaf, and season with salt and black pepper. Set over a high heat and bring to the boil. Simmer for 10 minutes and then add the potatoes. Stir the mixture thoroughly and bring it back to the boil.

Pre-heat the oven to 325°F/170°C/gas mark 3.

Meanwhile, butter a shallow earthenware or porcelain dish. Spoon half the potato mixture into it and sprinkle with the garlic. Season with salt, pepper and nutmeg and add the rest of the potatoes and cream, spreading the mixture evenly. Put in the oven and cook for 45–60 minutes until the top is blistered and bubbling. Check for tenderness with a small knife.

lyonnaise potatoes   *Serves 4*

The look of a dish of Lyonnaise Potatoes can often be deceptive; the taste of the thing is all. The potatoes never really become crusted and golden as the onions sort of get in the way during the frying process. Also, you need to allow the potatoes to soak up any onion flavour, as well as the fat in which they are cooked. Pork or bacon fat would be ideal here or, failing that, beef dripping, duck fat or, as a last resort but not really authentic in the Lyonnaise region, a mixture of olive oil and butter.

900 g waxy potatoes, such as Belle de   *2 medium onions, thinly sliced*
    Fontenay   *salt and pepper*
50 g fat (see above)   *1 heaped tbsp chopped flat-leaf parsley*

Cook the potatoes in their skins and, when they are cool enough to handle, peel and slice them 0.5 cm thick.

Choose a large frying pan or sauté dish – non-stick would be helpful here – and use half the fat to fry the onions until they are evenly golden. Add the potatoes, stir in, using a wooden spatula, with the rest of the fat and

chez gourmet   239

lyonnaise potatoes

cook over a low heat, continuing to stir and turn. Season and cook for several more minutes until the potatoes are tender. Stir in the parsley and serve immediately.

tomatoes à la provençale *Serves 4*

There is little point in making this dish unless the tomatoes are of fine quality. Similarly, it would seem pointless to eat them outside the summer months, as their flavour and the smell while they cook have almost nothing at all to do with wintry feelings.

There is nothing more to do with the tomatoes than cut them in half and strew them with the flavoured breadcrumbs. No blanching, skinning or de-seeding is necessary; just make sure that the tomatoes are fully cooked or you will end up with the sort of tomato that comes with your average provincial hotel breakfast: hard, warm and pitiful.

100 g fresh breadcrumbs
1 bunch flat-leaf parsley, leaves only
4 garlic cloves, peeled and chopped
thinly pared rind of 1 lemon, chopped

6 tbsp olive oil
8 ripe tomatoes, cut in half
salt and pepper

Pre-heat the oven to 360°F/180°C/gas mark 5.

Place the breadcrumbs in a food processor with the parsley, garlic and lemon rind. Blend them well – the crumbs will turn a lovely green colour – but don't overwork the mixture or it will become pasty.

Smear a shallow gratin dish with olive oil and arrange the tomato halves, cut side up, in it without crowding, and season with salt and pepper. Carefully spoon the breadcrumbs in little piles over each tomato, trying not to let any fall off. Generously dribble more olive oil over the tomatoes and bake them in the oven for 30–40 minutes, or until the breadcrumbs have browned and the tomatoes are cooked through. Flash under a pre-heated grill, if necessary, to further burnish them. Serve in the dish at room temperature.

brown bread ice cream

Serves 4

The quintessential ice cream Chez Gourmet. Brown bread ice cream is one of those quirky English ideas that is unearthed now and again, perhaps by a passionate cook/reader. It is the sort of recipe that someone like George Perry-Smith from the Hole in the Wall, Bath (see page 215), might have come across in a small collection of forgotten notes, gleaned initially, perhaps, from an old copy of Eliza Acton or Hannah Glasse.

One of the best interpretations was made by Michael Waterfield, a charming man who used to have a superb restaurant called the Wife of Bath in Wye, near Canterbury. It is interesting to note that he was also one of many cooks who trained with George Perry-Smith.

500 ml double cream
1 vanilla pod, split lengthways and seeds scraped out using the back of a sharp knife

75 g stale brown breadcrumbs
75 g soft brown sugar (light muscovado is good)
1 tbsp cognac

Make the ice-cream by whipping the cream and vanilla seeds lightly together. Turn it into a metal bowl, cover and put it in the freezer. As the mixture begins to harden round the edges, stir the sides into the middle.

Lay the breadcrumbs on an oiled baking tray and sprinkle with the brown sugar. Put them in a fairly hot oven (400°F/200°C/gas mark 6) or under the grill until the sugar caramelizes with the crumbs. Stir from time to time. When they are golden brown, leave them to cool, then break them up again into crumbs.

When the ice cream is semi-stiff, mix in the crumbs and the cognac. Spoon into a Tupperware container, put on the lid and return it to the freezer for another 2 hours. Before serving, put the ice cream in the fridge for 30 minutes to soften slightly.

chocolate roulade and mousse

Serves 6–8

One of the few puddings that has never really lost favour over the years. Perhaps it experienced a brief dip in popularity when the Black Forest Gâteau bludgeoned its way into our eating habits, but there has always been room for both – we all love chocolate in whatever form.

It is also possible that Chocolate Roulade was found more at home than in restaurants, although Peter Langan served a version (Mrs Langan's Chocolate Pudding) when he opened Odin's in London in the late sixties and it is still on the menu today. Its domestic popularity was probably due to one of the first recipes that appeared in the beloved *Cordon Bleu* magazines, published in the early seventies, which displayed a picture of it in all its calorific glory. Consequently, Chocolate Roulade became the darling of the dinner party rather than the temptress of the trolley. We give two versions of the basic recipe: one is the Odin's version, which is finished with a chocolate sauce, and the other, which we prefer, uses a rich chocolate mousse (recipe on page 191), which does need several hours' setting time before it can be used.

6 large eggs
75 g caster sugar
50 g cocoa
225 ml double cream
icing sugar
——

For the chocolate sauce:
150 g best quality bitter-sweet chocolate
50 g unsalted butter
——

For the chocolate mousse:
1 recipe (see page 191)

Pre-heat the oven to 350°F/180°C/gas mark 4.

Have ready a 2.5 cm deep 30 × 20 cm baking tray (a Swiss roll tin, in other words) buttered and lined with greaseproof paper, and the chocolate mousse if using.

Separate the eggs into two large mixing bowls. Beat the yolks with the caster sugar until thick. Sift over the cocoa and whisk it in until it is nicely mixed.

Whisk the egg whites into soft peaks, and loosen the chocolate mixture with a couple of spoonfuls, then slowly and gently cut and fold in the rest. Pour the mixture into the prepared tray and bake in the middle of the oven for 15 minutes exactly.

Remove the tray from the oven and cover the cake with a damp tea-towel (this stops the surface from cracking too much) and leave to cool – it will settle down into the tin.

Now make the chocolate sauce. Break the chocolate into squares and put it in a small bowl with the butter. Rest the bowl over a pan of gently boiling water and stir as the two ingredients melt and coagulate.

Whip the cream to soft peaks.

Lay a large piece of greaseproof paper on a work surface and dredge it thickly with icing sugar to roughly the same size as the baking tray. Carefully invert the cake so that it lands fair and square on the icing sugar and remove the greaseproof paper. Spread it with the chocolate sauce or mousse, leaving a 2 cm border and cover that with the cream. Now, using the greaseproof paper to help you, roll up the cake to make a stubby log. It's almost certain to crack a little as you roll but that's part of its charm. Slip the roulade on to a plate.

For best results, slice it with a thin, sharp knife, wiping between slices.

Serves 4 crème brûlée

It seems that Crème Brûlée is made differently these days. Once upon a time one was instructed to make the custard in the traditional way, cooked very gently in a pan until thick. However, we have noticed in more and more recipes recently that the cream, sugar and eggs are mixed together in the usual way but then poured directly into their pots and baked in the oven with the help of a bain-marie. This does not give the same texture as the stove-top method but, of course, it is much easier to gauge the exact cooking time.

We prefer the traditional mode, and although care should be taken as to when the custard reaches its optimum thickness, the resultant voluptuousness of the 'crème' is infinitely more satisfying.

600 ml double cream　　　　　　　　*1 tbsp caster sugar*
1 vanilla pod, split lengthways　　　*2–3 tbsp Demerara sugar*
5 large egg yolks

Chill a 700 ml capacity, straight-sided, round shallow dish, or four ramekins, in the freezer.

Heat together the cream and vanilla pod, whisking occasionally to disperse the vanilla seeds in the cream. Remove from the heat and leave to infuse for 10 minutes.

Lightly beat together the egg yolks and caster sugar. Strain in the cream and mix thoroughly. In a heavy-bottomed saucepan, heat the custard over a very low heat, stirring constantly with a wooden spoon. From time to time, stop stirring to see if the custard gives the odd tremor which indicates that it is starting to heat. When this happens, take a whisk and beat it energetically to disperse the heat throughout. Resume stirring. You may have to whisk again. The custard is ready when you achieve an almost jelly-like consistency. Begin testing after about 10 minutes by removing the pan from the heat and drawing the whisk to and fro across the surface of the custard. Give a final energetic whisk and pour the custard into the ice-cold dish or ramekins. Leave to set in the fridge for at least 8 hours or overnight.

Pre-heat an overhead grill to its highest temperature. Spread the Demerara sugar in an even layer over the surface of the custard and spray it with a little water (this helps the sugar to caramelize). Place the dish or ramekins as near to the grill as possible until the sugar has melted and caramelized. These days everybody seems to be using a blow-torch instead, so if you have one use it as it is, in fact, one of the most efficient ways to caramelize Crème Brûlée.

Return the Crème Brûlée to the fridge for 30 minutes before serving.

crêpes suzette

Now, come on, we know you're out there. Yes, you sad people who claim that Crêpes Suzette is not quite your sort of thing. You think it a touch vulgar, school of Saturday-night dinner-dance, with dubiously sexy waiters dancing around a rickety trolley looking for all the world like Arthur Brown, assuming, that is, that you can remember Arthur Brown.

Well, sorry, you're all wrong. No question about it. Crêpes Suzette is an astonishingly fine dish, intelligently thought out by the great Escoffier and as simple as can be. But, curiously, there is no mention of flames, flambé work, or any such thing in this, his original recipe:

The pancakes are cooked in the ordinary way and then finished at the table with the following sauce: 75 g butter, 75 g caster sugar, 3 tbsp Curaçao, juice of one tangerine, sugar (caster) for sprinkling. Cream the butter, add the sugar, beating well. Add the Curaçao and tangerine juice. Put the pancakes in a pan over a spirit stove, sprinkle with sugar, pour over and serve very hot.

His recipe, indeed, sounds so very nice, is so very economically written and supremely simple to make. However, if you wish to complicate matters, and require a more boozy and 'saucy' dish, try the following home-grown version.

Note: The pancake batter is fine for both recipes.

For the pancake batter:
100 g plain flour
a pinch of salt
1 whole egg
1 egg yolk
the rind of ½ an orange, finely grated
275 ml milk
50 g butter, melted
a little more butter for greasing the pan

———

For the sauce and final cooking:
8 sugar lumps
2 large juicy oranges
50 g caster sugar
100 g unsalted butter, room temperature
juice of 1 lemon
2 tbsp Cointreau
2 tbsp cognac
(a little extra orange juice may be
 necessary)

crêpes suzette

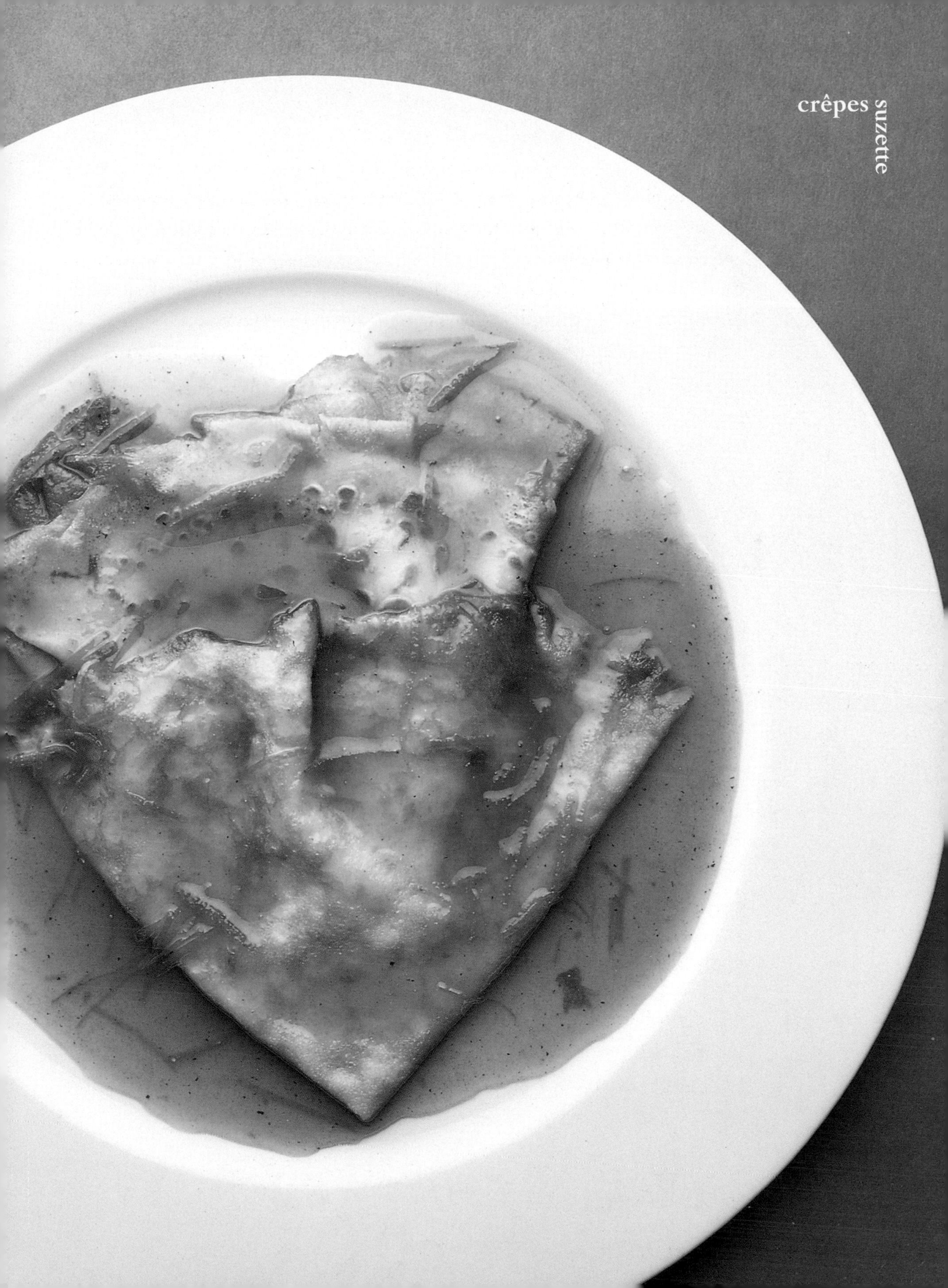

First, make the pancake batter. Simply put all the ingredients in a blender, blend well and allow to stand for at least 30 minutes. Take a 15 cm frying pan, melt a small amount of butter in it and allow it to sizzle. Pour in enough batter to just cover the base of the pan. The first pancake is often a bit of a mess; if so, chuck it out and start afresh. This is good for 'seasoning' the pan anyway.

You should not need to use too much extra butter in the pan as you cook the pancakes, just a trace now and again as the pan becomes dry (the melted butter in the mix usually adds sufficient lubrication). Make the pancakes as thin as you dare, flipping them over in the usual way with a palette knife. As each one is cooked lay it out on a dry tea-towel. The yield should be about 12 pancakes.

To make the sauce, first rub the sugar lumps over the orange skin until they start to collapse with saturation from the oil in the skins; do this over a large frying pan and drop the lumps into it once they are saturated. Squeeze the juice from the oranges and strain it through a sieve into a bowl.

Add the caster sugar to the lumps in the frying pan and set it over a medium heat. Carefully allow the sugar to melt in the otherwise empty pan; it will caramelize slowly and turn tawny. Once this has happened, pour in the orange juice, add half the butter and the lemon juice, and bring to a gentle simmer. Take one pancake, lay it in the sauce, then flip it on to the other side. Fold in half, then half again to form a triangle. Lay at one end of a lightly buttered, warmed dish (it is a good idea to keep the dish in a warm oven with the door ajar while you prepare the pancakes). Repeat with the other pancakes in the same fashion and lay them neatly in the dish, slightly overlapping.

You will notice that the sauce has reduced somewhat during this time and some will have soaked into the pancakes. If it looks too sticky, add a little more orange juice. Bring to a fast boil and add the rest of the butter in small amounts, swirling the pan as you go. When the sauce looks glossy, add the Cointreau and whisk together. Pour over the pancakes and leave them to soak for a few minutes. Then pour the cognac into a ladle and hold it over a flame to warm. Light with a match and pour immediately over the pancakes. Serve without delay.

pavlova

Serves 6

Some say that Pavlova was created by a hotel chef in the city of Perth, Western Australia, in the 1930s. It was named after the prima ballerina Anna Pavlova, whose tutu a perfect Pavlova is intended to represent in its shape and crisp lightness.

The chemical reaction of vinegar with cream of tartar produces the familiar marshmallow-like texture within the meringue, and is all important to the success of the dish. It is the great gooey show-stopper when well made, but don't overdo the fruit garnishes. The combination given here is one of the best of all: simply raspberries, whipped cream and passion fruit.

For the meringue:

6 egg whites

a pinch of salt

½ tsp cream of tartar

400 g caster sugar

2 tsp distilled white vinegar

For the filling:

300 ml double cream

1 tbsp raspberry eau de vie *(optional)*

250 g plump, ripe raspberries

6 passion fruit, flesh with seeds scooped out

Pre-heat the oven to 275°F/140°C/gas mark 1.

Whisk the egg whites with the salt and cream of tartar until frothy, then incorporate three-quarters of the sugar, beating until glossy, very firm and holding stiff peaks. Fold in the remaining sugar and the vinegar. Cut out a sheet of parchment paper to fit a heavy, flat baking sheet. Draw a 25 cm circle on the paper before damping it with a little water and placing it on the baking sheet. Spoon the egg whites on to the circle and smooth and shape into a nest, making sweeping scalloped edges with a damp tablespoon. Bake in the bottom of the pre-heated oven for 1–1½ hours until the meringue is crusty on the outside and just set on the inside. Allow it to cool then carefully peel off the paper and transfer the meringue to a serving plate.

Just before serving, lightly whip the cream (with the *eau de vie*, if using) to form soft peaks and spoon it into the middle of the meringue, spreading it out towards the edges. Decorate the Pavlova with raspberries and passion fruit.

chez gourmet   249

Serves 6

pears in red wine

It is well worth searching out a decent bottle of fruity red wine in which to cook these pears. A Beaujolais, or at least something made with the Gamay grape, is going to be the most suitable. Gentle slow cooking is the answer here so that the fruit has time to soak up the wine. Apart from imparting a lovely blackcurrant flavour, the addition of crème de cassis also deepens the colour of the syrup.

1 bottle red wine

150 g sugar or more to taste

4 cloves

2 black peppercorns

1 vanilla pod

1 cinnamon stick

1 strip orange peel, pith removed

6 large pears, not quite ripe

3 tablespoons crème de cassis

2 pieces of crystallized ginger, cut into
julienne shreds (optional)

thick cream or crème fraiche

Empty the wine into a stainless-steel or enamelled saucepan with the sugar, cloves, peppercorns, vanilla pod, cinnamon stick and orange peel. Bring the contents of the pan to the boil, then lower the heat and simmer gently for 20 minutes.

Remove the pan from the heat, cover, and leave it while you attend to the pears. Use a small sharp knife to cut out the end of the core to make a small triangular hole. Now peel the pear carefully, leaving the stalk intact. By the time you have finished, the pears will have started to discolour slightly; this doesn't matter, but can be prevented by rubbing them with lemon juice.

Stand or lay the pears in a pan that can hold them all submerged under the wine. Strain over the wine, tuck a sheet of greaseproof paper over the pears to keep them submerged and simmer gently for 15–20 minutes or until they are tender. Remove to a serving dish and stand them upright.

Add the crème de cassis to the pan and, if you are using it, the shredded ginger. Simmer the wine until syrupy and reduced by just over one-third. Pour the wine over the pears and chill.

Serve cold, dividing the wine between the helpings, with thick cream or crème fraiche.

syllabub

Serves 4

It is hard to believe that warm milk, freshly squeezed from the cow into a bucket of sweet white English wine (mead, possibly?), could have been whipped up into a creamy cloud of mousse-like consistency. But that's how the story goes. Surely it would have curdled in an instant, tasted pretty awful and could never have been served in a respectable restaurant, where it was spooned into a wine glass and served sitting on a side plate decorated with a paper doily . . .

Syllabub can be the most delicate of desserts, and it is possible for it to reach great heights of culinary skills if made with special care. The essential flavours are lemon, wine and sweetness, the latter preferably emanating from the use of sweet wine if the fragrance of the latter-day syllabub is to be cherished.

½ bottle sweet white wine, the more fragrant the better
50 g caster sugar
3 tbsp cognac
the rind of 2 small lemons, thinly pared (absolutely no pith; use a potato peeler) and their juice
300 ml double cream

Put the wine and sugar into a stainless-steel pan and reduce by half. Cool it, then add the cognac, lemon rind and lemon juice. Cover the pan with a lid or cling-film and leave it overnight to infuse.

The following day, strain the liquid through a fine sieve into a jug. Put the cream into the bowl of an electric mixer and slowly start to beat it (for an even better texture, hand-beat with a traditional wire balloon whisk). Add the wine infusion a little at a time, beating gently, until all the liquid has been absorbed. *Do not over-beat.* Pile into chilled glass dishes and chill again for 1–2 hours.

Note: There is an Italian drink called Limoncello. If you can find some, a teaspoon of the stuff, chilled and poured over each serving, works wonders.

Recipes with full instructions appear in the Recipe Index: other recipes mentioned appear in the General Index.

general index

Recipes mentioned appear in the General Index: recipes with full instructions appear in the Recipe Index.

First published 1997 by Macmillan General Books

an imprint of Macmillan Publishers Ltd
25 Eccleston Place London SW1W 9NF
and Basingstoke

Associated companies throughout the world

ISBN 0 333 68460 5

Copyright © 1997 Simon Hopkinson and Lindsey Bareham

The recipes on pages 141–3 grouped under the heading 'Pork Pie'
are copyright © Jane Grigson 1974

The right of Simon Hopkinson and Lindsey Bareham to be
identified as the authors of this work has been asserted by them
in accordance with the Copyright, Designs and Patents Act 1988.

9 8 7 6 5 4 3 2 1

A CIP catalogue record for this book is available
from the British Library.

Designed by Macmillan General Books Design Department
Photographic reproduction by Speedscan Ltd, Basildon, Essex
Typeset by SX Composing DTP, Rayleigh, Essex

Printed and bound in Italy by Manfrini S.p.a. Calliano (TN)